A TIME OF CONTRIVANCE FOR SAVING THE WORLD

A TIME OF CONTRIVANCE FOR SAVING THE WORLD

A WORLD FOR SAVING
AN UNCERTAIN FUTURE

Nigel Nicholas

ISBN:	Hardcover	978-1-7960-7360-7
	Softcover	978-1-7960-7359-1
	eBook	978-1-7960-7358-4

Print information available on the last page.

Rev. date: 11/22/2019

To order additional copies of this book, contact:
Xlibris
1-888-795-4274
www.Xlibris.com
Orders@Xlibris.com
805110

CONTENTS

CHAPTER 1

The Understanding from Which It Came

It came to me after I returned from England in the winter of 2008. I had a brilliant idea for perfect energy: the exhaust of the fuel was to be used in reconstructing the components for combustion. The idea of designer fuel was not widely known, but was a prominent topic among the chemists of the automobile industry from 2006 to 2007. The concept goes against all contemporary laws of energy conservation and physics. The idea of reconstructing a fuel was not very far-fetched since the breaking of bonds between atoms are very difficult to achieve. This requires complex chemicals as many of the nonmetals would break covalent bonds when induced with specific wavelengths and frequencies of electricity, allowing the partial and complete reconstruct of the initial compounds of the combustion processes. In other cases, wavelengths of light would assist in the complete breaking of bonds; this is the process known as photolysis. This was the birth of designer nonpolluting fuels. With these fuels, cost is limited to manufacturing leverages, and unlimited energy is achieved. The exhaust can be safely expelled into the atmosphere, making it a sustainable and reliable source of energy. The problem was the world of economics; the idea was sunk long with many proven formulas ready for testing.

It came to me seeking to change the future. It was a voice in my head speaking words in English, asking me to be patient with it. I was very afraid. I thought I should seek a psychiatrist; it startled me and asked to be its friend. I truly thought I was going mad. I thought that surely my career was over. I looked at myself and saw myself ending up in a loony bin or worse. I came to it, mustering all the strength I had. I had to face my fears and began speak. It asked how I was, and I began to cry. I was surely done for; all I could think about was I would be living on antipsychotics for the rest of my life.

I droned about my loft for the next few days, thinking of what to do. I looked at myself and saw that I was slipping into a dark place. I wondered where can I go and asked it why it was here. It said to lead the world into a new light. I cried thinking of my mental state. I am surely a delusional. I had no choice. I ran outside screaming to God asking him why. I could not believe myself that had I become a head case; my life was over. I thought I was not committed enough; I should have married my ex-girlfriend. I even thought I should have married my first girlfriend. It said to me, "You are now surely going mad." I began screaming at myself, thinking how could these things have happened. It said, "I am not a creation of your mind." I looked at the mirror, looking at the darkened rings around my eyes, thinking I had lost a lot of sleep. It said, "I will prove it to you." I could not help myself and I cried.

The next day, I awoke early in the morning lying in bed. The sun had not risen yet, and I listened to the birds chirping. It said to me, "That bird is a finch." I began to cry. I asked myself how could this be, what was wrong with me. It said, "Nothing is wrong with you, I will prove it to you."

I got up and made a cup of tea. I looked outside, and I felt my mind move toward the window. I walked to the window, and it said, "In thirty seconds, a truck filled with milk will come around the corner and stop in front of the building. A man with a blue shirt and a red hat will exit the vehicle and walk directly into the building." I stood there waiting for fifteen seconds, and I saw a truck come driving around the corner and stopping directly in front of the building. The truck was a Milkilver truck that delivers milk. The man immediately came out of the driver's seat with papers in his hands, wearing a dark blue company shirt and a red cap.

I immediately dropped my cup of hot tea, spilling it on the floor. I fell to the floor in fear, scrambling back inside, thinking it was an alien inside my brain. I immediately called the police; they came quickly to the loft asking me many questions. Finally they asked if I was on drugs. I was admitted into a hospital for three days. The doctors said it was sleep deprivation. I was reluctant to return to the loft so I checked myself into a hotel. I helped myself to the minibar and washed my problems away. It said to me, "We need to talk. I would like you to assist me with something." I thought, *Am I going crazy? Was this in my imagination?* I took a sip of the gin and continued watching the television.

The next day, I went back to my loft, I sat on my sofa and turned on the television. It said to me, "Hi, how are you?" I looked into myself and slumped deep within the sofa and began to cry. I went to the store and bought a huge chunk of chocolate. I felt like a middle-aged unmarried woman. I looked at myself; I had fallen. It said to me, "You need to pick yourself up—your actions are unhealthy. You will become a loony if that is the way we should speak. You need to think about your safety, and I am not in your imagination." It said to me, "I am an angel." I asked, "Like God's angel?" It said, "Yes, and I am coming to tell you of the destruction of the world."

I asked, "Why me?" It said, "I had to choose someone, and I chose you." I asked, "Why?" It said, "Because I thought you were handsome."

"Like what kind of handsome?"

It said, "Like a male model handsome."

I never thought of myself as a model type before. "What do you want with me?"

It said, "Let's talk for a bit." It spoke of things I was interested in—topics of science, atoms, chemistry, metals, and particles. It even showed me what an atom looked like and what atoms were. It spoke of the creation of the universe for which was the simple instant existence of matter, entirely created in less than a second; but in their world, time is not in the conventional sense as time in the way humans experience it. It was not a big bang theory as described; it was something more confounded.

It showed me images of other worlds and other beings that all lived on planets like ours, which their kind had access to. It showed me the earth, the distances between the planets and the earth, and what our solar system and universe really looked like. It showed our solar system that had more than twelve planets for which there were thousands of planets and planet-sized rocks in the asteroid belt. Farther away is another ring; this was a lot of planets, which is the rings near Pluto. Almost equidistant to that was another ring of planets with millions of other planets; all in all, there were four rings within our solar systems. These consist of many earth-sized planets, but they are very inhabitable by us.

The idea was our methods for observation in space was inadequate to observe the various celestial bodies. We use photons through photoelectric metals and radio waves in our devices for which the speed of photons deteriorate in space, especially when in a wavelike field of radiation. We are blinded to our solar system and the other universes; many of these carry life. Most of all of deep space that seemingly is a void is made of matter that our instruments cannot detect. These can be considered dark matter but in fact is altogether another type of matter. It was all fascinating at first, but then it seemed like the entire universe and all its beings were God-centric; they all served Gods. To me, it seemed like it was inclined to God over them, they were all devotees of under many names for different gods. It said, "God is in another place, and I did not create this." I was reluctant to continue, and I blanked my mind and its images, drank some liquor, and went to bed.

After a few days, it returned and politely described where it was from and what it was. It was comparable to a Chava, a being created by a god. It also explained it was made of atoms and was something tangible with immense power and abilities. A lot of humankind do not know what they know, and they live their lives taking their existence for granted. For where it lives, they are beloved things, and they should be proud in the presence of a God. I immediately became scared because it said it was not a God, and its ego flared.

It lives in our universe and is of the form of a quadruped. They are crafted by other beings outside of our universe that can recreate life. It went on to explain that the universe was created by a being that is designated to create universes. They have created many universes, and others were designated to create the beings that would shape and fill the necessary parlors with ancillaries and life. These beings were built by design for which there were parameters and laws; they also had a schedule for which their true purpose was unknown to.

These beings could not be destroyed as they moved across dimensions creating universes. They demonstrated immense power and only operate as instructed by their leader. Based on the purpose of the universe, the other relevant beings would populate and organize the variation of the inhabitants, creating the respective beings. The angels and daemons that would fill the world and teach these beings how to live exposes them to many situations, illustrating the differences within acceptable behavior. Any being that was outside of these behaviors were considered an anomaly, and they usually did survive the structure of the social environment.

Many would create beings and their lives, shaping their actions and their minds to what would be acceptable or in some cases what was pleasing. Upon their death, these beings were taken to many places for which we can describe as heaven or hell. As it described, it was not that simple; many religions have their own theories and belief. Not one sector of religion is accounted for entirely by one set of beliefs. In fact, all beings that were created, but not all, were collected, but all could be stored in one central place. They were not alive or dead but were stored in a state of semiconsciousness.

The universe was a multimetamorphosis of axisymmetric motifs within the structure of a dimensionally fasciated distribution of artesian spaces. Which is in a parabolic apperception of time and space. The psychology correspondence to spectrumnality of understandable and nonunderstandable matter and energy in complex motion is undefined because of parametric angles of perceptive effects. Matter and energy are subjected to parallax from our four-dimensional perceptions. Energy and its concentration are unaccounted for mental adjustments.

Differentiation in energy convectional oscillation, which is the alluvial mitosis of time, is the basis for man's perception. All of these are the universe to us for which it usually accumulates to our daily experience, our lives. The dimensions that are acknowledged and accepted by man are those that are measured in a specific way.

Time is considered energy in a sequence, light energy cosynchronizing with sound wave and other perceived sequences of energy accumulates to what is considered time. If one can mathematically account for all the energy transformations of a particular item as it exists in time, they can see the energy sequences. A ball that is thrown across a field, by a man, the arm of the man accelerates at 10 feet per second per second, as the ball is released its accelerates until it peaks and then decelerates as it moves across the field until terminal velocity is achieved. The energy can be observed in a sequence of spent energy. If we were to count instances of spent energy, we can observe the succession of energy that we define as time. A ball falls, and the energy or movement is perceived; the spent energy is no longer perceived. The ball is no longer moving. Its sequence of motion is erased or unperceived; it is described as the past.

The movement of the ball no longer exists to the human being, except in our memories. The human being itself is energy in a sequence, manifesting in specific types of matter. Energy manifesting in leptons, bosons, and quarks are defined as specific types of energy by contemporary fields of science, for example, radioactive energy. In fact, they are closer to specific types of matter rather than an energy at all. Matter is made of specific ties within the universe; the structure as it was explained goes from matter in perceived motions, which is termed energy. Energy in perceived motion of patterns is perceived as increments of time. For example, a man walks across the road. The energies that takes place to afford this situation are kinetic energy, which is afforded by chemical energy within his body. This is mediated by multiple energies acting upon masses that constitutes ambient forces. These potential energies work against man and are balanced by the force of gravity or gravitational energies. To define politely, forces can be defined as a mass multiplied by its acceleration. Acceleration is largely dependent on the energies acting upon the matter. The measure of time is increments of perceptions or experience; we perceive in increments of less than one second at a time.

Time and matter are reliant on our perception, which is based on our senses. Our senses are based on the absorption of particles in motion, which is transferred to our brain through our neural synapsis via electrical energy. The energy sequence of the perception of a sound or light is the kinetic energy of the photon or bosons and S or P wave formations among molecular structures of the ambient. These transfer the effects of kinetic energy to our eardrums or the rods and cones of our eyes. These induces an electric current, the neural electrical signaling of the brain, resulting in its reception within our cognitive functions.

Time is matter in motion perceived through our senses. Photons are matter in motion waves of sound, the effects of molecular motion, ideally compressibility within the atmosphere. These all stimulate our senses and are received by our brains via our neural synapses, which impact on our perceptions. The second is an increment of our perception, which is observed and measured by the parallel cosynchronization of a physical measuring stick, the sand in an hourglass. The increments of a second is truly the working mechanisms of the human brain; it is the amalgamation of all of its processes to produce a singularity in consciousness. The human brain is made of atoms; the atom and its orbitals are your thoughts, memories, ideas, and notions, the center of our perception.

The human being is one part of a much larger matter and energy scheme that exists simultaneously and simultaneously within the universe. A man that crosses the road at the crosswalk is seen by the natural eye. His atoms reflect and project molecules, bosons, quarks, and leptons, which creates pressure of motion and is received by our senses. We perceive the man crossing the road, the man that did not cross at the crosswalk was not perceived, it never happened. The situation that led to the man crossing outside of the crosswalk was not perceived. His ideas, the electrical impulses within his brain, did not accumulate to the effect of his decision of crossing outside of the crosswalk. It is not unnatural for a man to walk outside of the crosswalk. The man that did choose to walk outside of the crosswalk does exist and is not perceived. Atoms of the same energy regime react to each other. Atoms of different energy regimes are malignant or nonreactive. They do not react to each other because matter and atoms are a structure or pattern of many smaller particles in motion. These particles are not of the human perception.

Particle movements and distributions are parabolic across existing dimensions. Your memories only facilitate what your mind perceived. The mitosis of the future is based on increments of perception; photons expelled from the man at the traffic light does not reach or affect the eyes of the onlooker of a different energy regime. It does to the onlooker in the same timeline or the same energy regime. The man within the crosswalk is in an alternate dimension to the onlooker that sees the man outside of the crosswalk. The man at the crosswalk and the man outside of the crosswalk cannot be hit by an oncoming car outside of either energy regimes. The atoms are out of synchronization. Energy regimes are dimensions; these are planes where all the atoms are reactive to each other. Dimensions of time are called dendritics.

Dendritics are an important factor in the understanding of molecular and particle movements because they do no not partake in the conventions of temporal reactivity. Atoms are a structure of particles; in contemporary thinking, the atom is made up of protons, electrons, and neutrons. Atoms of specific numeration have very endogenous qualities. The protons and electrons of an atom that moves through space change in a way that the atom maintains its physical structure and reactivity to the particles within the ambient. Its changes are unobserved by humans; many would say these changes do not happen. As it moves through time, the atom is physically unchanged; its structure does not change or modify, but its energy regime changes so it is no longer observed.

All of its component particles exist simultaneously, interacting among themselves, but are depolarized to the other dimension. They become unreactive to its alluvial self; the atom that moves through time is unreactive to itself in the past. The atom in the car of the dimension where the man crossed at the crosswalk is unreactive to the same atom that is in the car where the man crossed outside of the crosswalk. In this, the atom maintains a continuous reactivity between the atom and its alter selves. The atom, as it moves through time, and its alter selves accommodate the stability of its structure, creating the ability to maintain motion.

Motion is defined or quantified by special parameters within temporal increments. In this, humans' inability to perceive all the changes and motions within an atom affects their knowledge of what their reality is. Atoms that change in energy regime move similar to atoms moving through different spatial matter matrices. They move in varying angles and trajectories, simultaneously in many physical places and time. An atom moving in one second has a pattern for presence in many dimensions and regimes' confluence assortment. One atom in motion is simultaneously present in the past and future as well as in alternate realities in a single state of equilibrium. One electron in motion is its parabolic distribution of its singular presence in the integration of its velocities across dimensions and time. This is also with its distribution of its differences across all alluvials within its mitosis, meaning, the electron is a mass projection of itself across all platforms.

The motion of an atom is the movement of the patterns for which many of its constituent particles are expelled. Water can be described as the facilitator of waves; the movement of one wave is the movement of a particular shape within a medium. An atom is the same idea—the movement of atoms is the movement of a shape within a field, a field of other moving things that are defined in the very same way. This is the very nature of all movement; movement by definition is tied to increments of time. Time is the human perception; motion is the ability to perceive a pattern as its energy shifts through the various phases across special platforms.

Motion is a pattern specifically tied to energy spectrums of alluvial mitosis. Motion is not considered motion in the conventional sense. If a person moves, the person is a pattern in a parabolic distribution of the integration of velocities through space and time, which is across all physical platforms. If a wave moves through water and its velocities does change, the shape of the wave changes, the structure of the wave becomes deformed. If a person moves through time and space, the thoughts of the person changes; their mind evolves toward their surroundings.

The wave in a body of water is just the same as a person in a city. A continuum of the deformation of behavior, this can be specifically calculated within the law of conservation of energy.

If one can perceive the movements of the wave, then the flow regimes are out of sync; the being is the wave that does or does not move as time flows past. As time flows, the being takes in air, food, and other particles. These are later expelled, just the same as the wave takes up water in the crest and trough cycles as it moves. If the being moves near radioactive material, it absorbs radioactive particles. The same can be said for all particles in the universe. If the being moves through time, its particle changes to accommodate the physical present time within the alluvial regimes. Advances to accommodate the general perceived present of the collective are automatically vectored to particle momentum and mass conservation principles, which prevents the out of synchronization with the collective present time.

Particle changes to accommodate the present by the collective conscious minds change in space and time to afford what is called the Frestution effect. If these particle changes do not occur, all the mass will fall out of sync, and the mass will simply disappear. It could be perceived as though it was destroyed, but the mass can no longer be perceived. In truth, the mass has simply shifted out of phase to a phase where it no longer interacts with the present temporal regime. The mass has crossed alluvial platforms. All the particle movements and the interaction of atoms affect the atom's orbital elliptical velocities.

The being's atoms and the structure of its atoms will change over time. In space, there would be temporary degradation. In time, there would be consecutive constitutive relation to deformations in accelerant gradients as they perturb mass conservation derivatives. Time and space can be considered the same; the being that traverses the alluvials of time can exert its energy to maneuver in the same way as space. The atom's structure in relation to its energy phases must remain in precise synchronization to accommodate the maintenance of molecular bonding. The atom's phase shift must proportionately maintain the potential conservation differences, which must accommodate the alluvial shift phases physically.

This is an important concept in understanding the Frestution for which the imbuement of one's atoms can allow existence outside of the sphere of atoms. The crossover phases into the Lecturaries and Feathecturaries are more complex. The atoms themselves possess radiants that are not of a perceived phase, just the same for the atoms that are out of sync.

The same can be said about spirits. There are many types of matter, for which not all are of the structure like atoms, which are mass structures of elliptical particles. Spirits are a weaving of Gurnesh and Furgeish energies from another dimension. They are both one and the same, a cooperative balance existing together in a comprehensive motion of energies, creating a medium.

The abilities of the mind to control energies of astral predominance and ascension are tied to the body's Gurnesh and Furgeish energies. It is the essential power that holds our thoughts in constant equilibrium. The human mind is physical and spiritual; the spiritual is more than just vigorously bonded to emotional and astral energies, both of which inhabit the human body and mind. A Bune is called one's spiritual self in the same way the ancient Egyptians described the Ka. It is the physical body of a person in its human form. It is entirely made of spiritual energies and matter, the Gurnesh and Furgeish. Without the spirit, the body appears to have no life; it fast becomes inanimate. A person's life signs will sustain for some time but will ultimately stop. Once the absence of a spirit continues, the person's mind will still be functional because of the presence of astral energies. These are responsible for the willing and upholding of thoughts within the human being.

The astral energies along with their subgroups of Maljoice, Stropoids, Trestorize, Pevestuiie, and Sizteme are all that makes up the intellect, the human cognitive function. The human body works in perfect synchronization with these energies to create the human mind. The mind without the human kundalini leaves the body in a scattered alignment. The kundalini is described as an energy that links the human mind, body, and soul together; it is responsible for the perfect synchronization of the person's diet to their body's functions and to their mind's predisposition.

The presence of and loss of these energies are the reason the body loses weight at the point of death. The energies within our bodies have changed; the combinations have reassorted and aligned themselves with external and internal energies, losing parts and restructuring to a malformed structure with an affinity to our atoms. This results in the atoms returning to its altered affected state, allowing effects such as rigor mortis and cooling of body temperatures, the darkening of the colors within the skin, and a temporary increase in body weight. The human body gains these energies from alternate dimensions and are specifically designed for cosynching and existing within the human body.

These energies are designed to do specific things; emotional energies are designed to guide a human's thought processes through situations. Emotional energies work in conjunction with the astral energies to produce a simultaneous result of behavior. Familiarity in conjunction with love meet with the acceptance of energies from a lover produces joy and happiness within the mind of an individual. If exposed to an environment of fear, the persons can create distrust and apathy. These energies are employed to control the thoughts of man; it is near impossible for humans to exist with these energies.

A being in space and time can no longer be considered just a moving wave. The increments of changes in space are generally unperceived, but the molecules, atoms, particles, and energies of our bodies are reacting to changes every second. The thoughts of the being are changed every second for which the being has changed the energies within its mind. These energies have the ability to move from one central acting point to another. The energies move simultaneously across all the beings of the alluvial in patterns of angles, concentrations, and proportions as they are distributed, resulting in a wider spread of the alluvial distribution. In our dimensions of time and space, they are tied together. A being walking a mile takes thirty minutes; if a being can traverse time, then it takes an instant to perceive its destination.

Beings that can perceive all things simultaneously are not subjected to time in the conventional sense; they are deemed to be timeless. They can traverse and perceive all time increments in a concordant way. A timeless being's perception is not measured in seconds, and they do not need to refer to a memory or look toward a future. They do not have a future in the same way as humans; they also do not have a past; in fact, the past and future is experienced in the present. This is called saellicise. Their minds' energies are not in a singularity of motion; one factor or component of the mind is not dependent on one facet or particle or energy or matter. They can be more described as multiple beings of one perception, perceiving all increments as a group, for all the group would constitute the entire being.

To further demonstrate a being of multiple perceptions, its ability is similar to a person driving a car, where the mind simultaneously focuses on the roads ahead and on the mirrors that shows the roads behind. These beings have significantly higher levels of energy regimes and are more complex in mass deformity force constants. They no longer need to traverse space in the conventional sense. They do not walk or use vehicles; they move temporally to their point of interest or their destination—in this case, space is time.

The human body is made of atoms and various forms of energy in many patterns and lattice structures. The body that is ours is a pattern of atoms designed to specifically account for the human experience. The atoms that make up the eyes are specifically designed to recognize the photons of this specific energy regime in a particular designed sequence. The man that chose to walk within the crosswalk is perceived, but the man that chose to walk outside of the crosswalk is out of sync.

His atomic energy structure changed or lessened and is no longer perceived. When this is perceived from a present tense, looking at the incident happening in the future it is called the continuous sinistrorse of mitosis of the future. In this, your mind can and does bend, creating alternatives of ideas and suppositions of reality, concatenate with the changes in alluvial reassortment. This is called the cognitive torsion; all the thoughts of a being are an amalgamation of your personality, ambient exposure, diet, and unaccounted-for energies.

Your brain's energy works in the very same way your electrons and brain chemistry form a nexus in time. The ideas you perceive versus the ideas you did not perceive are time-variant radiants that are energy dependent. If a car was driving in his direction over the speed limit, the man would have changed his decision of when to cross. This can be described as the energy balance in his brain being modified. In fact, the entire thought process is a web of energy ties beyond your control; this is the cause of our inevitability or our destiny.

It is not that the human being cannot help himself, but they are irrefutable tied to their energy sequence. The entire bodies are energy-accommodating conduits of physical motion and experience of perceptions. Unaware of their alter selves, the human being traverses his existence plane, partially aware that their minds and bodies are physically stitched together. The moments of energy and alluvial radiant particle movements afford the man that crossed within the crosswalk and his alter self to be linked via particle movement; they are also linked via energy displacement. The particles interact with each other regardless of how many dimensions are perceived; this is called anthropomorphic continuum palette within the human life.

If the man dies, his energy regimes change across all dimensions; particles and energies that move through his mitosis alluvial structures are now channeled differently. This results in a different alluvial distribution pattern; all of himself changes in perceived or unperceived ways. His life circuitry changes; his energies passes through the void that has become what is him, creating psychological Nirvikalpa and Vitarka, which affect the cycles of life, the Pricciuss. Spells of good or bad luck predicaments can become instantaneous, accident, travesties, or the simple act of increased precipitation the falling of rain can occur within the locale. This occurs because all human beings are interacting with the environment and each other simultaneously across all platforms. A nexus of intangible emotions, sentiments, passions, intuitions, and inclinations, expressed in conversations and interactions. An unveiling display of sentiments within our lives, the effects of the energies within our fabric. The human mind is more capable of doing remarkable things if it can perceive the effects of what it does within these spectrums.

A man that thinks of giving a gift exerts energies and particles that alter within all platforms within the alluvials in existence. He topples presidents, affords the growth of forests, and further along the timeline creates nations. In modern mysticism, this is described as his positive energies transcending throughout the universe. This is true, but it is unaccounted for. The mere thought releases particles that shift other particles within himself and in others shifting sometimes denying thoughts within their minds, affecting their destiny. Changing the present decisions can affect the cornucopia of alluvials and the links established in between and creates an interaction of the alluvials. This creates a kaleidoscope that turns specifically and mechanically that is quantifiable. All of our unified destinies are affected and realized simultaneously.

These effects can be physically controlled if one can perceive the links among himself, his intended objective, and the relevant alluvials that need to be affected. A man that wishes upon a specific event in fact can cause the event to not happen. The man plays the lottery, wishes, and does not win versus the man that feels he would win and does. That man that feels he would win, his alluvial patterns have suddenly come to a change; his alter selves may have been removed, creating voids within. The channels of the mass alluvial patterns create specific effects within their life cycles. The idea can be singularly described as their thoughts, which are the particle expulsion and energy synchronizations. The man that usually feels he would win the lottery is somewhat exposed to some degree of danger mainly because of the dangers afforded by having increased options. He is exposed to alluvial situations that afford the instantaneous availability of voids and void stations of his energy patterns.

People who surround themselves with certain frequencies of energies accommodate and harbor energies that cosynchronizes with the other alluvials. These give feelings and thoughts of good and bad, true and false, even feelings of who can come in contact with them. Some can feel the future of the other alluvials; a person who has recently lost a loved one can see them inside their homes. They hear their voices, smell their scent; their minds perceive an alluvial where they do exist. The death of this person has created the void that has channeled mass amounts of energies and particles that afford the brain and mind to perceive that individual, mostly momentarily or very faint.

People who have learned to channel, store, and operate these energies can feel the presence of the person for years. Some people can even communicate with them, gaining feelings, telling what he might have said. It is not a psychological effect of loss; it is the communication with those from other alluvials. Many humans from time to time have experienced the feeling of being warmed by the thoughts of their loved ones. Some might even transform the idea of hearing a loved one calling out to them, but they are not around. A father would think he heard his daughter call out to him or a mother thinking of a tragedy in her home while she is away. These are not figments of imaginations; they are events that have actually happened.

The daughter that called out to her father did experience an incident where she needed to call out to him; maybe he was in an accident. The mother that thought of the tragedy in her home felt the mind's waves from her children as the event took place. The voids that are created afford the crossover or transcendence of the energies that we perceive. The mind of our human body type affords the reception of specific types of energies, but can also afford or adapt to receiving a lot more if we take the time to practice using our minds. The average human mind is filled with thoughts and emotions from our daily lives. We do receive energies from an alternate alluvial line, but they are thought to be random ideas, intellections, and emotions. There is no such thing as a useless malignant notion; they are all part of the wider human self. People who meditate or follow a specific type of meditation are taught to channel their minds in specific ways, affording the reception of energies from specific alluvials.

Good energies emanate from alter selves that possess these good energies and feelings. The same is for bad energies and feelings. Creative and intuitive energies originate in specific places that possess an astral energy called Sarmuaisan, which is present throughout the universe. It is the source of all beauty and notions of wonder, the beginning of all questions. This energy is freely exposed and in motion, but many are not able to receive it through their lifestyles. The expansion of a person's mind affords the reception and expulsion of many energies that are used by us daily. Beauty is not actually in existence, but the mind's transcendence of beauty exists; the life that is loved is reflected upon by whoever loves it.

This life is not accepted by the loveless; this love is perceived by the mind as within beauty. Love and beauty within the mind are perceived in the same way but are not of the same energies or makeup, which are not from the same place, for love is of the heart. The heart can be controlled, and beauty cannot be controlled. Love is an energy, but love can also be classified not as an energy. Love transcends and spreads across all the alluvials and its facets, but it is only limited to beings. Love is only found within living beings. It is of the living construct for which it needs a being to traverse across the alluvials; in this, a rock cannot love. A man that loves a woman can feel each other's thoughts across continents; they know the inner workings of each other's minds. Love can permanently unify two beings to be as one.

A person who actively thinks of being loved finds love; a person who is the holder of more energy and thinks of being loved by a specific person can and does get the affection of that individual. The people who can actively expel and apply their energy are already in tuned with their alter selves across the alluvials. These people are those who remarkably apply their minds toward a specific thing in idea or emotions, and as time progressed, it occurs with little physical effort. This is called the synchronized marching of one alluvial selves within the matrices of the macroalluvial structures.

These energies within oneself can be pushed a bit further; a person with a high degree of success in exerting and applying one's energies should try to physically move matter. Ideally, they should try with very low-weighted objects, like the stopping of the movements of the clouds or the blowing of leaves. The particles and energies expelled from thoughts and emotions does afford the altering of atoms through the changing of their energy regimes. The energies and radiants that is expelled from thoughts is just enough to shift the phases, resulting in a time-shift special that is perceived by us. This has been achieved by humans who have expanded their minds through meditation and diet, for the foods we eat affect our minds, especially if they contain some amount of psychoactive compounds.

The underling particles, especially those relating to our sense, like sound particles, are timeless in the same way atomic movements are timeless. Sound stretches without the stress lines across the Nefectories within our universe like trees pulling energy from the roots and releasing at the leaves, reforming the resonance of one of those sleeves within the human ears, the cochlea, like dogs hearing a whistle. Humans temporarily hear activities of the latter energy regimes, like echoes spanning across a vast chasm of space. These echoes are channeled through the emotional spectrum and tie our alter selves to strange or frightful sounds that span across the alluvials.

A person in a forest at night hears sounds that seemingly jolt their imaginations. Their mind goes in directions that propagate these thoughts and energies associated with these ideas and emotions. These thoughts channel an influx of radiants and energies through the person's psyche and mental fabric, causing the expansion of fear and doubt across their alluvial alter selves, which can and does result in tragedy. A woman might hear the strange voice of a man or a soldier hearing the mechanical noises of a gun. They check to see if these noises are real, but in doing so and emotionally reacting to these noises, they allow more energies that are associated with the human void spectrums to enter our bodies and minds. These can result in conditions such as paranoia and schizophrenia.

Long-term exposure or acceptance of these types of energies results in permanent brain function abnormalities and chemical imbalances. Sound particles like many others are not only timeless but also dimensionless; the human ear receives particles from events before they even happen. Earthquakes, gunshots, and car accidents are the most invariable particles in radiant from tragedy received. It can be used like the sixth sense or can result in a severe case of dementia. Sound particle movements are very irregular across the multiverse of universes.

CHAPTER 2

The Universe and Its Constituents

Sound particle movement can be defined as in a circular pattern called the Rschour. The Rschour is a force that holds the circle together. This hints the expanse across the universe for which sound travels without bounds. It delineates the interaction of interaction among particles, which results in a never-ending cycle of actions from interactions. This originates from one single point in energy spreading across the alluvials in a vortex-like motion transposing the keys to its radiants through all the particles and energies within the universe.

The simple intention of a man is enough to spur his actions across one's multidimensional of selves. If something is done, it can never be erased; it is in existence somewhere within the nexus of alluvials. If something is thought, it has already been done; the mitosis of the alluvials allow for all to be accommodated within the parabolas of existence. The distribution of one's behaviors are non-Gaussian, meaning the thoughts of the latter side of one energy in its distribution across the alluvials are not symmetrical or concentric to the other side. If all energy spectrums are defined or distinguished in positive and negative, the idea's origin is statistically abnormal toward negative behavioral tendencies simply because of the human's mental design.

The idea of a hug and what the feelings associated with a hug does to the average person and their daily idea streams are in relation to the design of the human mind, arms, and the accumulated cultural perspective of the wider society. The effectiveness of hugs are dependent on the design of the mind and nerve centers that interprets nerve impulses received from the physical act of giving the hug. Social connotations associated with the hug help form feelings toward the acceptance of the idea associated with giving hugs and the interactions in between the people involved. The mass psychological trajectory that creates the alluvial that is dependent on individual decisions are dependent on factors that affect idea streams of individuals in their day-to-day lives. The use and cultural acceptance of psychoactively altering substances affect the alluvials in ways that alter the energy flows within the energy patterns. People that take drugs send specific types of energy combinations across their pattern of alluvial selves. Some individuals seem as though they are on drugs, but had never ingested one milligram of a psychoactive substance.

Each molecule has many energy and particle radiant signatures for which they all are associated with the fabrics of this universe, which our bodies are made of. A chemical compound and its effect on the human brain relates to its macroeffect within the universe. The mind of the human is acting upon and the minds of the beings that manage their existence. These beings are the angels of heaven and the others who wish to collect the souls of men. The minds of men and the decisions men make are pondered upon, and they affect the worlds of these beings. Each molecule that affects the human brain, within specific timelines of the human alluvials, do not always affect the alter selves of individuals within other alluvials.

Some molecules from time to time lose their effect on the human brain; other molecules become part of the human cell. Some form other molecules that dampen the effects of the substance; some transfer energies and spiritual end points to the human Ka. These radiant and energy structures that alter the emotions, minds, and thought streams of beings create tiers within the alluvials, creating aspect paths for personality within the alluvial channel delineations. These substances create a wavelike structure of fluctuation in energy pattern combinations within the Ajna or the coerced cognitive functions of astral energies within of the minds of humans. These energies and their patterns, combinations, and precise increments of traverse transcendence are recorded, mapped, and processed within a single dimension. These are sometimes found within the Paffarax and most often within the Mongadory.

Mongadory or Mongory can be described to humans as a library. Within this library, there are cartographic correlation of human psyches. This can be called the human synaptic mental vesicles or a psyche emulation. In fact, this is a place where all minds or a copy of the human responses are stored. The Mongadory is the single place within our construct or universe that actively collects all the minds of every living being that was ever in existence. It does so in specific ways that cannot be done in another way within all the possibilities of energy combinations within this universe.

The Mongadory is a dimension that is made of its own particular type of substrate; in this, the substrate is not matter. It is nonmatter in the sense that it cannot be acted upon and cannot be resisted. The base of the substrate spectrum of the Mongadory is not that of an energy like a mind or a spirit, but more of the idea of something that is truly inert, the effect of a thought within a mind, simply acting upon a molecule without any links or conduits to facilitate any action or motion. The idea is a spot of darkness among a backdrop of light. The darkness is not particle based; it is darkness in the sense of absence of light. This darkness cannot be acted upon by anything within its spectrum; no gravity and no forces equal no movement. Within the same parallel as the darkness, there is a void. The void is a description of a type of inert speck.

The void can be described as a reactive type of matter, which resembles a bubble. It resembles a bubble in the sense that it does not allow the surrounding constructs to enter in the same way water does not enter a bubble. If water does enter the bubble, it breaks apart. This void spectrum does not react to the darkness, which does not move. This void structure is constantly acted upon by a force that originates within the void, affording the configuration of the void, attracting other forces to its center. This void is constantly attracted to other forces, creating effects on other structures. A line moving to a center of the void creates a structure of many lines moving toward the centers. Let's call this entire configuration the structure, which is severely acted upon the darkness.

The structure energetically moves away from the darkness, resulting in the movement of the structure toward the void. The void moves away from the structure only at a specific distance, with mild increments of trembling as a result of its attracting and repelling forces. This results in a mass circuitry of movements and temporary coagulant among the void, structure, and darkness as they form larger reactant mass relationships. The movement of the void and structure's clockwork affords relationships and interactions that compound builds and resonances that residents to the summation of a particle. These particles exist within the time-distance parabolic distribution of interpolated reactions among the particle's occurrences.

The matter plane becomes aggregate similar to what we know. These three within a confined construct makes a dimension, which cannot react with ours in any way. It is immensely unperceivable. The Mongadory is one of the first-created paths within our dimension, outside of our own constructs. Within the Cesfuraedury, there are Andguarisier and Reshferthieughes, which can accommodate energy regimes. The subcategories are called the Jegreshures, the Ilechureshiers, and the Oleighuresh for which many can be used to house the various being of the universe. There are countless lesser categories of these dimensions that are ruled over and are sovereign from the larger macrosystem of governance.

The Calavary is a type of energy like a cloud, but the particles do not move in relation to each other. The particles are stationary and do not accommodate turbulence or any other form of internal movement. It is like a fire when it occurs inside the Paffarax. Fire and smoke are three detentions within its alluvial structures. The Calavary can also be a matrix of radiants, which is not energy; they are fixed in position and do not move in relation to each other. They are not completely stationary in position because of the various particles that orbit. The macrostructure itself moves in relation to these orbiting particle. They simply vibrate in very small increments, but these movements are translated to resonance frequencies within the larger structure.

They are of very specific signatures for which their relationships to their positions are precisely situated, and they are stagnant, rotating slowly toward equilibrium. This repositioning of smaller orbitals around their center causes vagaries within the energy regimes. These particle fluctuations causes perceivable and unperceivable matter variation, creating an alternating structure that mimics the alluvials of the universe. These sometimes form particles in circular motions to other ambient particles, which in timeless patterns of motions form other dimensions.

The Rhschour holds a circle of energy or radiants together. These are usually in a sequence that holds circles together. It is a series of pockets of particles, energies, or any type of conceptualization with an attractive force that are usually acting together. They usually move about thirty degrees to each other, forming a centripetal force of motion swirling constantly toward a center and expelling perpendicular to the lateral of the horizontal swirl. This forms a structure that accommodates the partial creation of spaces. Within these spaces, a slender formation of a dimension is created. These can be used to travel to different spaces in time. The sequence's roll and advances change in specific energies within the regimes. It creates movement and currents, making time waves that can be ridden by some forms of matter. These can take a person to a specific location in time without major changes into their energy regimes.

There are many particles that interplay with the swirls of the Rschour, reacting to the swirls in many ways. One such particle is the Vanscunda, which when in proximity to the Permenduis, creates an up and down movement in a mass structure of waves. This creates alluvials patterns that are similar to the Simnuclishes, a type of mind-based particle that is accelerated within the thought processes. The Simnuclishes percolate through the various alluvials and dendritics of the world. The way the particles move toward the various worlds is similar to the way the particles move in the Calavary, creating a dimension that can create the mind perception. It creates a precognition of thoughts within all beings across the entire dimension. The thoughts of a person can be received externally through the senses. The ambient releases the suspended sounds of a person's mind. These echoes burl, creating a mind's voice extrapolation that can be perceived like the reversing of a car wheel as it moves forward or the swirls of propeller.

This dimension can only be calmed by the Lexi-particles energy or Leximars. The Lex in the Lexi-particle group relates to the way the particle moves within the ambient fields. The particles usually takes an elastic fluidlike motion as they flow through the fields in an alluvial dispersion of nonlinear temporal motion. These particles are usually accompanied by an energy from an alternate dimension. These energies irradiate the particles into the range of the earth's ambient particles, creating a fresh new dimension of the verso alluvials.

The energy time shifts move in a negative distribution to the zero point from the nexus of physical perceptions. The mind in this instance reverts back to the physical state as clairvoyance. The mind mildly and sporadically echo in the directions of joyous energy as the dimension spikes to rebalance the particle wave structures. The Lexi-particles can be used to create shields for the various particles that are accelerated to dangerous velocities within the Calavary. The particles of a molecule that exits within the Calavary are met with traversing radiants from the alluvials, and a chain reaction occurs, creating a violent display of light and sound with some temperature fluctuations. These side effects could be used to various advantages but can be detrimental. The human can be fatally contaminated by radiant particles. The ambient reaction to the exiting particle could damage the cells and other parts of the matter in transit.

Leximar can be used in some areas among the Lexi-particles; they are smaller particles in sizes than the Zvestiuation and Revelutiuation particles. These can pass through many of the structures formed by the Lexi-particles. The Zvestiuation does not react with the particles of the Leximar, but they react with the Agrenthiuan particle in a way that moves southward. The Leximar reacts with the Lachaino particles in a way that diminishes its constituents and forms part of the greater

Baphorist horde of particles. They form partial dimensions of Agrea, Greadion, and some structures of Waridon. Many of these reactions to the particles form a semibarrier. The Leximar can be used like a shield for many energies, and particles cannot pass. The few things that can pass are very harmless to the internal matter molecules. These can and was used to protect many beings during the battles of the Shangri-la of Dieu.

Lexcurviur is a particle of the Lexi- particle group that can't pass through or go into the Matron. The Matron is a muon-sized particle that rains down over celestial bodies larger than earth. It was said that it does rain down on earth but in a form that is closer to antimatter rather than earth-spaced matter. It loses segments and reconstructs into smaller particles as it falls through the mesosphere. The Lexcurviur is the escutcheon of the lesser Gods; this is the particle of the Monomisa for which is the judge of the society. They fell out from the Frestution many Namimbian eras ago; they talked with the humans and eventually caused many sins upon the walk of man.

They thought they could help men, but caused many laws to fall upon them. This caused the demise, and they fell from grace. The fall of man caused many wars between many sectors among the lesser gods for which these particles were used along with many external energies to protect those that conspired against men. These particles react to each other in a synergistic way, creating an act or a scheme that is designed to create a scheme of particle movement that would create a specific reaction with the larger particles, which are the larger constituents of the Calavary regimes. These particles were tampered with and modified to be used by the gods, creating illusions within men as they are present.

These particles affect many other particles within the larger particle structures and allow for the movement of particles in a particular direction. The particles within the moving pattern flows toward the Lexcurviur, giving them power and strength in attraction as they traverse and collect more particles in this way. This relationship is a mathematical Fibonacci in relation to the moving pattern and the particles of Omensia, Kareidra, and the Reschular. These four particles can react together synergistically within a rotary structure to create a screen, excluding many other particles from passing through and along the moving structure.

These particles restructure internally and specifically to accommodate the microscale as they accumulate the external components of the restructuring rotary pattern. Many large portions are accelerated away from the moving patterns as a result of the formation of the byproducts of these interacting particles. Many of these particles are present in the various regimes and are forced to mimic other particles until they have become large enough. They eventually become impervious and sustain their own presence within the energy regimes of the spoldge alluvials.

Lexsguher particles are specifically negatively charged to most of the Lexi-particle group; these react like negatively charged magnets in close proximity to each other. These particles and those that precisely affect the larger particles in a chain of sequences causes the motions of physical and temporal change in energy regimes. This allows multidimentional travel between alluvial sequences. These particles are designed in such a way that they specifically release purses of smaller energetically modified radiants that change these larger particles precisely in such a way that the matter regime is absolutely controllable.

These particles are used to control the beings of their world, wage wars, create dimensions, and create other particles that are used to control the other variations of matter. These types of particles are in high demand and would be the basis of many wars within the Dieu. There are many particles that can be used to affect the physical ambient with little variation across the alluvials and the dimensional partitions within the universe. These particles are widely used with many variations existing and are used by the many beings of the Shangri-la.

Lexincos particles, like magnets, move in an elastic wavelike motion as they move toward each other. The motion of these particles are like water for the changes in the particles is a wavelike function in relation to their motion in a singularity of a spectrum within the multialluvial timeless structure. The pattern is like the motion of sound waves from one center to its dispersal zone, where there are many structures emanating from one particle center in a mass of time-variant conjoined structures. These motions within the matter are comparable to aggregate in fluid motion.

Spatial activity acts like pressure on the aggregate in motion, which reacts to the atmosphere like the spheres of the mind that are in consonance with the dimension's mental ambient atmosphere. The energies of the mind react like the boiling of a fluid that add pressure to the ambient, creating an exerted motion to the thoughts within the being. All thoughts add some specific types of particles to the atmosphere. The thoughts of any being can initiate motion to the wave structures, creating cycles to the matter that can be calibrated to the point of control. The particles that can be controlled are classified in specific ways by colors, spins, and compulsion.

Particle colors and change in spin can be described in color and radiations for which the radiation and the color is the internal mixture among components. The reactions are calculated specifically along the dimensions; they radiate 389 variant particles within this range. Particles that do exist outside of this range usually become part of a larger structure or disintegrate into smaller structures as the particles traverse the ambient.

Each particle can be used as a period of reference within the alluvials. If each particle is equivalent to a reference point in the time continuation, then the particles can be considered a bit. In this sense, it is used as a unit of memory or a point of reference. These particles are not allowed to fall below a level of 356 bits. The ambient allowing ability for particle immunity is hampered by the presence of the mass cumulative particles that are erosive. These particles can only agglomerate with specific combinations that are expelled from the latter mink particles of the ranges 133 to 226 of colors black to white with some pink. In the presence of erosive particles, these create excess compelling particles that reduces the imperviousness of the Lexincos particles.

These particles must be buffered by the green or orange particles in the bit ranges of 256 to 320 simultaneously, and they must move between 128 and 90 in a megalithic structure. This creates a dance-like sequence during the synchronizing of particle agglomeration and expulsion to balance the impervious ambient sequencing of the

Revelutiuation and the Mavardlian particles. The particles must be in the states of semidocile to prevent the dampening of the continued disturbances within the fields created by the presence of the Lexincos particles. Many of the variation to the Revelutiuation and the Mavardlian particles all correlate to the particle transposition radiant fields within the system. These Lexi-particles are the stitching and hinges to the doors within the universe. These can be affected to open and close the various compartments of the nexus of dendritics.

Within the circular motion of particles within the Calavary, there are five particles that move in similar motion. They move toward the direction of the Covelurty at all times. Their integrated motion in relationship to the general tone of the wider formations of the Deflagration dimension. This forms a dimension that is from an alternate reality with which many beings are partially constructed and are very similar to those in its host dimension. The beings inside are not of the same design but of a deflection of a particle that causes some construction like those of the host dimension.

The beings in the dimensions can be a hostile or friendlier version of that within the host dimension. The dimension is powered by the preceding dimension and is communicated by the same. The thoughts of the beings originate within the original dimension. The beings of the resulted dimension is not dependent on the factors that contribute to independent behaviors. The behavior within this dimensions is dependent on the particles' adhesion and reflection from the host dimension. All their behaviors originate from the original and are dependent on the links between these dimensions.

The lines of behavior between the dimensions are effected by Lexincos for which the beings are varied in demeanor. Alluvials of these dimensions are communicated across sine principles and particle intrusion, which are restricted by percolating frequency pulses. The particles move together parallel in a structure that coherently and simultaneously coagulates to create a parallel structure of alluvials that are the reflections of the host dimensions. These reflections are perpetuated among the dimensions, creating increased particle acceleration and ambient energy. These structures are the union between two circular forces, creating energy gradients or valleys on both sides of the formation of wave pulses of the cohesion between adjacent dimensions.

Columenisitionerray is another dimension that is of many of the correlated particles from the mass association of particles in the universe. It is a stationary structure of particles that creates a smokelike existence of a universe that is coexisting with the various rooms within the universe. The smoke is the presence of a Vangurthian that originates from the interaction of an Arutheaian. This exists within the interrelationships between many of the Lexi-particle's constituents as it is within the Calavary. This creates a geometrical pattern of equidistant particles that form a container for which the Columenisitionerray resides. The Columenisitionerray universe resides in a Moiré of covillatry rotary particle action. These interrelated particles spiral throughout the various rooms, affecting the various particles, creating an interacting web of reactions. This structure of interacting particles affect the particle's color and rotation, equaling to what can be called temperature. This action creates multidimensional coherence among these particles. The rooms created are not superior or inferior to each other.

These particles precipitate out from their room, expanding and creating the various tendons that actuate the dimensional crevices, allowing homeostasis within the Frestution. The interrelationship is dependent on Vangurthian presence in a semibonded state within the Mavardlian particle that behaves in a similar way to the Reschular. The Columenisitionerray particles are often of the colors of black to heated orange and usually expels an array of the Tendurouse particles. These creates a blast of white particles that quickly thickens and causes adhesion to the other particles. This action alters the behaviors and restructures the particles, causing increased pressurization. The formation of the particles are based on the latter versus the heated particles as they initiate adhesion to the formation of dormant alluvials. This particle formation flows and becomes a viscous and hydro scene.

The compository is made up of five particles; these particles are also made up of five particles. These particles are made of specific constituents that move in precise sequences in relation to each other. This creates a cyclical circular motion of matter within the intrinsic aggregate fields. These particles are mainly used to create beings that are able to traverse the dark fabrics. These beings have the abilities to utilize the many different changing colors of particles that are used by the compository. These beings are the men under the bridge from the fallen fences of Gurtheolem. They can be considered like the dead humans that have become daemons.

The particles used by these beings are one of the most stable particles in the universe. The particles are created and designed by the Gurtheolem of the clans of the circular flows within the upper reaches of the alluvials. The structure of these particles afford a circle uniformity of radiants that synchronizes the spins. This causes the macrostructure to roll, resulting in a cumulative circular production of force that agglomerates to specific bit and colors of ambient particles as they pass through the walls of the alluvials. Their resonance frequencies are increased as they approach and exit the walls of the various dendritics in multidimensional alluvials of the universe.

The Viskatearry is very similar to light energy. In conventional thinking, light was considered to be pure energy, but in fact, there is a constituent that is integral to the light energy that is the photon. The ability to see light is based on its movement or velocities. The Viskatearry is similar in the same way because of the lines that move in a very straight path and do not ever touch. The trajectory changes allow the regime's energy changes; this creates nonparallel movement within the alluvials. Other paths from alluvials cross dimensions and temporal delineations and change the macrostructure of the parallel patterns.

This creates a backdrop of particles as they move toward other dimensions. These particles are carried and varied along the interactions of the lines. They eventually collide, creating the mass energy fluctuations that transforms the matter and energize the particles. These energized particles constitute an energy regime affording a dimension. This dimension causes the blurring of lines that accentuate delineations between alluvials and dendritics. This can be a powerful place but can also lead to a lot of destruction. The power of the collisions created energy regimes and dimensions that contain pure energy. These energy regimes cannot be tamed but can be avoided if one knows the specifics of the angles of divergence within the pattern of lines from the original axis. There is a lot of power to be harnessed within these dimensions.

Brijuik is a wake of an energy that has already vanished; it is the stitching among the alluvials and are the formations of tubes between traverses among alluvials. These hold tunnels through the structures together and cement the crevices between the worlds. The effects of the Brijuik create worlds for other beings; these beings are within all rooms inside our universe. They correlate to the particles and various formations of the universe. The particles react in a semipeculiar way to the rooms and the patterns within the fabric of matter, creating a motif and paradigm wefts of systematical regimes. These greatly affect the frameworks for multidirectional particle flow, causing fluctuations within perception and operandi.

The alluvial phenomena displays a characteristic propensity away from morphology and toward criteria, mapping the behavioral patterns of schematic inclination for succession and from the variations in radiants. The tones of graphical modifications to the particle intrusion displays a tendency toward betterment of the beings. The particles within the Brijuik wake are in a congruent relationship between the Lexsguther and the Feisturode, which can only be undertowed by the Vangurthian Leximar particle combination.

The congruence of permutation for the platonic solid formations balance the quadrants of polyhedral structures. This forms disintegrating energy regime from the hexnominal flow of the five particles as they accumulate to create a triangle structure across angles of near obtuse to equilateral. Increased particle affinity replicates the structure to form a mass of superheated particle flows or an elastic fluid. The heat affects all the particles in a nominal infinitesimal function across all percolating platforms. This is usually induced by direct infiltration of particles or of resonance frequencies of action and inaction. This affects the direction of the network of particle substructural flows from one dimension to the next, stimulating the lattice structure of pathways to the compiling hexnominal structures. This can be compared to the principles of crystallography. These flows cause the radiation of corrosive Arutheaian particles, which could cause many fractures and openings within the energy regimes, causing matter adhesion to the alternate dimensions.

Furgurose energy is relatively indistinguishable when in a field of Leximar particles. They usually form a lattice structure with small openings that could cause the transcendence of many particles. These particles crystallizes within the presence of corrugated Lexincos particles, which are transforming into the Plusmonicular state of particle agitation. These superreactive particles to photons and temporal fibril matter oxidize and eclipse the Frestution voids. These are contaminated by the radiants from the Lexincos Plusmonicular particle states, creating the detonation of all particles in the crystalline structure. These are reduced to accelerated helix structure that behaves in a semiviscous corrosive structure that can dissolve all life and tensile in the crenellations of the cantilever of geometric crystals, which form a restructure of particle sequences that can be related to a binomial relationship between two constituent dimensions. The emanating particles result from the basis for which all the aggregate stands on.

The mortise of the matter space inside creates a special anomaly. The Furgurose energy created a reliant structure of matter that reacts to the Vexilamar and the Comestude, resulting in a hexnominal structure relating to five-particle adjacent dimensions. They are stabilized base structure and emanates particles of Lemnar and Vescunda. The formations are noncomponents of the multiverse and are dependent on the changes in the Furgurose energy. Its accumulation can be described as a progression in the number of particles that agglomerate into the larger matter structures, affording changes in sequence. This particle absorption relationship sequence determines the growth rate of the helix structures. These particles all compile together to simulate the effects of Paffaraxal energies that form the Paffarax dimension, which is very stable and is very difficult to affect since it is based on an infinite number of member particles and pattern donors.

Interaction sequences of the Zvestiuation, Lachaino, Omensia, Tendurouse, and Vescunda particles create a mixed effect of fluctuations within a pendulum permutation from corrosive actions to the release of radiant forces and nonconstricting concentrations of reacting particles.

These create deliberate effects on the macroparticle structures when induced a semiactivated version of the Lexi-particles. These effects are restricted to the dimensional aggregate. The alter dimensions that are created transform states of matter into a cyclical motion. The factors that affect the matter transformations and particle acceleration spinor transforms the alternate alluvials and dendritics.

This creates reciprocated dendritic presence fluctuations along the lines of interpolated gradients of the tensor deviations. This immensely affects the plane of existence and energy regimes delineating the present collective cognitive experience. The infinite series and functions associated with the movement of the collective cognitive experience of the present are the productions of the homogeneity of the patterns within the particle's collision and deflected trajectories and planes of reflection. This creates the latter roadways and cells that constitute many of the dimensions and alluvials within the Calavary. The mixing of radiants from the Calavary all interact to create a dynastic regime of collectibles of matter formations constituting all known presence in time and space simultaneously.

These matter types are the refuge of the single presence in the collective time cognizance. The emulative particle associates the past and future cognitive in perception; these are the particles used in predictions within the dimensions of the Calavary. These can be perpetuated with the Lemnar particles to an anchor, the Verosiunom forms of modification of foresight. Verosiunom modified particles have already been used to stabilize the alternate dendritics and dimensions removing the excess particles. This balances the particle integration and conjoint of alterations along the gradient of perspective and conscience in the particle-accelerated resonance.

These patterns created can be used to create modifications for bodies and dimensions with the ability to affect and alter regimes of the Omensia and the Vanscunda particles. They can cross many dimensions and can affect the particles of the Dragnma. The Dragnma can cross all dimensions in the latter to middle portions formed within the universe. These energies are usually bonded to particles and each other to form the various types of matter. They can be very dangerous and are the Holy Grail of the wars of the systems.

The Paffarax is a parallax of parallel dimensions. It is another dimension of particles unlike time. A lot like fire, it is the synchronized with the horizontal and tandem flaking of the parallel dimensions that anchors the gravity or base particle direction. These are equal to or nearly equivalent to the commensuration of the total symmetry of the corresponding particle agglomeration. This forms a dimension called the Paffarax. The Paffarax is an alternate of parallels in the simultaneous duplication of parallax existence of realities. These combined creates an epicenters for resonance of replicates of all the realities within the divergent affinities from the anchors of the dimensions. All the dimensions and alluvials within the Paffarax are anchored simultaneously at angled trajectories to the horizontal commensuration of the total symmetry of the flow of the larger particle agglomerations.

The Rschour all contribute coefficients and particle confluence, which creates its own structure and energy regime that slightly pulses. The pulses-caused regime induces particle simulation that creates its own regime chain and anchor conduits, making a mueonopolle of dimensions. The Fievesturode, the Fievestornod, and the Fiestnormeed are various alternatives in color and movement for which they possess many orbiting particles. These are not present within the voids of light and Spectrumite, orbiting the particles from the Vexilimnar, Leximar, the Vanscunda, and the Simnuclishes.

Osmordhileia, Surmerdhilia, Carfrensdia, Berthieldhia, and Freindghurilia are the main orbital within the Rschour that react to create regimes within the parallax of dimensions adjacent to the Paffarax. This creates five distinguishing dimensions for which each dimension has a nexus of nexuses of realities. These range from Parallax dimensions to coinciding dimensions. Parallax dimensions are different from other dimensions because of mental views, where coinciding dimensions are the same because of very precise increments of particle similarities.

A prism is formed from the particle adhesion of realities and dimensions magnifying the alluvials and dendritics that distribute the realities of shifting geoid surfaces. This creates a refractive index of land spaces spanning across the matter distribution. A flow space is created for particles that shift alternatively across diagonals of distribution. This intermittently dispensing energies influence personalities as it distributes particles that affect the geoid space in a trinomial manner. These geoid spaces are created through the rotation and evolution of Zvestiuation particles. The formation curves of divergence causes charging variations that accommodates agglomeration with the Lexi-particle and Vangurthian particle formations that stimulate the adjacent affinities.

The tunnel ways created through the voids are created and filled with rare particle formations that eventually form usual matter spaces. They simultaneously move in combinations of dextrorotary and levorotatory from the static position of the nucleus of existence. This is usually centered in perception around one's cornerstone for perception as one enters the Paffarax. Accessing the alter parallels of perceptions are based on the incandescence of the Vangurthian, Arutheanian, and Tendurouse particles that are channeled through and around the presence of the Viskatenarinan particles. These are usually the first and third orbitals of the nucleus and can erode the perceptive particles of external dimensions.

CHAPTER 3

The Landscape of Their Home

Within the universe, there are many partitions that can constitute rooms for which a room is not time or space in the conventional sense. Time can be perceived as dendritic within a river, but many beings perceive time as a linear continuum. Their space becomes an instrument that is acted upon by multidimensional energy regimes. Every choice fosters a tributary; a split in time makes the fabrics of mitosis adhesive. This multidimensional time-constant variable coagulates with the various waves that abscond the structures of the being's existence. Time movement unlike spatial movement cannot be easily afforded for them.

These beings live within different facets and structures that are afforded by the different effects of particle interactions. The beings are made of different things; humans are made of atoms, which are made of particles in an orbital pattern. There are many types of matter that coexist with atoms but not affected entirely by the presence of atoms. They are made of many types of reactive matter that do not constitute atoms in the conventional way. The other existing matter or energy variants are interlinking in a relativistic array of energy variants. This translates to beings in the same places but never perceived by each other. In the sphere of perception, they are not in the same place; the same is said for the various dendritics of time. Time and place is and is not the same in this instance, for time and place are results of perception and the mind's functions.

These beings live in a place where there are trillions of solar systems, galaxies, and nebulas. They are not machinery dependent; they can apply themselves to their environments physically. They can cross dimensions and interact with the many types matter that make up the universe. They can change the matter and alternatively the energy types of all Nefectries of this universe. They are timeless beings for time is not of their cognitive function but within their physical anatomy. There is no past or future; they can be described as always being in the present.

Time is omnispective; perceiving all within energy regimes simultaneously irradiates the notions of past and future. They live in an omnipresence of reality where there is no suffering, needs, mistakes, discomfort, or accidents. They are always prepared or rather always in the present of all occurrences about their reality. In this, they experience all simultaneously; nothing cannot be changed. This affords the deterioration of concepts pertaining to empathy, patience, benevolence, acumen, possession, affection, dependability, equitability, and serendipity; everything and everyone becomes transparent. All particles in motion that control their thoughts and ideas are in perfect synchronization. The energy sequences and cosynchronization of beings are like gears at the event of their interactions. They simultaneously maneuver the alluvials of their interactions. They see and know all that happiness before it happens in that they cannot lie or convince anyone. Their worlds are very fragile along the social structures and connotations associated with their norms; behavior is paramount.

The social interactions of timeless beings is a complex one. Social learning is vast and accelerated in comparison to human beings. Observation is not only limited to sight for observation is also acquisition. If one can see something in time, they have already experienced it; they have already experienced that point in time. Time is place, and the mitosis of responses are the relationships in time. This is displayed across the alluvials and are dependent on one's ability to expand on their rational and cognitive functions. The distribution of their behavioral traits are elastic for the mitosis of their behavior is experienced in the third person from a perspective point of view. This is a cause of a lot of concepts that grow within the subconscious of these beings, resulting in deep-rooted aggressions influencing their abilities.

With all of their abilities, they are allowed to capture and utilize the beings of the latent Nefectries. They can or are allowed to harness the powers of all types of matter and energies that exist inside our universe. This ability affords the reincarnation of their captured prized beings. They are superpowerful to the being, and this power has afforded a culture that is subjugating and enslaving of lesser beings, especially toward human beings and animals. Within their ways and laws affording their culture, they consider the human to be an incomplete scrip of verses within life; they are one line among the summation of all the beings that exists. To them, the human being needs to be guided.

To them, the human being is an incomplete being that cannot generally help himself. Within the vast oceans of existence, humans need to be taken care of. They need to follow and learn from a source that knows the inner working of the wider spectrum. This is just one article in their philosophy among many others delineating the appropriation of human behavior. Another philosophical delineation is that all men must serve a god for which the souls of all men belong to those that are of power. The lives of men must follow their natural cycles for serving a god must be a part of their diurnal routine. These and some of the laws within their constituency afford the expulsion or deaths of millions of human beings annually. The mass influx of collected beings across all systems results in an ever-growing population of a few trillion a day.

With the high demand for the dead, their laws are centered around the collection schemes from planets like ours. The royals, the business owners, and the judges within this system would pay high prices for a human or animal souls among other parts from the systems. The economy is vast, and its vastness is its flaw; it is very fragile. One shift in belief, which is not a shift in the belief in God but in social morals, could result in losses beyond compare. The laws of collection are eccentric surrounding land occupation and fields of movement. With methods of demise and choice of spouse, the offspring is accounted for or collected by ruling or presiding facet of the economy.

It duly determines where a being might be placed or the price they might go for. Another factor is the state of the mind upon demise, for which reclamation practices can be applied for a fee. Ideally, the collection of spirits, souls, memories, and kundalinis and parts of our mind are high-valued products within all cities of their civilization. The prices are dependent on availability of the disposition or moral structure or the city for which a being would be sold to. The availability of moral structure on earth is very dependent on what happens within the societies on earth; the economic distribution on earth has shifted vastly within the last eight hundred years.

The exploration of the West by Christopher Columbus has resulted in a population rise, the distribution of human alliances, which has shifted education in a direction outside of the favor for the royals. This accommodated the explosion of egocentrically inclined humans, which dominate their markets. This thought pattern is now dominating Africa, the Middle East, and Asia, resulting in losses by the billions. This was said to be a big problem. These modern personality types are not desired by the royals. Ideally honest and authority-honoring individuals are in high demand and are conventionally favored. These types of contemporary, sophisticated, educated professionals are sold to the middle-class cities. The demand has grown considerably and caused inflation in conventional God-fearing routine devotees. Some business owners seek to shift the delta in their favor; the collecting of soldiers, gangsters, and serial killers have risen. This caused an induction of many of these types of personalities, which would fetch a hefty price.

The royals are not pleased with the collecting schemes and the personality types that have been afforded to grow within the system. They have enforced new laws on the system, which would change the social climates of the worlds to accommodate more devotee-oriented beings across the systems. This has resulted in mass trembling of the royals that could gain favor in the other courts across the board. The board of trustees have linked their good favors to their vindicators and bailed out the arbitrators and sovereign nations, leaving the systems because of the entanglement that was to come.

The royals usually dominate the markets, and as the balance shifts, their stature in the society also shifts, resulting in the favor of the markets being passed to a successive group. The business owners and the large underworld groups can now have a chance to rule. The shift on earth and the restructuring of some systems have caused many downstream effects on the wider economy. The restructuring of the human lifestyles and well-being has caused collection delays and the procurement of alternative cognitive traits; this is an attempt to accommodate for the reduction in mind types.

This has caused major upheavals within their society for which these must be rectified; it has been pinpointed to the single cause, the internet. With the advent of the internet, man's trajectory has shifted more than ninety degrees toward knowledge and information center, which has spawned a global revolution of self-absorption and egocentrism. The birth of the cellular telephone has exacerbated this information influx effect. Information on the go gives a human being everything he or she could want at the touch of a button in the palm of their hands. Human innovation has changed the way the collection businesses have worked. The poorer classes of beings now have the advantages in the laws. It has been blatantly described as a wreck. Human being are quickly becoming knowledge-absorbing sponges that are fascinated by the facts surrounding their daily lives. The technologies of human beings are centered around the idea of making their lives easier, creating a mass subliminal movement for laziness and procrastination. These trends are quickly becoming a technology-hogging status quo of the privileged sectors within society while simultaneously creating a vast amount of technological waste that fills the ponds in the minds of the ecoconscious citizens, creating mass concerns and paranoia for the global environmental health.

The knowledge needed to advance and alter existing technologies are at the push of a button to anyone who has access to the internet. The information age cannot be stopped or hampered from orders within their courts for there are laws against the reduction of the human population. Man's population greatly depends on his lifestyle; removing or the internet would compromise the economic growth of the system.

This is more than just a problem for the ruling classes. This can cause the destruction of many cities due to a reshift in the balance of the distribution patterns of the human societies. This reshift could and have already caused wars over this productive resource. Many have died, and many beings have already been confiscated and remade to new families; the industry for used beings has taken off and is greatly invested upon.

Human beings upon their deaths are collected by the owners of the presiding religious sector, for which they are remade in the likeness of their god or leader. They are usually made with slight alterations to the human figure. The cities they are taken to are usually those that require workers and are populous. Some individuals within those cities require friends; these individuals are those who are of highborn lineage but are of low ranking. They usually wish to embellish themselves with the souls of men. Of the specialty orders, the lovers and soulmates are the precious of the collected beings. These are usually the men, women, and children who are remade into aesthetically pleasing figures. Their minds are to be reclaimed to be the devout lover of an individual that executes the wishes over their inamorata without question and with enjoyment for as long as their inamorata would have them.

The people who are usually chosen for this are people who live solitary lives, with little or no lovers for long periods of time. The most expensive and sought after are the adult virgins. They are considered the purest among all the categories of people who become inamorata. This person who is to become inamorata, under the jurisdiction of sex segregation, are under strict laws of behavior and conduct. These laws state that the inamorato has the right to do whatever he or she pleases with the inamorata. The inamorato is absolutely responsible for the actions of the inamorata. This is especially true for homosexuals and teenage girls who die before maturity. It is a well-developed industry, for which many years of history and culture have afforded the prudish nature of their laws, especially in areas of divorce, mind reclamation, and the reconstruction of a beloved being. It is not uncommon for a reincarnated human to search the earth for a soul mate; many people who feel or believe there is a soul mate for them are usually right. The soul mate is either in another system or on earth.

There are many beings in this universe who pair up humans in an attempt to dampen the industry of inamorata collection because of misconduct, abuse, and even in some cases slavery. Many of those who wish to expand on the inamorata industry induce ideas of cheating and sexual addiction, as well as low self-esteem and nonbelief in love. Most humans in their midtwenties change their mind-sets toward love and the way they choose a mate. Among those are the true hearted; those that would become soul mates are those that think of the afterlife with their spouse. It is not in the favor of the collected being to be chosen as an inamorata; the situation for the contemporary inamorata has become closer to slavery.

A soul mate is a mate for life for which it is rare to survive or escape. It is wisest to transcend to the afterlife with a soul mate. The industry has become like a conscientious loop of extravagance. In fact, it is a complex social circuitry of servitude to your allotted inamorato, which is bolstered by the appeal of good looks and grandeur as one is adorned with status and wealth. The patrons of these schemes often proclaimed this as the beauty within all the worlds, just the same as existence is the purpose of the universe. There are often large public hearings and meetings held to proclaim and celebrate the joys and beauties of their purpose and the endeavor of knowing the true meaning of love from the creators of the creators.

CHAPTER 4

The World as They Know It

Its purpose is to change the future of man; its plan is to create a world war, burning earth's major cities to the ground, destroying all technology that would afford the distraction of man. The execution of many coupled with the selection of humbled religious people would allow the right changes in cultural trajectories that would not cause humans to fall. Their behaviors would not cause the in application of the collectibles in the law; all of mankind would no longer be collected by the lesser beings among the schemes. The destruction of the guiders, belonging to the other collectors, who influence or inspire men to do the work of executing his desires is needed. The other cities of collection are the influencers of men, resulting in their change in behavior. It is said that man has to be destroyed for their ways have become sinful and disgusting in the sight of the gods. It has come to destroy the world through the inventions man has measured himself against.

This war has already begun, World War III; it is called the Fall of Man. All of mankind is unaware that this being is upon them. The only hint that can spell this was World War II and its intended demise of the Jews. For they were a religious kind, under an ancient royal city. World War I was about the declaration of land between the rulers of the German and French collection cities, in which there were many disputes about collection among those groups. Even the demise of the French royalty and German chancellors were surrounding the fragility of the laws of the collection schemes associated with that area.

The intention of this war is to induce separation of powers within the chambers of commerce by splitting the human bloodlines that occupy the lands, ideally induced racism and classism. Mixed lines cause entanglement within the law, which leads to appeasement in collection. In the beginnings of their wars, a declaration must be stated, for which the details surrounding the duration, psychological angles, appropriation of the land destruction, and the pruning of the lines. If the war was agreed upon by both cities, the field operators are to be informed. This is followed by the setting of the stage psychologically, which allows for integrity and balance at the beginning of the war. To us, the war has begun because of two leaders who cannot settle their differences within peaceful grounds. Usually, we place blame on a particular side; our justification exactly reflects this. To them, it is a procedure in law that reduces bureaucratic clutter and blockage that allow free movement of collection of souls.

The Roman Empire of the first and second centuries were one of the expansions and one of the already notable-sized cities, which was a sovereignty that was illegal in the courts. The Roman Empire expanded to almost all of modern Europe and to most of North Africa, which they colonized and civilized the people along the lines within a specific culture. This was a travesty within the laws; the royal family responsible for the Romans said they were within the lines of the laws of willful creative fulfilment, meaning it was the desires of the human beings.

The collection cities for the aboriginal European settlers were somewhat penny pitched and agreed to temporarily accept the Roman influx of culture and technological advancement. The reward or incentive of an increased population was satisfactory, but the laws of maximum allowable population for land size had to be fringed legally. This could not be avoided so a war was decided upon; this would allow increased collection until the due date for the application of the removal of the Roman influence on the collection regulations.

This meant that if the humans remain of a purely Roman-controlled religion, they would now have to be legally collected by the Roman royal cities. The maximum allowable period for the infringement of land occupation was 1,000 system years. This gave the humans enough time to relocate and readjust while emotionally erasing the effects of the incidents surrounding the relocation or removal. The beginning of the fall of the Roman Empire was the nearing of the due date for the application of the law, for the removal of the Dieu Roman royal's city on the aboriginal European and African human cities. The first were the Ferderatti cities and the Latini tribe people who attack the Roman municipalities, sacking the emperor.

This carried on for the next 800 years until the sacking of Siegfried, the Danish king who abruptly died in the fall months of 798, who was later succeeded by King Gufford. King Gufford was killed by a nobleman over his wife in 810; he was replaced by King Hemming in the same year. In December of 800, the Roman Empire ensured a new emperor, an emperor that would ensure the reclamation of the old Roman Empire, Emperor Charlemagne. Charlemagne was the son of Pepin who was the first of the kind to become king.

Upon his father's mysterious death, Charlemagne and his brother Carloman ruled together until his brother died mysteriously within the castle walls, and he became the absolute ruler. He continued his crusades against the many fighting posts of the Roman Empire factions, for which many succumbed to his rule. As the annexed emperor of the Holy Roman Empire, as it came together, he brought the law of the Roman system upon the people. They could not marry without their lord's consent, and children were not allowed to perform their own tasks without the lord's removal of bondage. Peasant status remained hereditary; he induced hard physical punishment on the peasants, and they were owned by the lords. Because of their lords, slaves were jealous of the peasant's status. This caused the introduction of imperial authorities that resulted in changes, which were generally in the direction of ecclesiastic Bible religions.

Charlemagne was viewed as the father of Europe because of his endeavors to reclaim the broken cities of the old Roman Empire. The

Eastern Orthodox Church viewed him a hetero-orthodox because he recognized the pope and the Roman Empire and not Athens Byzantine Empire. His address was not greatly received by the countrymen, resulting in even more wars and disgust for the Roman churches. The treaty of Heiligen, was signed by the Danish king Hemming and Charlemagne in 810, delineating the boundaries of the Danish sovereign to the edges of the Eider River. King Hemming was killed in 812 by the noblemen of his country, and Charlemagne was killed in 814. This marked the beginning of the end of the Roman Empire, as the Roman royal city within the Dieu must release their rights to collect souls of the aboriginal lines of the European regions.

Pope Leo III was the sole conspirator of these assassinations; this would shape the future of Europe for all time, ensuring that all of Europe would rule the world. This was to be short-lived since there was no law to accommodate the Roman Empire in its legal jurisdiction. Rome had to fall; his renaissance revitalized the true Roman culture of the Western churches. That incident on earth led to the murder of Princess Anatelli by the orator for the Roman royal imperial cities. The lower courts of adjudicators were weakened by the abundance of investments within their collection schemes; this was the beginning of the great war of the second royals.

The royals ruling the Danish Empire were concerned about the legitimacy of claims over lines that were of the then diminishing Holy Roman Empire. Their claim was that most of the people under the empire came from the Lithuanian origin and cities more than twenty thousand years ago. The lines that the Romans conquered were belonged to the Danish and Polish sectors of that city within the Dieu. These were heavily protested by their royals in charge over the Roman invasions. The declaration was displayed to the wider Dieu population and the Danish royals, who stated that the proclamation was to be litigated by the courts of avail. This matter was to be discussed, the question of what was to be done to the remaining installments of the Roman lines within the cities. The Roman royals declined, claiming to sack the cities and erase the lines, which was the best course of action. This plan was followed without dispute because of acts of willful perseverance, which in civil disobedience would alleviate an indifferent disposition in part of the later collection litigation hearings.

The lead up to the French Revolution was the beginning of the removal of the remaining aristocrats of the Roman Empire's bloodlines. The House of Capet in France ruled the region from 987 to 1328, for which Louis VII was marked as the beginning of the reclamation of the European lands from the previous owners. This was ungratefully received by the collection under the Roman royal cities of the Dieu. Thus, the House of Carpet was sacked with the death of Charles IV. This led to a hundred years of war in the human world and an overturn of laws of many cities that would lead to the French House of Bourbon and the House of Valois among others to lose the existence of their male lines.

There was a major restructure of the human lines from the end of the Italian war of 1499 where Louis XII was to sire the lines of Milan and Naples, which was rejected by the female royals under the Roman royals of collection in the Dieu. This led to a personal agreement outside the touch of the courts, to sack the lines of Florence and France. This was the beginning of a secret illegal pact that would be considered misconduct in courts of law within the general court of the royals. This was the beginning of the War of the Leagues of Cambrai.

In 1559, Henry II ended the Italian war with France, England, Spain, Austria, Sardinia, Naples, and Sicily. The treaties that were signed afford the presence of French troops to remain in Italy, resulting in the mixing of the lines that were present in the Italian country. This was a sack of schemes for the various collection cities under the Roman royals' courtship to the French cities of collection. As a result, Henry II was killed in 1559; his successor Francis II was killed in 1560. Charles IX took the throne, and the collection cities under the religious teaching court of the Act of Acton took action, gaining control of the Italian council within the human hierarchy, resulting in the French religious wars, ideally the Massacre of Vassay, which led to the death of many nobles within the houses. By the time the St. Bartholomew's Day massacre occurred, the religious teaching court was tired, and their willingness to change the situation of the land occupation of the cities within Europe had dwindled.

The Roman royals tried to breed out the Protestant by the marriage of Margaret of Valois and Henry of Navarre, which would immediately reinstate the strength of the collection claims to line aristocracy. The hand of Margaret of Valois to Henry of Navarre was signature for the union of all Protestants to marry back into the lines of the churches. The St. Bartholomew's Day massacre was a low-handed trick by a rival city under the court of Deceivership Tactics, which was a foreign council for collection. They killed and harvested many souls from the Huguenots. Charles IX ordered a siege on the city, which resulted in the deaths of thousands until the signing of the Edict of Pacification of Boulogne and the Peace of La Rochelle. Charles IX was executed in fine style by the assassins under the pope in 1574 by the inducing of tuberculosis.

The Roman royals of the Dieu attempted to provoke the law by openly stating their rights to claim and collect souls through the laws of collection associated with the rights to lineage. They too had rights to collect the souls of the lines of the Huguenots, but were met with fierce objection by the courts under the religious teaching sectors. The religious wars of France was declared to be over by 1598, but this was far from true; the court of religious teachings was discontent with the actions of the Roman royal cities and their address to the laws of land occupation and population. They further induced wars throughout the Holy Roman Empire. The Thirty Years' War was the foundation of a catapult that would send mankind into a state of repeal, removing the legitimacy of the claims of the Roman royal cities to the throne of claim over the lines from the Holy Roman Empire.

Almost all of Europe went into a state of disrepute against the Catholic Church. The bulk of the fallout was under the jurisdiction of the royals of Denmark who were the original collectors from the lines of Lithuania. The citizens of the Holy Roman Empire, Prague, Austria, Hungary, and Poland demonstrated disdain for decisions by the church, creating wars against Catholicizing of the people. This war officially ended in 1648 with records of little resistance from the

Protestant movements, but was heavily resisted in Prague, Poland, Nitra, and Bratislava up until the 1720s. The wealthiest collection schemes were of the religious signs groups and who were too displeased by the domination of the churches by the Roman royals. The houses of Hungary elected a new Habsburg to bring peace to all of Hungary and later detached themselves from the Holy Roman Empire entirely. This spawned disgust for the royals of Denmark for they preceded the law and cast the afterbirth of responsibility to the royals of the Romans to clean up their messes.

The Roman cities under the royals soon manipulated the minds of the aristocrats in France in an attempt to take back the people from being freed from subversion to their king, resulting in France and other countries, invading lands belonging to the Danish royal's cities, killing millions by 1720. The court of the religious teachings implemented acts of famine and the poisoning of water throughout Europe. This exacerbated the wars and drew disgust for the thrones. Alternate philosophies spread teaching and inspired the people while instilling discontent, which drew animosity among its people, frustrating them to rebel.

The Roman royal cities controlled the minds of the Spanish and instigated the war of the Quadruple Alliance. The collection cities of Spain were not involved or disputing the legitimacy of collection of the Spanish people, with regards to Roman or aboriginal bloodlines. The Roman royals needed help. The Spanish armies would take Sicily and Sardinia in 1718, which led to a powerful treaty among George I of Britain and Louis XV of France, but it was said that the treaty was with the French Peacongh, William IV of the Dutch republic and Emperor Charles VI of Austria. It was said that the treaty was partly a lie since there were many Italian nationals that were not mentioned.

The 1720s was cast in a war in Middle and Eastern Europe. The land exploded with violence, resulting in the overturn of houses and growing disgust for the thrones. This was an attempt by the court of religious teachings to initiate the removal of the remnants of the Holy Roman Empire within the cities belonging to the Danish royals. The Roman royals in the Dieu restructured their aristocrats and their thrones with the war for Austrian succession. This war forced the court of religious teachings to operate outside of what is now known to be Belgium and Austria. Louis XV endeavored to take the Austrian Netherlands and was successful. Violence spiraled through the cities, forcing many to relocate. The French armies sacked Ghent, Oudenaarde, Dendermonde, and Ostend.

The war took siege with the intention to invade Liearge, pushing the rebellious forces west, farther into the Holy Roman Empire while taking parts of the Austrian Netherlands. Charles XVI of Austria was killed in 1740, leaving his daughter, Archduchess Maria Theresa, the heir to the throne; but she could not proceed to the throne because of Salic law, which forbid royal inheritance by a woman. This was an upheaval for the Roman royals and their allies since Austrian law was not fully a part of the empire of the Roman royal's schemes for collection. The court for religious teachings could only use this to their advantage and help press the issue of a woman ruling on the throne. There were some rebellions in France and the southern states of the Holy Roman Empire to her rule; she took the throne in 1748 for which France was already on the warpath with Austria. The Roman royals were regaining strength in Europe, but this was illegal and was in poor strategy to discuss the legality at the present time because of the operation.

In 1760, the Seven Years' War had already started. The court of religious teachings was already on the move to remove the monarchy and the implementation of a better and more socially acceptable system. The Roman royals were already on the move to building a unified Europe that would conquer the entire world. The wars in the New World were already on the way. The Spanish-American War, the Palmares war, the Guarani war, and the so-called Fantastic war, which signified the breakup of Spain to Portugal and was temporarily in the form of a gesture to the new court of issues, which were already shaping the New World. The world was to become the cultural likeness to the descendants of Rome.

The cities under the Roman royals were seemingly not giving up the lands and people occupying Europe, meaning the law of Septerio Nemacade was to gain effect, which shifts the balance of rights to claim out of the grasps of the Roman royals in the Dieu. Charles Edward, steward of the Jacobite rebellion in 1745, began as a letter to the Roman royal's court, who was the son of King James, for which they already accepted the James Durian letter or the James Bible, meaning they were no longer accepting the Roman ideological God within their collection schemes. The rebellion signified the retake of the people to that of their original God structures. Charles Edward Stewart and the rest of Scotland was of the Icelandic bloodlines that originated in Lithuania through Northern Norway and Finland. The Roman royals ended with claims from their nobles conquering Lithuania. James Francis Edward Stuart passed away in 1766 by the hands of their god as a full stop to the dialogue.

The war for Polish succession had already been on the way, meaning that the Danish royals were of the intention to use the law of Valkurin Valdermis or fight for the right of the people. The so-called Seven Years' War stretched across Asia and the Pacific, pushing the issue among the Roman and Danish royals to a courtwide debate among all stakeholders within the system. As the Iberian nations of Europe were at siege with the tribe of the Native Americans, a halt in the Holy Roman Empire had to be begun. The religious teaching court had to be ameliorated to be in the correct stance to state claims against the conquests that were launched by the court of the Roman royals. This is now a global issue, an issue for all that operates on the system, those of the courts and those of the freestanding schemes.

This was a great help for the royals of the Danish court because it was already noted that the Roman courts were of the begrudging stance within the laws of collection. The spreading of the Roman line was their claim to collection through the laws of city building and beloved collections. The sacking of tribespeople can only be overshadowed in correct stance by the collection of a royal for personal and emotional satisfaction. The war for Polish succession was a long-standing letter, a piece of enactment that constitutes articles of law in a series that would pertain to larger acts of law. These laws require or demand specific behaviors in action to be recognized by the emperors of the larger kingdoms. The situation has now been forwarded to a higher court of the Areopagus.

The letter was complex in which the treaty of Vienna was irremovably linked to the consort of Vienna, for which the treaty of Vienna was one of the last major pieces of law documents that was to be written in Latin. This marked the end of the use of the Romans' original language. The Polish king Stanislaw Leszczynski renounced his throne, acknowledging Augustus III as king. Augustus III was of some Saxon blood for which Leszczynski was the same, but he was representative of the first Lithuanian lines, meaning that the Romans have drowned the original lines of the regions.

The name given to Leszczynski was Stanislaw, or in Polish Stanislavic, meaning "man of good faith," for which he gave up his throne, silently asking the Roman royal cities if they should give up the throne of rights to collect their beings. Leszczynski was given the duchy of Lorraine as compensation for his removal from his throne. He too, like James Francis Edward Stuart, was killed in 1766, for which the duchy was awarded to France in honor, a betrayal within the courts under the emperor of Salzhear. The French under the Roman royals wrote a letter in Spanish by sacking the remainder of Polish guards in 1798, meaning the death of their hope. Poland gave up Livonia, which was their last statement to the Roman royals. They immediately left; Poland became largely influenced by the Russian territories.

The duchy of Italy requested a meeting with Louis XV in 1770 concerning the wars with Prague and the Slavic territories; she was displeased by his ability to achieve their goals, and their meeting did not end kindly. Louis was killed in 1774, leaving his son Louis XVI to the throne. The already stretched-thin France had to be replenished as the wars in the New World and Europe was taking its toll on the French people and its so-called economy. By 1778, the American War of Independence was in full flight. As a result, many dependent resources were redirected to easier and safer outlets to be sold. The starving of goods to the European nations caused even more riots to a near war-torn Europe.

The court of religious teaching used this to their advantage and implemented more starvation and deprivation of goods in stable nations. This would result in a near global riot within the system, forcing the law of malpractice and endangerment upon the Roman royals. This with legal restraints for the Roman royals resulted in the French Revolution, where all the French aristocrats were killed at the hands of the citizens. The court of religious teaching used this as a marker for the permanent removal of the Roman kings and their bloodlines from the lands in Europe.

This was to be short-lived; the families of Austria were now chosen by the Roman royals to stake their claim to the right of collecting the people of Europe. The Danish royals' court used the French Revolution to further incite war to the neighboring Prussian states, for which the English and Scottish supporters greatly influenced the thinking of the French and southwestern Prussian population. As the court for religious teachings, this inspired men to think along the lines of res republic and good thinking citizenry. The Roman royals instilled ideas of economy and well-thinking pragmatics with the importance of economy. This brought a split to the people of that region's spewing further war. Socialism grew among its people, throwing classes to the floor. This was a major problem within the social structure of the people, toppling the hierarchy in the command letters of that time.

This could have changed the outlook of the eclectic toward the favor of the Roman royals. It was said the phrase used in making the decision was made in the stance of a guest preponderance, which in court could be revoked.

The court of religious teaching had no choice but to implement the enlightenment of inclination, meaning think of one's actions in the presence of God. The implementation of famine, plagues, and natural disasters followed in that area. This was little to no avail, and the church had to be reformed along the lines of Catholics among a very restless and rioting people of various religions breaking off from the Roman Catholic—a deception for the court of religious teachings since the use of the church in that region was quashed to the point of near benign.

The sacking of Louis XVI was the mark of the end of the reign of the Roman Empire on Europe. The true death of Louis XVI was hidden to the world, but it was said that Louis XVI was killed by an ax on August 3, 1783, in a prison under the Rue de Galley. There were a few French nobles who were executed publicly as Louis XVI, but Louis XVI was never caught and was betrayed by his brother, who thought he could tame the duchess of Euluvois. Louis XVI and most of his family were killed with the exception of his daughter Marie Therese, who was sold to Austria, and his cousin Peopien who left for Ardennes immediately after the conflict.

Marie was not seen again since the Austrians knew of what was to come. They hid her, spreading rumors of her death and her ascension as she could never be found again. This was the last remaining line from her beloved parents. The Austrian people and some of the members of the Holy Roman Empire knew that their reign over Europe would end. The Roman royals implemented lodge houses and meetings with metaphysical beings to guide these people through the next few hundred years of war. This would result in many wars and ideas surrounding legitimacy to many titles and claims within the European kingdoms.

The knowledge parted in these meetings would be of technology and metaphysical powers, which would spew technological advancements that would inflate the Austrian people to that of a superior race among men. This was the intention of the Roman royals as they moved forward in diamante parlance of their collection scheme. The Danish royals knew this was the mark of the return of Gaustik, an old butler under the Roman royal kings. They reduced their chatter with the Roman royals and simply sought to change the churches and its ideological framework of man. They tried to encourage men to accept the benefits of socialism and fairness for all, but they were of Roman bloodlines. They had no choice but to accept the terms surrounding the laws of lineage fecundity appropriation until this situation and stance could be resolved.

The Roman royals seemingly made an error, or was it the humans that made the error? The Caparia state was captured by France in 1769, for which these people are under a different jurisdiction to the existing peoples among the courts. The Caparia people was one of a God-fearing people who did not belong to the royals of the emperor under the Raija. They were of the Constantuplyght of the emperor, the cousin to the Ethiopian royal. This was an unsightly act, but the Roman royals recognized they could use this to their advantage, which was noticed by a queen that could be seen as an obliteration of goodwill.

The British courts referred to the capture of Caparia as a crisis; it was the willful destruction of a civilized nation by the French rulers. In the courts of the Dieu, this was an infringement of the law of intently endangerment of the system. The Roman royals cannot legally prolong the implementation of the laws of reasons for much longer as their endeavors have put a strain on the legal architectural framework.

The British courts were heavily controlled by the court of religious teachings under the Danish royals; they communicated a scene of sympathy for the Corsican collection schemes. With this scene in play, the Roman royals controlled the British, leading to the creation of the Anglo-Corsican kingdom, which would create racial tensions within the society and agglomerate the ethno-franchise of the European bloodline. Pasqualcal Pauli was said to be in exile in Great Britain, but this was a diversionary tactic; he secretly left for Africa instead. This was a message to the Roman royals as to where they got their aristocracy and lines from. They were the remains of the lost cities of what is now called Egypt, meaning their legitimacy to the claim of lines can be quashed, dampened, and they can even be ordered to distribute the line by the prede collectors of those lines.

The Roman royals stated openly that this could not be and fostered the act of Fescaaluris Perfulis or the act of natural born, which states, "If a man is borne of his own tribe three times, he is no longer of the tribe of his fathers." The Romans are more than fifty generations away from their Egyptian ancestors by nature and by interbreeding. The courts agree in some cases, but the stipulation of sire-to-dame nomenclature stance states that one must declare the right to a new tribe in the office of his registrar. This is to be displayed among the system's court of details. The Roman royals replied that the emperor does not need to display, meaning the emperor does what he pleases within season.

The African lines of the Roman kings are of purer stock from the Egyptians than that of the kings of the Holy Roman Empire, from which many are the descendants of interbreeding with the nobles of the African regions within the Holy Roman Empire. These lands are not for discussion since the African cities of collection are the land, line, and proprietary holders of that sector of the Holy Roman Empire. All that was collected by Rome had to be returned to the African cities of collection; the law of operating within those lands had to be obeyed. This was to be true for most of the islands and land masses within the Mediterranean Sea.

The Roman royals foresaw a situation that was not in their favor, and if the African collection cities joined with the Danish royals, their efforts could be delayed, resulting in the retraction of all applicable laws to the jurisdiction of the Italian peninsula. The Danish royals could not have invited the alliance of the African cities just at this instance since it can be deemed as a fervent advantage over Italy. They humbly invited the city that operated in Corsica, the African cities of collection, and to a larger extent all the African councils to their place of discussion.

The Roman royals were not pleased and saw the outmaneuvering of their tactics and sought help from the cities that operated within southern to eastern Asia. To the majority, this was not an issue of winning, but an issue of the problems that could be held and the repercussions of the law within collection and system health. The Siberian cities of collection looked on with acknowledgment of incidents that took place to the detriment of the system of a similar legal situation of adjudication. They did not openly decline the invitation to the Roman royals but issued advice: one should be careful for the future could not be of prosperity and assemblage.

The African city's council issued a statement for good measure, where the rights for human women should be awarded in this era. This was a good measure from the Roman royals' city, for the Corsican people were very favored in female rights and suffrage. The Romans stewed within and looked at the system and that saw this could be a great idea, but was short-lived by France and Austrian cities under its control. The court for religious teaching could use this to their advantage since the people of that time were not of accepting women as part of a larger ruling scheme.

The war for Corsica ended with the termination of the Corsican constitution that implemented women suffrage. Women's suffrage was abandoned by the new French rulers and was used as a message to all members of the new court who favored good faith within the system. The European section of royal cities who collected women were very displeased and in fact submitted a motion against the Roman royals for better conditions for all women within the system by an adamant due date of 2515, where they must comply or face the penalties of the law of facto de constitutionality for reclamation.

The Roman royals were not pleased since almost all the Holy Roman Empire treated women and children poorly for many centuries; this was not good, especially for the Austrians who were chosen to reclaim the European territories. This was a sign that the issue of equitable treatment of the constituents within the system would come back into discussion. The fall of North African traditions was because of the law of religious servitude, where the men closest to God were revered as king or gods themselves, for which they would have many followers and servants if they choose.

These chosen men could have taught anything; they could have math, science, philosophy, medicine, anatomy, and many others. This was the law of follower constitutionalists for which many kings are descendants of these chosen people by the old gods. The fall of the old civilizations was one of disparity, where the descendants of the chosen men grew egotistical and viewed men as lesser beings and undesirable. They soon wished not to be among them and sought to exile and even destroy them, naming themselves differently from their ancestral origins.

This was the work of the collection cities in an attempt to regain claims to the collection of the descendants of the chosen. The Roman cities of collection knew they were guilty of perjury and larceny. The true Roman human societies could not have a king in the imperial sense. This was because of the laws of their relationships with the old kingdoms. The laws of old kings state that a king can only be killed by another king of a greater line, meaning a descendant of a chosen line. A descendant of a God can only be killed by the descendant of a God of greater standing within the domains of all languages. Consequently, Alexander had to be killed in Africa or India; he could not have been killed anywhere else.

This meant the conquest to India by the British could not have been legal within the Dieu. Britain had to lose and regive what was pillaged back to the Indian region. The losses incurred had to be settled between the gods where India had to claim lands within the mainland of Britain. This was a significant problem in the laws of collection since the laws of India are surrounding gods and religious teachings, which was not of rulership and peasantry. This led to the issue of the commoners and the concept of a commoner, which India does not have, but they could be found throughout the Holy Roman Empire.

A commoner was a person not of or of little royal lineage, which was deemed a lesser being by ethnicity or line. Land laws associated with ascension cannot be placed or implemented. The choice of a person to inform the populace of the presence or atmosphere of a god can be chosen among any human within a specific region at any time. These laws could be implemented without adherence to the laws of the era or season. The human stance of a commoner degraded the psychological acceptance of God's message, presence, and ideas. This could not be compared to other existing laws, where a member of a lesser race was chosen to inform the people who were among other accepted races. The commoner is specifically a race of people, but it is also a demarcation of a lesser and worthless people.

The treatment of commoners was also an issue for the court of African cities and the African council of religious teachings. The commoner was treated as less than slaves for which the laws of slavery state that a slave should only work more than two-tenths of its day. They should not work for all the days of their lives with no possibility of freedom. The human cities had already broken many laws surrounding slavery. They had also broken the laws pertaining to the lines that could become slaves. Slavery in the Western world has already taken the descendants of gods as slaves. The creation of new slaves was also an issue since the Western European nations funded the capture of existing peoples of the cities within Northern Africa to be enslaved.

This is an issue for the Roman court of appeals where their infractions along the lines of the laws of infringement had to be discussed with the African court of religious teachings. The Roman royals had no choice but to implement a new court, the court of ethical communications. All actions surrounding the treatment of human beings had to be lawfully discussed before the implementation of any action within the human cities. This was a major problem for the Roman royals since the laws of human control would now take effect to control intentional use of human intention for which the emperors of the cities did not issue any such orders. The Romans were displeased and sought to adjourn the entire session, leaving the Holy Roman Empire to stand on its own. Among those courts and royals that were present whose direction of the human being was decided upon, they all agreed upon freedom of choice for all of mankind. The adjacent cities of collection to the Roman royals were all that was left to continue the intent of the Roman royals.

The Ottoman Empire in 1788 engaged in war with the Russian Empire over lands it had lost through the wars that took place among the people during the last few centuries. The royals and collection cities of the Ottoman Empire could not be found; no one within their parliamentary range could give any details of who these were. The Danish Court of Royals grew weary, for they did not know who was responsible for the Russian-Turkish war. The adjacent Roman cities tried to manipulate the minds of the Turkish men but could not do so. The court of issues wondered and called for the right of acknowledgment surrounding the collection's population consensus. The Ottoman Empire had no answer; this was in violation of many laws under the emperors for which the emperors realized that this was not of the cities of their ancestors.

CHAPTER 5

The Ottoman Empire

Unknowing what to do, the emperors imitated the law of expansionism but had knowledge of the enemy to engage with. The emperor above the Roman royals immediately gave an order to the Roman royals to destroy the Ottoman Empire and the surrounding countries. The Danish royals did not know what to do since this meant that the Roman royals could still operate with some degree of legal immunity. Austria was immediately sent to the Ottoman Empire and fought on the opposite side of the Russian Empire, both to the destruction of the cities of the Ottoman landmasses. This was to some avail: the Roman cities of collection requested a meeting, wishing to know who they could be. The Ethiopians said it could be the Zvazvians for which those civilizations were destroyed immediately. The Ottoman Empire still remained with their full strength. The emperor was saddened, and the remaining Zvazvian allies immediately disappeared.

The emperor immediately called the cities responsible for the nations of the Middle East, to see who could come to his aid, for which the Salute war, Annoukute war, and the invasion by the tribespeople of Syria and Najaf occurred. The people of the desert as well as the Holy Roman Empire all attacked the Ottoman Empire during the period of 1790 to 1845. The area had not seen peace for a very long time, for which all collection cities involved wondered who collected the large number of dead from these wars. The emperors stirred and grew weary and eventually tired of the ambiguity of the Ottoman Empire.

This seemingly was no longer a threat; the only link to this illusive city was the humans that belonged to the Ottoman Empire. The Roman royals and their allies of the cities sought to silently chip away at the Ottoman Empire, creating wars and inciting the tribesmen to wage against the sultan, resulting in the breaking off of many nations within that region. Within this, they sought to rob the people of their rich history and knowledge with the sacking of tombs and destruction of monuments and historical artifacts; many were stolen and taken to northern Europe as prizes.

The tomb of Abdul Hamid was raided for jewelry, and under the tomb was a library with books dating back to the second to tenth centuries, with books about God and man and the origin of men. During this period, the Austrians stumbled upon the presence and historical artifacts of the ancient Jews, artifacts that posed metaphysical power. These artifacts were kept a secret and was widely sought after by those who knew; this spawned the secret wars within Austria and France. Fifteen years later, these libraries were found by the French and caused the Tripolitan civil war. On hearing this, the Austrians invaded the city looking for these tombs, and many looked for it to no avail for the owner of the Ottoman Empire stayed hidden.

The Austrians stayed there for some time, even after the Treaty of Tabouli, looking for evidence of a library. With the raiding of Abdul Hamid's tomb, the creation of the Hafiz Ahmed Agha Library was implemented by the owner of the Ottoman Empire. With knowledge of the opening of this library, the Austrians went to investigate what could be in this library; they searched for years for evidence of a secret chamber. They sought to confront Hafiz Ahmed Agha but was deluded, and Hafiz Ahmed Agha disappeared a few years later. It was proposed that Hafiz Hamid Agha died on a journey to Mecca.

The Austrians sought to gather information from the Jews; they gained knowledge of what these libraries could have held. Upon acquiring artifacts, the Jews were captured and investigated in an attempt to understand these artifacts and how they can be used. This led to the assemblage of the Jewish court of councils to the court of issues. The Roman royals acknowledged the Jews' long-standing history of lineage purity and sought to interbreed the two lines, for the Jewish lines were stronger in the plausibility of law to the applicability of Vandis schemes within the system. The Jews declined, stating the Austrians were of Roman descent, and those lines were under investigation for reclamation from the Egyptian remnants. The Roman royals allowed the Austrians to interbreed regardless of what was to come. In some cases, they forced pregnancy upon them and combed their lines against the will of the Jewish court.

The Roman royals had little option of sanitizing their lines so they silently influenced the building of new mosques and churches in the early nineteenth century before 1810. These mosques would institute the day of Jumu'ah, which would eventually replace the Zchurhu prayer. It is required for one to pray five times a day as the sun traverses the sky. This was a religious sacking of the native Islamic traditions and a bridge gap into Christianity, for which the day of Jumu'ah will be and was associated with the creation of Adam. It is proclaimed a day for celebrations, and the charity given on that day is greater than any other day. It is a day for which the Muslims will serve as though they serve Allah but will eventually serve the Roman royals as their god.

The day of Jumu'ah is synonymous or comparable with Sunday church or the Sabbath of the Jewish day of rest. In 1806, the assimilation of the Islamic people into Christianity had begun; they would eventually be inducted or abducted into the Roman royals' court of traditions. Unfortunately, the people of the Ottoman Empire were of the Saleem bloodlines and were under the laws of lineage collection, which could not have been discussed with the owner of the Ottoman Empire. The standard practice for some of these lines present in the empire were of absolute impregnability or physically could not be touched.

This meant the Ottoman Empire was a powerhouse in law for the old and antiquated laws of collection still stand in sight of legal infringement as the abilities support the endeavor. The Danish court wondered if this was a possible ally, but considering the Russian nation had already attacked the Ottoman Empire, would they vouch for a partnership? The African courts presumed that the answer would be no since they did not openly engage in dialogue with anyone within our region. This led to a discussion of how many cities of collection of this system were still unknown. An investigation led to undesirable findings; there were approximately thirty nations or tribes of people, where there was not one legally accountable nation. The collection of those people and their components are not on any known list of proprietors. This was not what the emperors had in mind for the appropriation of a better collection scheme; the laws accounted for everyone on the systems, but not everyone was present or participated in the drafting of the laws. The upper courts of the emperors could not stand in shame of doubt or unknowingness; it could be illegal.

The emperors thought of the unknowing dangers of the collection cities and sought to gain an alliance with the many powerhouses within the schemes, for which old grievances took the helm of the cities, waging wars for seditions and soliciting of souls and other collection components. This was a mistake that led to the fall of one city that had to be persuaded to reform. This accident led to the need for an alliance with the Jewish royal court, for which upon request stated that their royal court is not of royals in the conventional sense. The royals were simply representative of a far older regime, for which only the emperors could know the origins. It was their law, meaning none of the foreign laws of the emperors could be applied to the Jewish collection policies. It is simply not permitted; in fact, the emperors that sought power through the alliances with others could not be indemnified or realized.

The emperors were maddened and attacked the Jewish city of Avnar Anja and failed miserably, almost losing half of their citizens. The Jews humbly apologized to the Roman royals and other present company and moved left of their present-time presence. A member of the African council said it was exactly this behavior that caused the disappearance of many tribes; in fact, it was this decorum that pushed people to ignore the courts. They wondered if there were other courts out there and how to gain assemblage. One such court answered no; it was the court under the Ethiopian warrior cities. The emperors were barbaric and were the descendants of the Raija who slaughtered their way into the schemes. The arcane law was still for justice and redress for their actions. The emperors asked for the allowance of a truce among members, and many members answered that debts must be paid. They looked at each other, smiled, and continued on with the earthly wars.

The creation of Serbia was borne from this article, for which Serbia was chosen to conquer all of Asia, but this could not have been for the lines of Saleem could not have allowed it. The emperors shrugged and ended their presence in the Courts of Issues, allowing the cities to carry out their duties of resolving the situations of law. In 1793, the Serbian cities were removed from the Ottoman Empire, which was occupied by Austria. France was sent in 1799 to further capture the Ottoman Empire with full-scale invasions to Syria, Lebanon, Egypt, and Jordan in an attempt to capture all of what was the empire under the sultan. The Roman royal courts grew even wearier of this new adversary and wished for peace, but this could not be because the Danish court was soon to create disturbances in Europe with the Russian nations.

The Danish council ordered the Russian Empire to engage in war against the Prussian Empire in 1804. France was already at war with Prussia and Austria in 1803, where France ceded the River Rhine. Napoleon had relaunched an attack in 1803 after the breakdown of the treaties with France during the conflicts within the parliaments. Napoleon abolished almost all of the ecclesiastic's smaller religions and smaller states, freeing the cities under imperial rule—this act was illegal. In 1806, the Holy Roman Empire was dissolved with the Austrian ruler Francis II. The confederation of the River Rhine was the first French empire under Napoleon after he took sixteen Holy Roman Empire states.

This caused some European and Middle Eastern countries to attempt to regain their lands from the Russian Empire. The Russian Empire then invaded Persia, Wallachia, and Moldovia. Many of the royals for these collection cities were unaccounted for and was presumed to be that of the owners of the Ottoman Empire. The bloodlines of the people of that area were of the same origin to that of the Ottoman Empire or were hidden by the Mongadorian library. In 1812, the Russian-Turkish wars were nearly over, resulting in their conflict with the French forces, leading to a partnership between France and Russia. They were to fight alongside each other within their endeavors in the Middle East and Africa. This was not reflective of any partnership between the Roman royals and the Danish royals, for there were many issues to be resolved between them. There was mass neglect for the actions of the humans engaging in wars in this region. This created more issues for the collection cities of the Middle East and Northern African courts.

The African courts of address brought an issue to the Danish royals. The Russians and the other lines were very much in behavior like the Roman lines. They were avaricious and covetous for land and territory. The laws of lineage approximation state that the similarity of behaviors could fall within the lines of the donor collection cities, possibly giving the Roman royals the right to preside and collect. An example was brought to the court where the extrication of the minds of the Russian leaders was in an attempt to observe. The Russians naturally invaded Finland and Sweden in 1808; this was not a good result for the lines possessed the temperament of the Roman aristocrats. They were unscrupulous and self-absorbed with an appetite for invasion and conquering with force even to their loyal allies. They displayed tendencies toward prevarication, lies, and deceit. The lines had to be refined; one court of a warrior city suggested that this could be used to an advantage until the disbanding of the Holy Roman Alliance within the reaches of the Danish court's jurisdiction.

In 1812, France invaded Russia, a war which they lost; this was a terrible defeat for the Roman royals for this was a sign that they could no longer occupy the land of the Danish royals and, to a wider extent, the lands of Europe. In 1815, a court under the Roman royals implemented a congress called the Congress of Vienna, which would attempt to stabilize wars and conflicts in the region and achieve long-term prosperity and good faith within Europe. The problem was the court was headed by an Austrian statesman, for which Austria was the chosen people to conquer and dominate all of Europe. The treaty achieved from this congress would return territories gained during the many years of conflicts among the nations while returning and maintaining the status quo among the European highborn.

The congress afforded the magnification of relationships among statesmen of many capital nations, which quickly boiled feuds and conspiracies of murder, betrayal, and eventually, plots of war. The congress never did become a court or governing body even though it superseded the laws and orders of the existing parliaments and courts of participating nations. The consort of Europe was the remaining participants of what was left among the dialogue from the period of 1815 to 1848. The consort of Europe sought to balance the powers within Europe, meaning if one nation gained military might over its neighbors, it has to ensure the peace between them. This led to many wars and smaller conflicts among the Protestant and Reformationists.

This reformation could only spell even more conflict for the Ottoman Empire, for which both the Danish royals and the Roman royals continuously invaded the Ottoman Empire. In 1852, the sultan confirmed the supremacy of the Catholic Church to the Holy lands; this was a turning point for the people of that area since the church would now enact their religion wholly upon the people. This meant that the people belonging to the Ottoman Empire would soon have to be collected by the Roman royal cities but was short-lived since the Danish royals also had claim to the lineage.

In 1853, the Ottoman Empire declared war on the Russian Empire. The following year, France and Britain declared war on the Russian Empire, aiding the Ottoman people. The war was largely based on land occupation, but was gestured along the lines of the church for which the court of religious teachings was against the Roman royals' court of religious teachings. France and Britain supported the Roman Catholic inhabitants of Ottoman while Russia supported the Eastern Orthodox churches. The Islamic people including the sultan and his families moved east to Iran and Arabia. The Crimean war ended in 1856; France continued to wage war against Europe, North Africa, and the Middle East while uprisings took place against the Russian rulers.

The Danish courts perceived that the Roman royals would eventually make a move to retake all of Europe under one governing body sometime soon. The congress of Vienna and the consort of Europe was already on the move to take parts of Europe and legally engage in wars. Meanwhile, the French nationals were protagonists in the attempt to take lands from the people of the kingdoms of Wurttemberg, the then name for the Prussian Empire. There were a series of attacks until 1870 where the French consort declared a full-scale war on the kingdom of Wurttemberg.

The French rulers were surprised at the fighting forces met in Wurttemberg and were largely overwhelmed, leading to the treaty of Frankfurt in 1871. In 1883, the French consort told the aristocrats of Belgium to attack the cities of Wurttemberg. This resulted in the 1886 riots near the border with the kingdom of Wurttemberg; this war silently continued until 1901. The French government publicized many claims against the then kingdom of Wurttemberg's government, with claims of threatening attacks and war-scare complications. The war secretly took place near the border of France and Belgium, with Russia strengthening its relations with France in the 1870s. France proceeded to encourage wars between Russia and the kingdom of Wurttemberg. This led to degradation of the German-Russian relations, strengthening the triple alliance of 1882. France's diplomatic alliance with Russia grew with great financial benefit from their alliance; the wars to the north became worse. Germany politically joined the triple alliance in 1882 along with Italy and Austrian Hungary.

By 1887, there were new complications between France and the kingdom of Wurttemberg, for which France appealed to Russia for aid. During the 1890s, Russia and Germany had many discrepancies between them, for which economic repercussions had an effect on both the people of Wurttemberg and on France. This led to protests and rallies among the citizens of then Wurttemberg, resulting in movements for radicalism and war for the territories to the north. The early 1900s war was already the prescription for the people of the kingdom of Wurttemberg. The French among them reported their findings to the parliaments and sought to sabotage their protests with explosions and urban fires.

The sabotage of public utilities and induced food shortages was an attempt to weaken the unifying Germanic people. The kingdom of Wurttemberg moved toward socialism in an attempt to support themselves. The added pressures from discrimination from the Austrian people created wars with Austria while eroding their alliances within the other European nations. Eventually, war broke out, resulting in what was called the First World War. The French and many others had learned the skillful arts of espionage, which led to the secret wars of Europe. Many of the accounts for these wars were hidden, and documentation by the enemy was destroyed. World war ended in 1924 with the death of Knzatzchen Gustien in south Germany. The German people after World War I was uncomfortable and would not stand for rulership from the British for which they seek World War II; they had foreseen this war and pushed for technological advancement.

Peace between France and Germany came with the Armistice of 1918, for the court of religious teachings did not accept the terms in kind stance. They immediately propagated the flu virus in 1918, which killed millions globally. France and the Roman royals kept the southeastern lands belonging to the falling kingdom of Wurttemberg. Russia to the west also did the same; this war was to be short-lived since talks of France reassembling their forces took place nearly five years after the end of the war.

In 1924, France launched an incursion into Germany; they claimed they were looking for documents of importance, but it was a ridicule to the noble families of southern Germany, ideally the Nazis. They were looking for the Glitzchen family that were related to the French aristocrats. This was a sign that France would later return and destroy their bloodlines since some of them were descendants of Louis XV. To the wider world, all the aristocrats of the French line to Louis had perished, but this was far from the truth, with many living in Germany, Belgium, and England today.

To the royal cities, this was a situation where the humans had to choose for themselves; the war in Europe could end, but the wars in the Americas could continue and exacerbate to global proportions. With the history of France, the Germans chose war; they saw efficacy in death prompting the fervent need for technological advancement. The humans became technology-seeking warriors of survival; this was not a bad psychological stance for collection. It could mean prosperity for the system; the royals chose to allow the human decisions. The Roman royals were more than displeased; their best chance for European domination was stopped with the assassination of Franz Ferdinand or Archduke Franz Ferdinand Carl Ludwig Joseph Maria Austria of Austrian Hungary, where he was killed in 1914 by a group of Serbian militants aided by a secret group of assassins called the Black Hand.

The Black Hand was a subsidiary group of the league of assassins under the pope. These assassins had worked with the pope since the Vicar of Christ. Franz Ferdinand was assassinated by Pope Giacomo Paolo Giavanni Batista Della Chiesa. The pope was and still is in charge of a group of ancient elite assassins called the Seekers of Death or Ferrum Sacris Initiatorum the Hooded Blade. They became servants to Rome via Legio Secunda Parthica in AD 197. They worked with Parthica I and Perthica III, who were stationed near Castra Albana. Their presence in Italy dates back to 3000 years BC.

They lived and operated in regions of high populations, observing cultures and human psychology. Their main goals were to search for the presence of artifacts that date back to the beginning of man's existence. Throughout the existence of Rome and Greece, they were responsible for many assassinations since the art of war was their lifestyle. They were of ancient African origin, but interbred with many ethnic groups to hide their true identity. Their children were chosen from age two to start their training in vocabulary and mathematics, in which they were proficient. They also recruited captured slaves and runaways into their secret order. They performed acts of murder for high-ranking officials of major cities as these could facilitate the undetected presence of their order.

They helped shape the contours of the Roman Empire with the murder of many of the emperors from Severus Alexander, who was presumed to be killed by his own guard, and Elagabalus, who was killed in a field by an unknown soldier to Otto III in Castilallana. The styles of the assassins were mixed when assassins of the Italian order met with different clans during the Jagurthine war in 112 BC. All members of the assassins' secret order knew a single common esoteric language, which has remained the same until today. They were known to keep secrets and set up stations wherever they worked. It is said they still exist under the pope today; many of the popes were assassinated because of the actions of these assassins. Pope John Paul, like many others, were assassinated and replaced by look-alikes as not to cause public distress.

In 1920, Paul Deschanel became president of France. France at that time was ruled by a group of secret societies under the old crown of the descendants of Louis XVI, in which many of the politicians at the time were executed for their incompetence. Many of these wealthy elites perceived the wars of 1850s and the loss of the war with Prussia in the 1870s. They chose to move to Russia during the triple alliance's revitalization; they secretly planned the incursion into the kingdom of Wurttemburg and fled, sustaining no losses at all during the First World War. Paul Deschanel only knew of this when he became president, for which they had already planned the resurgence into Germany in 1923. France launched an attack on the cities of the River Rhine and the Rhur area in Belgium, resulting in agitation of the German people that caused Second World War.

Paul Deschanel was said to be going mad at the beginning of his term in office, but was to be executed by a descendant of one of these secret assassins as France had a long-standing relationship with the Catholic Church. He protested heavily for which he could not publicly disclaim his situation for the safety of his family was at risk. Paul Deschanel was replaced by Alexander Millerand and left office in September 1920; he was placed in a mental institution for some time and then was killed in 1922 by the assassin of the ruling secret monarchs of France. By 1924, the war in Germany near the River Rhine and the cities of Rhur and Malmedy were under siege from the French forces.

The German people knew that they had little time, so they strengthened nationalism, safety from political misconduct, and social upheavals that were common during the mid-1920s. By 1924, with the French army on German soil, the United States and the allies were in negotiations of remuneration for World War I, putting the Dawes plan into operation. In 1925, German statesmen Gustav Stresseman,

Austen Chamberlain, and Aristide Briand negotiated and conceded to the Lacarno treaties, which were seven treaties. These discussed the reinstatement of German prestiges and privileges. The mutual guarantee of the frontier of Belgium, France, and Germany, similarly Germany to Poland and Germany to Czechoslovakia and the reconstitution of the Dawes plan.

Germany had not made a single payment to that date in 1926. Germany was pressured into the League of Nations. France had already taken over most of the northern territories of Germany and, to a lesser extent, southwestern Belgium. Two years before the German election of 1930, France made its way into influential positions with the statesmen of the German national parliament. Stresseman was killed in 1929, and others were suspected as being pro-French idealist, including Gustav Ritter Von Khar. The wars with France, the Young Plan, and sabotage from the French, Jewish, and Kurdish businessmen put the German economy to a near depression.

International treaty agreements were not in the favor of the German people since the remuneration of Germany to France and Belgium. Simultaneously, Germany was being invaded by these said nations. This caused the parliament and its people to be decisively prudent with the choice of their leaders. In the election of 1932, the statesmen seats were shared unequally and resulted in a reelection in early 1933. This eventually led to many discussions and incidents surrounding the leader of Germany until the elections of December 1933 where Adolf Hitler won. In mid-1934, Adolf Hitler went to the cabinet of Reichstag and implemented new laws to protect the people from foreigners.

There were many attempts on Hitler's life by the SS and the SA, but it was said that the SS that attacked Hitler was not the Waffen SS, or the Schutzstaffel, in fact, was a part of a smaller Nazi party of the Heimerich people. The SA who were the Sturmabteilung or the Nazi party's Sturmtruppen or Braunhemden, who were the same periodically, were responsible for Hitler's many assassinations attempts. They were responsible for many left-wing organizations and revolts in the next following years. In 1935, Hitler announced the rearmament of Germany, which signifies the moving forward of the German people. Following this, there were two attempts on his life for which the investigation led to the belief that the Austrian and the French were behind the plots.

This led to an invasion of Austria in 1938 and the destruction of the Jewish and foreign business by the German SA and civilian populations. The pogrom conducted was of Austrian, Russian, and French nationals within the German populace, which later spread to all Jews and even later to all non-Germans. The French were agitated by these actions and invaded Germany in 1939. This same year, Germany and the Soviet Union signed the Molotov Ribbentrop Pact, where there was to be no aggression between the two. The invasion of Poland soon took place. In December 1939, Germany launched a mass invasion of France, Belgium, Luxemburg, and Netherlands, destroying the border cites.

The French population was pushed back to near central France, occupying almost all of Northern France. Ending the bloodlines of that area, Austria lost nearly half of what was official Austria with genocide of their elite lines for crimes against the German people in the sixteenth, seventeenth, and eighteenth centuries; the same was done in Poland. The French nobles that lived or hid in Russia moved farther into Russia. That same year, the Russian Empire executed more than twenty-seven thousand Polish prisoners and signed peace treaties with Japan, Finland, and Bessarabia. Lithuania, Latvia, and Estonia became part of the Soviet Socialist Republic while joining forces with Moldavia and Bukovina.

This was a situation where the people of Europe can trajectory in many directions. The Roman royals were tempted to regain the hold on the European nations, but their hands were tied. So they focused on the African region through Italy, which was heavily tied with coequal collection, but they were relatively unmatched in military might. The Roman royals joined forces, influencing the German Nazi movement. The Danish royal cities sought to unify its territories through Russia as France and England were distracted by the actions of Germany.

The union was not one of great intelligence on behalf of the Danish royals for the African courts was an ally in the court of issues. The German people could not have engaged too deeply into the conquests of Africa alongside the Roman royals. It would seem as though the Danish royals had won and the Roman royals had lost most of their footing in the European regions. The Roman royals had to finally admit their defeat; they had stated their intentions to move to Argentina and retook Greece and Albania, with Bulgaria invading the Ottoman Empire.

It would seem to the Danish and African courts that both agreed that the activity was just to engage in war, which could be accepted in the stance as a harvesting event, but was a political reshuffle. The Danish court despaired at the deaths of the human populations. They could live terrible lives of suffering, so in an attempt to encourage human wellness, they gave the responsibility of the human inspiration to a lesser city of collection the court for the education and understanding of the ambient. This court would help teach man to understand his world in a scientific way, teaching men to specifically channel their ideas and upstanding their environments, for which they would teach the humans how to meet their needs. In 1941, the Zuse 3 was built as the world's first functioning computer. The Roman royals accepted their shame, for the affairs that took place in the world also gave their remaining stock of the Italian population to the court for the education and understanding of the ambient.

The Roman royals had a parting gift for the court of issues; they influenced the minds of the German and Austrian leaders of the 1940s and instilled the idea of the Jews having a master plan. This, combined with what was found in Vienna, surround the metaphysical abilities of the Jews within the Ottoman Empire. Scared were the nationals of the German and Austrian Hungarian region, in which the balance of power theory enraged the German people, forcing discrimination and further hate for the Jewish people. By 1945, the final solution debate took place with the wide issue of what to do with the Jews and the Jewish revolt. The Nazi government voted to exterminate the Jews, carrying out their intentions. The royals of the Danish cities showed great disgust for the acts of the Roman royals. The German people proceeded to eliminate the large populace of Jewish descendants within Europe, from the middle of France to the eastern edges of Bulgaria and far north as Russia, sacking all cities in their path.

This was a travesty for which the Jews were exterminated, and the human nations looked on, mainly defending France. The Jewish cities of collection had no reply when asked about their stand toward the incursion brought against their people. In an attempt to help the Jewish people, the court of religious teachings moved the surviving Jews to a land of their forefathers via the ideas by the United Kingdom. Unfortunately, the land they were moved to was not their original land where their ancestors lived. In fact, that land was 1,040 miles west of their current position.

This was not a good idea for the people of that region, for war would take place less than twenty years after their arrival. It seemed the Roman royals were determined to keep the Jewish court involved in the issues associated with misconduct within the systems collectors. The African courts looked on at the travesty that was to become on earth and said no, the earth would not become that. Global wars, stretching from one century to the next, the human being would not see peace for more than a thousand years. The breaking of many laws resulted in the propagation of a culture that affords an appetite for war within the human worlds. This was bolstered by the excuse that the humans were given free will; this was the "fine china" of the gods. Man would not be able to enjoy this freedom but cause the frenzy of gods; something must be done.

The Jewish courts were not pleased but remained humble; the Danish Court of Royals simply looked on as the German and Russian people fought. The English and Americans planned their strikes and built new weapons that would ensure their victory. The birth of weapons of mass destruction, the very first human replica robot, hydrogen-propelled airplanes, and the world's first rocket all came from the German people as they marched on toward their freedom from the remaining cultural effects of the post–Holy Roman Empire rule.

They all wondered if this was healthy for all of mankind, what will their intentions be as they trajectory further into war and conflict resolution in an atmosphere of war. The African court stewed, saying this batch of humans will produce more violent and aggressive cities within the Dieu. By 1945, it was reported that Hitler was dead. With the near defeat of the German cities, the war was soon coming to an end. The Russian forces swarmed the city of Berlin, capturing the capital. The remaining German forces were scattered and captured many cities within Poland and Austria, putting up a front against the allied forces. It was also rumored that Hitler moved to one of these cities, where he was never seen again. The war against the Jewish people continued for more than twelve years after 1945, for which Austria continued Jewish genocide until near the 1960s.

The Danish royals saw what the Roman royals were planning in the United States and England. They sought to garner their nations under one umbrella. In 1945, the Russian Empire captured Warsaw, Budapest, and Prague among many other Eastern European countries. With this, the prospects of the Soviet Union had to be reshaped. The idea of Western ideology was soon to be the agenda for global thinking. Looking forward from that point, the future of man was not one of prosperity but one of war. The nations that spread capitalism were on a global agenda for prosperity, ideally spreading philosophies that originated out of the fall of the French monarchy. These concepts were geared along the lines of ensuring their survival and success through economic means. The problem was they were not very tolerant of others and their ways of thinking, especially toward non-Saxon groups.

The Slavic and neighboring lines were of the socialist and communist ideologies who ensured their survival through military might. The seeming cultural effects of thousands of years of war show correspondence for the balance of power theory. This theory existed in Europe for many years. The balance of power theory suggests that states should ensure their survival by preventing any one state from gaining enough power to dominate all others, where it has been realized that the neighboring nations of greater military might will surely invade a nation of lesser military might. The Western philosophy of survival through economic means has proven to be unrealistic in the environment of ethnic tensions and domination among the European lines.

This environment has remained socially volatile with propensity toward war since the Roman era. Europe has been at war for the past two thousand years. War during the Soviet Union after its fall was for peace and for resources. The human being has become a war-philosophizing being. The human being has been at war for the past ten thousand years with pockets of sporadic intervals of relative peace. The Danish royals were disheartened, and the African royals said it is the vicissitudes of their lives. It was decided upon to ensure the free choice of man; what was conveyed was the question of if they would choose wisely. Everyone agreed they will eventually choose war.

The laws of collection permit the propagation of human ideas to the avail of the enjoyment of their world. Their ideal world must be in correlation with the laws of the larger collection schemes. The laws of free choice in the world cannot allow the human likeness for their world, to exceed the cognitive development signal's restriction for the allowable maximum levels for gleeful and joyous indulgence. A man can only express his ideas of the architecture for his world momentarily until the restructuring of his physical anatomy. It should and could not be allowed that the total responsibility of the assemblage of law associated with the human cognitive function be the total responsibility of one particular group within the Dieu. The responsibility of managing the human ideas should be designated to a court of responsibility. Ideally, a general architectural steward must be put in place, the Danish and African councils agreed, but the members of the courts were not in favor of an arbitrator of law within the system at this time.

CHAPTER 6

The Human Mind and Their Gain

The human will has changed. Within the last eight hundred years, the desires of men are no longer along the lines of love and emotions, but of physical accomplishments, permanent safety, and status of accomplishment. If men were allowed to execute their own will, their world would become that of a race for achievement. Their world would be centered around physical gain powered by economics. This is not good for the collection schemes as well as the mental health of the humans within the system. Nearly all the courts agree that in the 1960s, families who were middle to lower class were now middle to upper class. By the mid-1980s, the minds of the individuals had become goal oriented. This is largely becoming a problem; by the time the mid-1990s occurred, families of upper-middle to lower-upper classes felt or believed that they were underprivileged or even poor.

The gentrification assimilation of the mind of these individuals were not of a conventional classification dispositions. The laws of collection state that if a mind is measurable, closer to that of a particular type collected by a city, it should be awarded to that city with consideration for line and land applicability. This type of system leaves some degree of problems for the average collectors operating within the usual laws of the system. If a steward is to be awarded, the laws must be adapted to the choices of the human beings as they are allowed to evolve. Many disagreed and voted for the destruction of the human civilization that were outside of the laws. This meant that many of the gods and cities of collection were against the applicability of the law of freedom of choice for mankind.

The ideal sections of law are surrounding agrarian and warrior societies for which man has lived for thousands of year. The law rarely accounts for or prepares amendments for technological societies. A man of German lineage who flies to Beijing, China, and marries a woman of Ming lineage is possible in today's world. The laws that account for such situations in an agrarian society are centered around the type of person who can be present in China. For example, the man who can travel to China is usually very rich, an aristocratic, a soldier, or a merchant. These men are permitted to do so within the legal framework of affordability and access, which occurs in a controlled manner. In contemporary societies, a single event can cause the influx of more than 100,000 people to one area or nation. A global event like the World Cup or the Olympics causes tens of millions of tourists to one country. One hundred years ago, this was not possible. During these events, many children are born from the visiting citizens. This mixing of the lines creates complexities within the collection schemes among the cities, leaving conflicts and unresolved issues surrounding stances within the laws of lineage.

This was not possible without technology, the invention of mechanical engines used in trains and airplanes have afforded the mass transit of human beings across the globe. In fact, a trip that would take months by horse or foot would now take a few hours. Technology has significantly advanced within the last one hundred years, for which a person no longer needs to visit a place to see or speak to an individual. The invention of the cell phone is no more than forty years old while electricity is no more than three hundred years old. The basis of this law issue sits upon this acceleration of technological growth; this has spilled a lot of traditional collection laws on the floors of the council's halls. With more and more discoveries into radioactive uses, technology could revamp almost all laws surrounding man in the favor of the businessmen pirates within the Dieu.

The future of man seems bleak to say the least, for many of the religious texts predict the destruction of man at an appointed hour. The collection of man has become entangled along the bloodlines and among the landowners of the schemes. The course of collection had become advantageous to the cities and emperors; if the world of man continued on this path, the emperors would surely dominate the collection schemes. This is not to be since man's advancement in technology was a temporary measure to ease his suffering from the wars of the Holy Roman Empire. The laws of de facto states that "a man does as a man can," creating a chain that is his train line to his destination, the means to his end. This leads to the statement that man shall destroy himself. The court of issues agreed and voted for a rest. The collection schemes should be applicable along the lines of chronological succession with preference to lineage and then of land occupation; all other schemes should be at rest. All the royal cities agreed with some nonroyal cities, voting for a reassembly.

The smaller cities asked many questions, which was to the availment of reopening dialogue to change the decision on lineage collection. The question was, should man be allowed to pursue technology that would exacerbate the endowment of his fruitfulness until such time of his ultimate demise? The royals acceded to the point, meaning if man's technology grows to a point of his absolute destruction, the laws of system termination must be applied. It was also said that man could discover a lot from cellphones in the direction of radioactivity and the conduction of gamma rays and waves. This could exacerbate space travel, exploding the system's productivity while simultaneously antiquating the laws of the land occupation. A travesty to die for; this meant more beings, less right of collection.

It was asked that if man does gain territory in space, what are the laws for collection since man was under the rights of his own willful endeavors? No one answered because no city wanted the responsibility for the allowance of the expansion of the system without notice; this usually leads to war among the cities. The royals and the businessmen were on a scheme to fix these issue before it becomes a race or a public spectacle. The expansion of the human system could cause the fall of many great empires; the entanglement of the already existing bloodlines would cause great contention as the populations grew. The emperor's councils immediately stated in formal stance that they would rather see the destruction of the system than to stand losses on an astral scale.

It is willing to do so adamantly to the destruction of all subsidiary cities before they could finish the smaller cities expelled that was enough. There is already too much violence over the collection schemes. The Danish royals said that our world is in trouble and we will see the destruction of ourselves. The understanding gained from living in a society like this results in mass paranoia, leading to the destruction of all that one has worked for and to the appointment of a temporary replacement of yourself until such time has come.

Looking at the human world, a tribal world is not as bad, considering the states of other systems. Human beings are more inclined toward caring and looking out for each other. Values and morals are predominant; the human being is far more civilized than a few thousand years ago. Love, honor, and respect are prevalent. Compassion, art, and music all contribute toward a healthy human being. Their direction is one of war and self-impalement. We are inclined to inspire men, but this would only result in more war within the Dieu because of the leverage of the other cities and the applicability of our laws.

The human society is group centered; they are beings that feel the need to join or create larger groups. If left alone, the human being will create a group with inanimate objects, which it holds dearly. This was the innate nature of the human being. They were once the envy of the systems. They were a beloved being in the Dieu because of the way they loved their god and the way they loved each other. The way they cared for each other is by expressing their emotions and thoughts, which made them the center of many collection markets.

Modern humans are busy and are always on the go, for work or school. Family time is spent periodically, usually on holidays and weekends. The human beings quickly become ugly, purposeful, and intently the beings of the Dieu, with a disposition to resolve their issues with war and mayhem. They had become the ugly product that fell to the gutters. Many humans today see no evidence or acknowledge the presence of God. The influence of the Roman royals have drowned the cultures of the last millennium. All the world's societies are quickly becoming cultured in a variation socialism that is centered around economic and academic achievement. The world has quickly become cultured along the lines of achievements that were the milestones that rectified the errs associated with European history.

Scientific thinking, theories, and viewpoints have taken over; the age of invention is upon man. Thinking along the lines of what is now known to be Dadaism will perish. Many of the ancient style of thinking has already perished with the advent of globalization, which the Gods are displeased. To the Gods, humans have become undesirable and presumptuous, for hypothesis and conclusion have caused many forms of conclusive thinking that fills the global economy. The downside to technology and this way of thinking is that the entire world has to adopt this style of thinking in order for the world to move forward. The economy has formed a system that puts the world in a tight situation where if it stops causes mass repercussions to a large portion of the human population. In this, humans are creating fragility within the human population as they move toward stability in the global economic community.

Many agreed the humans have become more than undesirable, and it was the fault of the Roman royals' influence on the social environment of the earth. The humans would and did lose their sense of self as they were exposed to the forceful acceptance of European cultures. Many indigenous people had to abandon their aboriginal customs and adopt the ways of their new rulers. This caused a mass identity crisis among the various peoples of the world, creating a global identity crisis as their original God's presence perished. This also meant increased profits for those who could collect souls from mixed lines and in some cases the benefits from powerful political alliances. This could also mean the positive change for many cities as well as the way the collection laws are applied. The way penalties were issued was changed because man could choose his own destiny. This brought forward issues for a long-desired change from the barbarism of the emperors; this single event could change the Dieu. The African cities agreed that this could lead to a more civilized relationship among the cities.

Many of the smaller cities said to the court, "Look around, what do you see?" The wars caused the city's structure to be in shambles; the people and the culture has become more than rooted in fear and forced respect for those with wealth. The mentality of the young are traumatized, and their general outlook is dark and is of the cold reality that their world could end at any instance. Hope is far and a dream for many who are held in cages until they are rebuilt to new homes. Escaping is a dream because of the bounties placed on runaways; the price is simply too great.

The rich live lavishly and wallow in the deals that are afforded by the power and leverage created by the bond that are made and broken over this large influx of souls. The riches, the glory, the glimmer, the affluence, the exorbitant opulence of the royals' success push their egos to new limits. They simply remove economies because they are no longer aesthetically pleasing. Public statements delineating the success of the royals tarnish the reputations of officials leading to their removal, and this caused many wars within the Dieu. Many officials were replaced by foreigners who were seeking the office of the kings and queens to earn a percentage of the lavish embellishments acquired during the restructure of the systems. While our worlds are falling apart, your crown jewels, the human world, is your biggest concern. We are the remainder of the destroyed royals and emperors, and we are by no means surviving; we are simply waiting for our moment of departure.

The Danish royals replied that just as prosperity is rearing its head among the cities, so is discrimination and hate finding itself among the hearts of the people. The law and its provisions are being exercised. The rights of many to the souls and stocks of others are being redeemed. The sorrow and cries of the poorer classes are but a temporary condition for change.

The wealthy will become greedy and self-loathing for which there is little that can be done about this showing off and showboating. The ignorance of the compassion for social good constructs that held the wider society together has fallen apart. Many moved to repay what they owe as a form of keeping their lives and their soul or souls of their loved ones. Many have cried and moved to replace the lost loves with lower-class designs. Some have made moves to acquire upper-class designs and move to better positions within their society. Others have taken modifications with the intention to repay, some have taken power as a means to hide their losses, and others were simply assassinated because of gaining too much wealth too quickly.

The classes have become weary because they too may be rebuilt to a new city in the modification of schemes. The loss of subordinates has spawned mass ascension, jerking the hierarchy trending the thrones. Servants became kings, kings were betrayed by their masters that rose to wealth. The honor and respect, the haggle and bagel of the successful over the unsuccessful quieted the wealthy within the shanty towns. The death of the advantageous rulers spell freedom for mass numbers, spawning millions of revolutions with new ideas in philosophy, economy, and social application theories.

The stench of the rich was no more, the cheers of the free filled the environment. Many of the rich were executed, with many of their workers and servants becoming exiles or slaves. These trends cause many of the citizens of the Dieu to take their own lives. Some fled to ally cities while the guilty had gone to the poorer cities to maintain their lavish lives. The smart became wealthier than those of their neighboring cities while the auspicious plotted for opportunities of compensation from the free.

Conglomerates that were formed toppled the powerhouses, with mass public execution taking place daily, millions and millions of planets destroyed. Billions of citizens were remade to new cities every minute, with no remorse or consideration for their freedoms and rights to claims. Some are exorbitantly pleased with the way the societies are going. The laws have made provisions for temporary stands in remediation of the dead. Policies surrounding the systems have afforded accommodations for temporary residence in participating cities. Many are protesting the reclamation of soul exercises, but this was absolutely legal in these ways and seasons.

Laws of deserved places and lost loved ones have been amended; both lost loved ones from the remade dead and those whose loved ones were new arrivals from the systems are to be stored in a nondemonstrating city. Laws of conventional collection schemes are being ignored and overlooked. Cities that fell lost their business collection license or privileges, and these license were now being used by those cities that recently could not have operated on the systems. Laws for duration in operation teenier have taken over. Cities were sacking other cities for the right to operate on the systems. The free human dead have been taken over by the animal cities, for which the animal dead now owns the human dead. They are gaining law review that would allow the permanent placement of these people within the system; these practices can now be made legal.

The entire restructuring of the world has caused too much damage to the systems; laws of overpopulation in some cities have already taken effect. The large influx of collected dead have caused problems of social stratification and the inappropriate treatment of specific classes of beings leading to convictions and rebuilt cites. Laws of improper and inappropriate relocation of collected dead must be revamped. Many men and women have found life mates from reclaimed cities; the restructured collection schemes allow for the easy transition of illegally acquired souls into the systems. The marriage council have changed the way they had to bond pairs together; many have used stolen souls and other components to make wives or husbands.

The issue has become what must be done humanely to the wives or husbands that were created from stolen components. The cities have put a band on the bonding of pair that have used uncertified components, which has led to the appearance of a rogue marriage scheme done in secret in the far reaches of the systems. People who marry in this way have gained favor from the masses and some of the nobles who believe in love, as it is known as a rouge or unlicensed marriage. The restructuring of the cities have caused the large influx of request for weddings. These have lengthened the waiting process, creating a lot of incidents of fraud in collection certificates from the cities of origin. Fraud has taken a toll on the cities for which they have little choice but to repeal the laws, preventing the acceptance of the newcomers wishing to marry in the Cacoethes cities.

CHAPTER 7

Their Ways of Life and the Way They Want Men To Be

The societies are structured similar to that of worldly royals of earth; however, life is based around misfeasance execution. There are thousands of royal societies who were started by the Khazar, who were descendants of one of the founding races created by the first beings of the Dieu. The Khazar philosophized that worldly beings should live in benevolence in the Dieu for all eternity. They sought to reincarnate many of the collected dead, as they can be well and commune in fellowship. Death to many beings was a part of life for which choice is the elevation. Among the descendants of these created the most active, and seemingly the largest of these are the emperor's Houses of Colnobis, the Tokhar, the Nefelleis, and the Idayama for which all are of the same nobility and power.

The emperors of the House of Colnobis are the most active in the collection of the dead; they are the most secularized and structured in law. There are twelve houses within the emperor's house: the House of Colnobis; Ishtkhar; Nozhar; Maizher; Ishzaha; Foszha; Dzusueazha; Itshoukher; Kheazhar; the Natoukshar, which houses the women of the Inamorata; Rhazkshar, House of Holds; the Huzueszhar, the House of Crowns; and the Beazhear, the House of Brothers. These houses are in constant power struggle for the right to collect. It is said that they dominated 13 percent of all systems in existence. Their laws are very strict and precise for their languages are in constant evolution. To remain clear in the law, their languages have become a snare; foreigners attempting to waiver legal standing causes the reshuffle of the scheme's distribution and collection. This causes many to accede to such laws as a sovereign city; this could mean the redistribution of many.

Colnobis was a reincarnated warrior king of the Pompadour systems, late in the Neagian era. This was an era of war and bloodshed, with mass exterminations and genocide across the systems. Upon his reincarnation, he sought to rebuild his empire in all the glory and splendor that it once was and in the regalia of the Dieu. He pledged loyalty to the Masheinghigh, an older race created by the Khazar in an attempt to gain a footing in the ways of the then Dieu. After collecting his second and third in command, he began to rebuild his empire, raising an army that was vast and powerful. This army was dangerous enough to negotiate the release of his first in command from the Rhuscur clan; they openly stated they wanted no part of what was to come. He took over all the smaller cities that were overlooked as useless and middle class. They grew and prospered under his rule; at the end of thirty eras, his house was almost as large as the Masheinghigh, exponentially eighty million times its original population. Upon this time span, he had to be promoted to Iaikido, which means he must sit at the high table in the council of the Ofitami; they are the consort to an emperor. He was not pleased, but he had no choice for disrespect to an emperor was death.

Colnobis grew weary and split his house into twelve subservient houses: the Ishtkhar, the House of Beloved Things; Nozhar, the House of Tangibles; Maizher, the House of Waste; Ishzaha, the House of Oath; Foszha, the House of Perfection; Dzusueazha, the House of Directives; Itshoukher, the House of Prevalence; Kheazhar, the House of Hands; Natoukshar, House of the Women of the Inamorata; Rhazkshar, House of Holds; the Huzueszhar, the House of Crowns; and the Beazhear, the House of Brothers. This was a message to the emperors that ruled over him, for which his decisions were barred. He sought after wisdom and found light; he displayed love to his people as he improved his kingdom.

He wrote philosophy and poetry, describing the beauty of the cities of the Dieu and the love for all things seraphic.

He grew deeply saddened by the laws that governed the cities and devised a system of governance that incorporated all laws simultaneously in an attempt to escape the undertow of bias within the court systems. This system of governance was not one of free choice but one of evolution, for the way of evolution is the strength of the courts toward the exploitation of the amendments of the laws. He instilled within the people habitual thinking that would facilitate the avoidance of pathways leading to application of the law. This in concurrence with controlled habits of decision-making in cultural dissimilated concepts and moving toward societal eccentricity that counteracts the qualification of persons within the society to the application of external laws. This would undermine the court and the democratic processes associated with decision-making, leading to the debilitation of the law.

The emperor was angered by his conundrum, and he was called into a meeting with the emperor for the very first time. The emperor wanted to know specifically and tactically how can this be. He answered in one word—*Instructables*. Instantly, Colnobis understood what the emperor was—a man that can be had, a man that could be controlled. He secretly started a clan, a brand-new city, simply by selling and channeling animal dead to a place of residence and fertilize its endowment. The size of the hamlet became an issue for the courts, but animal cities were not allowed to be a part of the emperor's court. So he sought to enhance the court's laws to embellish the cities, but was turned down; he displayed signs of empathy and sadness to its people.

The people then sought after another Iaikido, for which they could not gain any help. He leveraged the court to gain standing and was denied; some time had passed, and the cities exploded with an excess of population and success. The lack of legal standing allowed many persons to have the ability to operate within unaccounted-for limits of some irregular activities with no legal repercussions. The problem was the laws of the court; they simply did not account these positions that were being occupied by the animals. The emperor was not sure what was about, but he knew Colnobis was the architect. The laws of region states that the laws for the impoverishment of communities must be the responsibility of the emperor, for which the emperor was now in violation. Colnobis knew he started the city under the law of the Khazar for which all things should be in fellowship and be well with each other. Colnobis could not be blamed for starting an animal city in the stance of love and fellowship.

Upon this news, the emperor looked at him and saw that he was behind it. The emperor looked at Colnobis's past and saw the capabilities of his mind and instantly thought of a meeting, saying, "Summon Colnobis." Colnobis knew he could win. The emperor observed him and studied what he saw. He pondered how a man so young could be so constructive. The emperor, triggered, looked at Colnobis's system and contemplated it. It was the combination of lifestyles and the history of people that afforded that type of mind and psychological grade.

The emperor secretly sought to change his past. The moment his past was touched, Colnobis instantly shifted and changed the Lukai systems of the Raija, a mass collection scheme. A Lukai system or Louki system is a system where inhabitants of the system are in search of a host of leaders; it is usually a system that is rooted in violence and feudalism. The emperor was maddened and had no choice to physically assassinate Colnobis. Talk of the emperor's position spread throughout his kingdom and many others, creating a war that Colnobis and the Masheinghigh clans were always prepared for. Their cities became outlaws and outcasts under the emperor, but they were not enough to wage war against the emperor. Their forces could have run thin, so they sought rest and increased their footing in the collection schemes. This was incorporated into their national anthems; their cities became respected and feared when in a royal stance.

The middle to larger kingdoms grew weary and frightened of what was to come. The balance of powers are to be shifted in the temporary favor of Colnobis. He grew tired as he saw the Amongu, an ally of the emperor taking the victory, not for the emperor but for the entire society. So he wondered, if winning this battle means losing one's true place in society, losing the war means the loss of one's people. The hopeful idea of reinstituting one's status or one's place in society is a temporary indulgence of family and delectation. The best for our people is to live by the laws of the Khazar. The best position for my people is the best of all possible wins.

He attacked an old enemy, partially destroying their cities. The emperor wondered, saellicise, and saw the alliance of Colnobis with the emperor of Salzhear and immediately called upon his council, for which Colnobis knew was a wrong decision. He called upon the council of a would-be enemy, Princess Cuszhar, an outcast from the Immanizhar clans, a distant cousin of the Khazar, which spelled the destruction of all the emperors, the wars that spawned the fall of the old cities and first-created beings were to be restarted.

The emperor saellicise and saw the destruction of many cities and the fall of many first-created beings; the old cities of the first beings had already begun to be destroyed. The emperors immediately sought the council of Colnobis, but he had already pledged his forces to Princess Cuszhar, for he and thirty thousand of Masheinghigh allied clans have already begun the war. He was simply too powerful to be defeated; they immediately took over all of the smaller unallied cities. The only cities left were those under the first-created beings and those who don't believe in war.

Thirteen eras have passed, and the emperors watched the wars with bitter disdain, wondering what could have been done better. The emperor looked at the growth of Colnobis with a wrenching heart: how could this man be this proficient and successful? Colnobis wondered how the emperor's demarcation of himself could be greatly moronic and unenlightening as he was surprised of his military tactics. The emperors saw Colnobis's thoughts, and they all decided Colnobis must die; the nobles of the lesser cities also agreed he must die. "Colnobis must die" became a chant among the collectors of the cities of schemes. He noticed many people who wanted his life to end; he immediately looked at his people and saw they all loved him dearly. So he thought, *Even though our battle has been raging, we are strong and we can arise.*

The emperor looked in scorn upon an empty planetary system and wished upon the death of Colnobis. Immediately, he vestured an answer: why not create new beings in the same way we create modifications for ourselves? They wondered how can this be achieved and saw the answer in the future. Immediately, a strange new voice said to them, "You are right, and you are the brightest among you." They frightened and searched for the origin of that voice, and instead the voice said, "I am before the Zhar, a mother, for which all of them are my descendants. Go forth and shed light in this world. Do as you would do."

They filled the empty sectors with these new beings and gave them all the powers and abilities they had. Their instructions were go to war and destroy Colnobis, destroy the Princess Cuszhar, destroy the Masheinghigh and all their allies, and they did so adamantly. Colnobis could not avoid this attack; the battle was fierce, changing the past, shifting the matter phases, destroying the future, mitosising the present that people did not know who they were. The cities became distant; their world became unknown and strange with strange new faces, and they became alien in an unexplained reality.

Colnobis stopped and watched these new combatants, these new design of beings, and wondered how could they be in existence. He looked at the other clans and saw they did not care for how they could have come into existence, only caring for surviving the battle; they were almost on their last stand. He looked at the newly created beings and saw that their one purpose was to kill him, to see his end, and to see his destruction. Colnobis thought, *How could we destroy these?* Every advancement in the battle affords the situation to create more. In doing so, he realized that defeating his enemies does not take intelligence or strategy or tactics. It takes impetus; only the drive to win was important. The men were broken and tired; options were becoming scarce.

Colnobis knew he had to do something quickly; the only thing he could do was what the emperor did—create living beings. He looked hard into the emperor and could not see how he did it. Colnobis thought he could not exactly create a new being but could create a mind or consciousness that only does one thing—focus. Princess Cuszhar called him from the future and gave him a design to build; he instantly knew this was the end of the war. These beings were superior to Colnobis in every way; their minds worked not only timeless but dimensionless as well as their cognitive functions perceived no alluvials but seamless coagulation of all existence simultaneously. Colnobis realized he could not understand their focus; he immediately deployed them into the war, and they started to push the time parallels to what would be described as a scale for which the enemies would have to balance their effects on the alluvials of time. He was unsure of what was to come, for time has become unrecognizable. This was his last hope for defeating these beings.

The men recognized what they were doing and coordinated their attacks in an assault of the home territory of the emperor's beings. In doing so, they were distracted; they could not comprehend what Colnobis's beings were doing, so they did exactly what was needed, a time energy shift. Colnobis realized they were powerful, but they were not intelligent logical calculators. He made variations of the princess's design, and these beings made a lattice structure of minds calculating in a sequence of consciousness, accounting for almost all types of matter in the battlefield. They exerted time shifts on every part of their physical world, restricting their phase shift movements. He made more of these beings, which would attack the focus of the more complex combinations of cognitive functions within the opposing forces, with the sole purpose of breaking their will.

He vastly realized that the world had become strange, and they both did not recognize what was the ambient or where they were within the multiplex of the universe. Combinations of matter and obscure perceptions had acted upon time which bents the fabric and structure of the prenetial fluvials, causing mass mental time fluctuations, something they had never experienced before. He immediately attacked the forces with a more complex sequence of consciousness, causing the mental and physical destruction of many of the emperor's created beings. He was soon left alone with his creations in this newly perceived reality. He saellicise for a way to return to his reality and saw that he was alone with a strange being.

Before he could ask, the being answered, "I will show you the way home." The being showed him a reversing sequence of time that took him back to his kingdom to a point only a few hours after he shifted out of phase during the battle.

Upon his return, he looked at his people and yelled, "Victory!" His armies roared, chanting, "Victory, victory, victory! We are victorious, we are undisputed!" The men immediately started reincarnating the dead and rebuilding the cities, for which less than a year they were back to full strength. All the kingdoms within their allied empires congratulated each other of the victory, the Princess Cuszhar visited Colnobis personally to speak of the future of our allied nations. She said our day was strong, but the battles wage on, the wars of old are not yet over, and our lives have just begun. We should be wise as we are strong, for our day of judgment can and will be sung. Colnobis saellicise and saw that he had given his world a gift, a monument of their accomplishments. He had created a pair of beings that were a reminder of how they won this war, a symbol of their triumph. They passed a law among all the kingdoms—no one is allowed to prohibit the creation of life.

Some time had passed, and Colnobis realized that the beauty of his city had faded. He saellicise and saw the destruction of the world, not through physical means of war but through the temperament and psychological effect on the society from these new beings. Their popularity grew a doltish nature within society in the same way he installed a drunken evolution of rebelliousness within his people. He looked at all the allied cities and realized that the same was true for all who had created these new beings; he called a meeting among the rulers. His allies pondered and searched for an answer, for it was not a matter of pollution but humanitarian attitude. A strange voice said to them, "Stop and observe your people." He immediately realized he could not see who it was or where the voice came from. He started to see images of a strange race of people; he saw the birth of an idea. This idea spawned immense change within their society, the creation of a world without sin. A world without the issues and flaws of their own was actualized in the creation of a new species of life; this was the beginning of the end of their society.

Those that created life created more, for which those who were created, created many others, spawning generations of created beings. It quickly became emblematic pleasantry. Their existence changed all the social norms, affecting the culture and overall behavior of individuals within the society. He knew what this meant—mass cultural change leading to the eventual change in law. The trajectory of the society could lead to one of social collapse. He knew what to do, but did not know what to do with himself. Implementing laws to effect change was no longer his portfolio, and he could not be seen constraining the laws of creation, especially to the world of collection. He showed what he saw to the people and the enemy who were the descendants of these created things, saw that they were not the only beings to be created for war. They ran to the outskirts of their world, seeking these beings for answers to their state of existence. His cities stopped the remaining wars in an attempt to observe themselves. "Have we become of the wicked?" they asked. Colnobis said, "No, our wars have been too long."

He wondered what does life mean to them. Colnobis created a city purely of new designs in being architecture as a promise to his people to fix the social and moral problems. In doing so, he realized that the interpretation of oneself is largely dependent on society. To the bereavement of one's habits, one must learn to accept the inability of change without loss or judgment within himself. We are our world for our world is us; our culture can be our ideas of ourselves and the acceptance of our society. The actualization of our attitude to others is our manners and our coordinate interactions. The abundance of our minds is our handle on our society. Colnobis ran out of answers and sought to revisit the memories of those that spoke to him. He searched the past for societies and cities that had fallen but could not find what he truly desired.

He revisited his own past and analyzed his mistakes; he revisited the wars with the emperor and looked at what he could have changed and why. Looking at a different side to his ideas about life and existence, he decided to leave his kingdom, appointing a steward and physically traveling to a very distant planetary system, where he looked at beings he created and found that he was trapped within the constituents of his personality. He was trapped within who he was and knows now that he is oblivious to what is outside of his own perception and self-embellishments.

He dawned upon the selfishness of men, for all men relish in their own desires sometimes to the avail and retrenchment of their self-awareness. We all seek to change what we have regrettably done, but cannot without the self-changing exploration of who we are and who we would like to be. Where is the balance between selflessness and selfishness, where is the balance of a being? Many people of the other cities disagreed with Colnobis's theories and saw selflessness as a form of insanity; it is a form of being untrue to oneself. It is like selfless people are pretenders or deceitful liars, believing in their own imaginations. His own people's diagnosis of him was that the war created mass trauma, for which they do not know how to deal with the stress.

Colnobis was saddened and returned to his kingdom, where he met a cheerful royal welcome. He was named Emperor Colnobis, for his people no longer cared for the laws of governing titles from the above clans. He was their emperor, and they loved him for it. He taught them all that he knew and discussed publicly what he and the others have found; he sought to change the worlds of the collected systems. He endeavored to teach men of the enlightenment within knowledge and the benefits of enlightenment. What found was intentions was to be short-lived. The old ways of collection was still an important system in the way things are done in the collected worlds. He looked forward and saw the dangers and wondered what was best. The Princess Cuszhar saellicise and immediately changed his status among the cities to Armadadan, for he was still a proficient military tactician.

He saw the danger the beings of the collected world were in and hastened the rate of collection of the dead. Shifting the collection schemes in their favor, he knew the life and thought of one collected being causing an entire shift in our world. This was not to be; the clauses within their laws could not be applicable in many systems. The title of Armadadan was an intimidating symbol of his accomplishments; many of the larger clans have little or no tolerance for a member of a participating group whose first impulse is to initiate war for collections.

He decided to leave the collection schemes to his cities; he turned his back on the beings from the collected world with respect and love because his hands were tied. He saw the weakness within himself, the weakness the system propagates in one's character, the weakness he first saw in the emperor. In his final message to his kingdom, he describes the ways the laws abuse a person, resulting in weakness and hesitation in decision-making. The weaknesses of the struggle is the weakness we must display in triumph and how they can use these weakness against others. Colnobis left, thinking of himself and what he did not know, knowing that he is a multispectral being. He wondered what were the limits of his mind, how could one free himself from himself?

Colnobis left the cities in search of an ancient civilization; for many centuries, it remained a mystery to him until he met a being shaped like a butterfly but made of stars that was huge beyond compare. Colnobis had to keep his distance because of the share size and immense energy it radiates. Just looking at the being can cause the transmutation of a person's physical anatomy. The being asked, "Who do you seek?" Colnobis replied, "To find the ancients." It answered, "No one." Colnobis saellicise and saw nothing, not even himself, and wondered what this was. Colnobis asked, "Is this the beginning of another war?" It replied that it was a formality.

His senses drifted to an end, and he wondered, *Who are you?* And it answered, "The Ulterer." For the first time, Colnobis did not know what to do; he was disoriented. The Ulterer asked Colnobis in a female voice, "How can I find the ancient people?" Colnobis wondered what was the Ulterer. Colnobis answered the Ulterer in a female voice, "They have never existed." Colnobis knew something was happening but could not tell what it was. Colnobis noticed his mind becoming something else; his thoughts became alien to him, his ideas and strings of thoughts became that of a female, and this was very obvious. The Ulterer asked why the ancients destroyed the Ashmend, and Colnobis answered in the female voice, "Because of their creations, because of the creation of a mind, the idea of quantifiable construction of thoughts."

Colnobis realized that his disoriented mind split into two. He could observe with his own mind and experience the minds of others simultaneously. The Ulterer asked, "What of the quantification of your own mind?" Colnobis answered, "Our minds are not quantifiable but measurable in a continuous string of cultivated ideas, not of perception but of retention." Colnobis realized that the woman was of the ancient peoples, and their minds are not of the same kinds of those of the collected systems. The Ulterer began to reorganize the disorienting factions of Colnobis's mind.

Colnobis ask the Ulterer who was she, and the Ulterer replied through his own voice in a gravel-like tone that she was the Princess Mastsika of Ashmend, the commander of a vast army during the wars against their own creation. The Ulterer asked a question to himself through the voice of Colnobis, "Why are you doing this to me?" And Colnobis wondered, "What is the Ulterer?" The Ulterer replied, "I am showing you what you seek. The things you wish to know are what you cannot perceive. The perspective of others is your friend, and in that, you will find many enemies."

Colnobis raged, and in his rage, he saw and experienced the minds of those whom he sought. He became them while he was still himself; he became a being of beings. The Ulterer asked, "How can you be a being that does not know what is outside of your own perception?" A female voice inside Colnobis's newly given abilities said, "I have never been someone else." Colnobis screamed and realized that his mind had many factions added within his mental functions. The Ulterer released him from his disorienting daze. He stopped and looked at the Ulterer. The Ulterer said, "Become me." Colnobis became the Ulterer's mind where he saw the destruction of those he seek; he saw that their destruction was not temporal but infernal. The Ulterer said to him, "A being is not a being for beings are made like a fabric. Instead, a being is a mind for a mind is eternal." Colnobis realized that his idea of what is life was all wrong; his approach to his questions led him to his loss.

The misconceptions of his ideas in the address of his affairs led to his state of mind, affecting his reality; he had never thought to become someone else, and in that, he saw a lot that he never thought to see. This being was something special to Colnobis for he was freed of his own perceptions. The Ulterer acknowledged Colnobis's notion as incorrect. Colnobis was not freed of his own perceptions, but within himself, he had self-actualizing ideas of his own mind. In fact, Colnobis perceived that he can only perceive within the limits of his own mind. Mentally,

Colnobis restricted himself and his limits, constricting his capabilities by lowering his confidence.

He asked what this could mean; is it the acceptance of self? The Ulterer said, "No, this is just the language you use to describe of delineating traits within yourself. When you understand a mind, it is far more dynamic than that of quantifiable mathematics and mechanical interrelationships between ideas and factors surrounding thoughts. You would then see that the way you think a mind works are misleading theories within your analysis of the situation, leading to the decisions that landed you here." The Ulterer displayed within herself the destruction of a world, the destruction of Colnobis, saying, "Your mind is your reality. It is your window to this universe."

He tried but could not comprehend what was meant; he saellicise and saw nothing. He looked back and saw nothing. He immediately shifted, and the Ulterer showed him a child inside himself. This was a child he had never seen before; the child was standing with an inquisitive face and said to him, "The levy of pounds is unweighted to the sound of a heart cast in metal." He instantly thought of what he could not perceive and looked at the Ulterer in understanding of what it meant. He looked inside the Ulterer and saw the movement of the stars that constitute its fabric and its makeup. He asked the Ulterer, "Am I going to die?" The Ulterer said yes.

"Yes is the answer to all things knowing, but unexplainable is all that is not to the knowing. No, you would not die. You would never die, but live on through releasing the holds on yourself. That which do not exist is found where?" The Ulterer said, "Yes, it is found in a place that is conceived. The place you see does not exist physically but exists only in the minds of those who seek it. Hidden from those who seek to destroy it, remove your mind and you will find yourself there." This baffled Colnobis, and he had no choice but to continue his travels. The Ulterer seemed to be knowledgeable but unreachable in thought. Colnobis realized that what things are, are what we label them to be. The Ulterer was beyond beautiful and intelligent for her intelligence was beyond him.

He continued for a while, wondering on how to remove one's mind or what was truly meant. Then suddenly he heard a voice: "How far have you traveled, Colnobis?" He looked and saw a woman, a very strange woman dressed in black built of something he had never seen before. He answered, "Far along the ends of the collection systems." She asked, "Do you think you would reach the old civilizations?" He said it has not been seen. She said, "Saellicise now," and he saw his destruction. He shifted, but she was still there and saw that he could not shift away from her. He paused and asked, "Why are you here?" She said, "To end the wars of the Prophentheid."

He did not know what she spoke of; he looked forward and saw that there was nothing he could do. She said the first civilizations are unkind, and they are prohibited from destroying the reincarnated things. They are also prohibited from reincarnating the collected dead; he instantly became her mind and saw that she was from a place where she and others were created to do the work of something greater. He said to her, "You are surely not a collected being." She replied, "The sound of a string is not spilled by the pound of water."

He thought she was surely insane, saying, "Why speak of these for you are a new created thing?" She said no and gave him the thought that he was not enough. He said, "Those that are sure will see the rise of their sun, but those that are blind are never sure and will never hear the melodies given by water, for blindness and water are not of sound." She replied, "You are just one, Colnobis, and you will leave now." She instantly struck him with fatal precision. He fell out of space, falling to an unknown surface.

As he was dying, she said, "How can the sun rise and fall without collective assemblage? It is the mechanics of the Dieu." He looked at her and said, "The unyielding will of self." Then he instantly shattered his own atoms, destroying his fabric.

His first in command immediately looked at him and saw a void and looked at the woman and saw the unusualness of her body type, something he had never seen before. Princess Cuszhar immediately looked at Colnobis's first and said, "I have never seen a being of that type before. We should be wise for what she told him was that the war was thought to be ended." His second immediately hid his last location and made it unreachable to all lower than them. The clans all came together and decided that this should never be spoken of, for many still did not know that Colnobis was dead. Caution and incognito was the main motive among all the houses. No one knew who this woman was, for she was an assassin of a hidden clan.

CHAPTER 8

The Emperor and the House of Chambers

The emperors under the chambers are the elites of the modern cities of the collection schemes. The chambers is a court and policing body that gives directives or guidelines who are directly under Cahrpulhar, the being governing the era of Ashghner. The emperors are the rulers of the kingdoms where all the collected dead reside. The laws of secular hand dictates that the lives of the collected dead are to be controlled in a manner that permits the unusual occurrence of reorder or reshift within the distribution of souls in the event the law changes or a remediation act was enacted. The collection schemes are separated periodically with different laws dictating the rules of collection, allowing a check-balance buffer zone to minimize the effects of the changes within the law. The period of collection are described to be that of months for which each has vastly different and specific laws.

The month of collection in this physical period states that the houses and the laws of the houses must be organized in a military strategic stance until the renaissance period has ended. The laws of the houses of the emperors state that all emperor's houses must have three subordinates Marakhilbos, which are prepared or thought of as like the children of the emperor. They are the Michilo, Hitoichi, and Kurtanuran.

A Michilo is a squire to the emperor, often considered the sweet child for the emperor. They are allowed many children for which they must have an Akichino, a master law man. The Akiabo is an acute system manipulator who teaches and instructs the constituents of the system when and where to apply law and approve housing for new residence. The last of the emperor's children is the Malasi, a master of information and an expert in recon and intel. He or she is the assistant to the Kailo, who is a specialist expert in concealment.

The second of the emperor's children is a Hitoichi, a master psychologist and possessor. He controls the people in public office to discreetly get what the emperor wants. Among his children, there must be a Cartessei, a lawyer that is responsible for royal court cases. The Ulsesas is another of the Hitoichi's children, who is responsible for the acidification of the status of the royal's stance in law. The third is the Eresesas, the keeper of the knowledge of the networks of the old kingdoms.

The Urkeyoik is the concierge to the largest cities of collection. He pays and controls the larger cities' aristocrats, maintaining the influence of the emperor. He also controls the Penesesas, the regulator of the abilities of the cities. Alexasdas and the Kerkglouster acknowledge the dominance of the Urkeyoik over the city. The Alexasdas is in charge of the face of the cities and the faces of others in court. The Kerkglouster monitors and controls the elasticity of the cities' debts and markets, gaining the favorable positions and boxing out their competition.

The Kurtanuran is the executioner of the emperor. He is rarely even seen by the average citizens and is not a title one should discuss in public. The Kurtanuran must have a wife, for many have tried to offer soul mates in exchange for their lives. The Kurtanuran must be a skilled practitioner in his field. They sometimes lose to foes that have risen above the emperors. The emperors usually encounter revolts and wars for independence where the courts order the execution of the Kurtanuran or the emperor themselves. The Kurtanuran must be wise to remain unknown to all the courts, and for this, he is not allowed to have any children.

The Kurtanuran has a second in command, a Dainichi who can only collect souls and cannot be paid in currency. He allows the Kurtanuran to possess his creations, which become his disguises and avatars. Of these, there are three known types: a Hatsumatsu who wages war over souls. One must possess a soul if he or she is brought before the council. The Neighou creates and inflates the status surrounding the collection; he also publicly decapitates the highest-ranking officials to ensure the order remains in absolute control. The Higaraito is the last of the Dainichi's known avatars for the Kurtanuran. The Higaraito is an enforcer of legal confiscation; he or she forcefully collects souls from those who seemingly acquired souls legally in the form of weekly taxes.

The Kurtanuran cannot have a stance in collection, for his obligations cannot be of the affairs of the systems. The collection stance of all houses during the Ashghner era is not allowed to stand legally as their own and must be appointed by a leader under the emperor. The Kurtanuran cannot be chosen by the emperor to become a leader of a house of standing. A Schougnar is usually appointed by the emperor for these reasons, which he must rule with a military stance. The Daimyos must follow his leadership without question. The Schougnar's forces must be divided mainly into factions, the Schgaumrech and Dimerech. The Schgaumrech are the main fighting forces that executes his will perfectly. The Dimerech are the supporting teams that aid the Schgaumrech in the endeavors. The Daimyos controls the other aristocrats in order to avoid conflicts between the Schgaumrech and the lower-designated classes.

These classes are the Aimusitu who are the remainder of the Bokkaiyo clans, an old fighting society that was very misunderstood; they were once under the Himulin kin and even considered the same at one point. These were the hunter cities of the chaos seekers for the Schougnar of Jinsimnu during the Himulin period of the current emperor. The execution of Schougnar of Jinsimnu led to the joining of the Yogoi Jin and the original Aimusitu clans. They had no choice but to inhabit the home worlds of the Aimusitu; they eventually attempted to rule over Aimusitu and change their ways of life. The emperor was displeased and ordered the Yogoi Jin to destroy the Aimusitu, which they did. Almost all of their royalty was stored in a hidden vault until the change of the era. The Yogoi Jin attempted to win the war with the remaining Aimusitu but could not defeat the Bokkaiyo; they were simply too weak and was outmaneuvered.

The Himulin was given more physical abilities to defeat the Bokkaiyo. The creator of the ancestor of the Bokkaiyo removed their presence from the cities immediately, leaving behind just a few Aimusitu of no more than 100 million. The remaining Aimusitu today are proud but disgraced by their battle against the current emperor. They were cast to the slums, and they moved from city to city like vagrants as the eras changed. Like the vicious dogs of the barren lands, they fight for scraps from the emperor's tables. Their claim is very similar to their distant relatives, the Oshotoshk and the Sastuman, who are said to be those who lived in space before the children of the suns. These are legendary clans that claim the solace or inspiration of the sun.

The Etarhara are a smaller clan of the Eduro. The Eduro are a people that ran away from the cities near Jinsimnu during the cleansing of the allies. The rumors of the silencing of officials and the entanglement of Rhashid's hands who was their leader was to gain favor in the court of appeasement, but resulted in the destruction of their people. They abandoned the population and chose to be outcast. Heresy was their occupation within the newly created wilderness. They lived within the lowest reaches of the systems, creating pejorative and prejudice as a means of defense. The laws were abandoned and the termed neutralism within the Burachunin.

The Mekaija tried to abolish the acts that caused the fall of the Eduro but abandoned these to the courts. Many complained that the fall of the Eduro had created ghettoes in Burachunin. The law creates a vine that spreads throughout the security forces; many citizens are still forced to live in poor conditions. Eduro openly refused contact with or employment in the court's occupational schedules and were advising its people to avoid the courts.

Nonofficial consensus of segregation in varsity and esteemed driven sectors was recommended; the wealth of society played a major role in allegations brought against the Eduro. Financial themes were forbidden, and the Burakumin had a problem with their foreign origin. Population and scholarly consensus is now their original Burakumin interests to the Orthodox Veintio Bandhehism. The Eduro was severely tarnished without scorn and disdain, with little regard for the promise of their ascension to Auphiluteous Esluthiate. Feudal law was banned by the Eduro during the Ahefimensa era; this was to the anger of the emperor, with castes of segregation because of occupational forced badges were banned. Opposites are used in law with avoidance of others in an attempt to demystify the pinnacle of poisonous missiles of court.

One of the Burakumin met with the organization of levelers, who were employed to stratify the societies. They studied the effects and the scouts of the tax collectors in an attempt to persuade them to abandon their endeavor. This resulted in more military and political taxation collection organizations, leading to the Burakumin Zanzohu War. The Durekai society integration and liberal act created a third world dietary supplement, resulting in a barbaric assimilation of the society. The organization of the Zunhukuidu Burakumin created a liberation movement to topple the Burakumin masters. The Etarhara, seeing all of their known associates killed, ran to a time-shift void. Their presence in that void tinkles the time-shift barriers, bringing another tyrant master to the top of another shaking ladder. This tyrant was from a foreign alluvial and would cause the fall of systems. Upon the appearance of the foreign tyrant, they abandoned the Eduro people and with it the abandonment of the known time alluvial, uttering these last words. Time is no man's friend.

The Hidurin are the reckoning of the disappearance of the Etarhara emerging from the low classes within the courts, which their names signify were civilized. They were cast out of the Etarhara family during the wars, who were forced to do political polluting, controlled begging, street performances, and assassinations. This afforded confiscation and stealing of body parts, the empowerment of Frestution radiant types, and simplifying the modification of mental components. They wore banners coming to the end of the wars when they thought they had gained control of the cities. The courts under the emperors were wrong and were fooled by the Eduro and Etarhara.

They were forced to use violent means on the cities, which both sides abandoned all civil acts and Eduro returned to dilapidated states of poverty. The Eduro were considered an artistic race until this point for which they were thrown into the Bulsarian classes, which were considered a consequential rapscallion mix of beings. They were taken in by Sorvchens; they became exploiters, which became their prison. The Etarhara eluded all facets of the emperors royal authorities, remaining free, and were once noted to be outlaws until the extent of their power was displayed in the battle for the freedom of the Himulin.

Their quest was to separate the Himulin from the rest of the outcasts, and if they were successful, the Hisabetsu would take them in and give them a place among the socioeconomic majority. Speaking the languages of the old Schougnar, they were shunned to be among the outcast societies. They were forced to imitate the respected clans to avoid detection, but this caused many members of the Himulin to become criminalized, making them a marked race with a propensity toward breaking the law. They created replicas of the Etarhara and Eduro among many others, which they used to perform acts of heresy and murder. They were shunned and considered disgraceful for this. The Himulin were considered permanently unreclaimable, and they gave up on their ascension to glory and respect as they turned their backs on the emperors and the Raija. The criminal tanning edge of the Schougnar's sword must be stifled, returning the Dieu to the tranquil ways of the Dulis untouchables and the in situ classes of the Himulin.

They were given jobs of entrapment, for which they were banned from four main castles. These castles were consumed slowly by the lower classes, the victims of circumstance. Those among them that joined high-status groups were executed. They were sent underground for security by the Samaheai, the keeper of words. The Chiekeraba, the library, and the Sheakeila are the custodians of the scholarly living quarters. They were sent away to be killed by the hands of an angry Schgaumrech, an underhanded technique known as Tohidon Ahideyos, which causes the attention of those in authority. The authority would think to eliminate the ascended based on their appropriate ideal behavior.

Among those are the outcasts, the scorned tribes that have committed crimes that are not fully warranting of the death. Their entire population has been shamed and disgraced, resulting in banishment. These were from the Burakumin; they are a low-level class of soldiers that returned to their society and met an outcast group of rebels that were their countrymen. Falling to the bottom of the traditional social order, they were made to serve the victims of war. They refused and severe discrimination and ostracism befell on their city. Those that chose to fix the mistakes of their elders worked and grew discontent, angry, and hateful of others. This was a consequence of working with fallen high-level individuals of the executioner cities.

These individuals are those who were touched by very powerful assassins but were just strong enough to escape death. They are considered impure and tainted by death; they worked with executioners, undertakers, and torture houses, which left marks of deep punishments on their minds. They are attached to the illegitimate helmets; this is where the disgraced Burakumin lived. A helmet is an energy sphere that is built like a mind. The energy regimes that thoughts are made of constitutes the building blocks of this world. It was thought as an impervious city from the Schgaumrech attack, and the attacks from those that they were obligated to help. The walls were breached, and the inhabitants were killed, enslaved, and ruled by Vandiscumles at the end of the Jinsougin Jin Schougnar Era.

There was a power struggle within the Burakumin, for which there was the outlaw who committed murders against executioners of the court. The law's Freus was his name; he killed all within the laws of access to serve, for which many abandoned the Burakumin and joined the Juhatszu membership. The Tokatsu Burakumin incident was the hushing up of officials. Then the manipulation of their minds to instill conformity ideas created a war they call the end of all that is law. The Burake library threw out all books of laws that contained the controlling of minds. The aristocrat Burkuran banished themselves from the helmet and created religious aristocrat discrimination among the newcomers. They established new links with other nonatomic clans who gave them the ability to change their biology to nonkorin. They had no choice but to move to alternate energy regimes: the Brasissers, Demascarghs, and the Heirschulories.

The Schougnin are not really outcasts or scorned; they are the remainders of fallen armies or frightening men who would not accept another leader, especially of foreign origin. The word *Schougnin* literally means Schougnar. The Schougnar are usually fallen due to the wars for the end of law or the war for the right to dominate. They are the remainder of a fallen emperor and would never accept a foreign ruler. These are the bounty hunters of the Tokatsu Burakumin. The illegal dismemberment of the courts forced the remaining Burakumin soldiers to be executed; those that fled were highly desired fugitives.

The Rhedir are the lowest class under the emperor and fought to keep themselves unseen and untouched by the courts and councils to his ear. They wished not to rise, for they are colloquially a hooking clan that destroys other clans by destroying their images. They have a derisive demeanor and are very powerful with vacuous understatements written all over their faces. They are very undesirable to be among the Rhedir. They are the weapons of the wealthy, and their price is the key to their legitimacy of claims. They are very skilled in Opprobrium outbreaks, the twisting of societies' vituperation, condemnation, disapprobation, and common considerations within understanding.

The Rhedir was created by Herra or Hrea of Samir, a queen of many gods, and is not a new broker but an entitled beloved connoisseur among the royals. The Rhedir are experts in forced ascension for which a clan is elevated and praised, then sacked for the fall from which they have taken. They were given notoriety and acclaim, prominence, stature, notability, and public position for the sake of being known and then defamed, making them a target for the lesser cities who wish to rise to power. They are given wealth and distinctions of elegance for which they will enjoy the spoils of their accomplishments but will ultimately make mistakes, like exorbitant spending during an economic shift. They are eventually blamed for their lack of éclat of knowledge and indulgence in irresponsibility. Their rise to power too quickly is their detriment. Their increase in beauty and poise is the pedestal, which becomes their gibbet they will be hung from. This type of sacking is called Illustrious Besmir Fratricide, and it is admired and adorned as a preferred style of murder by the wealthy and discreet. The euphemistical optimists or the ambitious protagonist professionals seeking redress or standing in a decision-making court are usually the targets.

Legal status vanishes from a kingdom once touched by the Rhedir. The toxic benefit of the presence of high-ranking officials causes the acidic knowledge of the systems and its laws, which leave many people wealthier than they previously were. This created new upper-classed schemes pushing the entire city into a new tax bracket. The tannic beauty of poise and stance as the public domain creates tension around the city, creating an eerie atmosphere of responsibility. Tension for clairvoyant decision-making and fear of misjudgment and carelessness builds. The cities become anguished by the added pressures associated with the responsibilities. It was deemed legally unfair, as many of the citizens were executed for malpractice and negligence, causing the destruction of their environment and the ills of gentrification.

They are skilled executioners to the point that many who recognize the axe simply congratulate the queen and pay homage to her accomplishments. She is the creator of her own realm, an accomplished queen, the Gaicga Orunus her vault in the sky. She sees all and navigates all to the greatness of esteem and power; she is the conqueror of Celebe, the father of shies, for he tried to stop the Graija and lost. He had no choice but to stay within her vault.

His poorer classes were loved by their oppressor for their failures. They chose rather than to stop the Gaicga; they obligated their servants to the mills of the courts, which meant they had to retain their own vault, causing the changes of best practice for the prerequisites of owning and operating a vault. The words of her last victim were, "The changes have afforded our loss, for the beloved of the courts have ruled against us. We are found noncompus mentus and abstruse." The Rhedir are a dangerously beloved clan; they hold the favor for all swordsmen within the Dieu.

The devastation from the wars have spawned many new cities that fight to become rich. Some wish to become greater than they are; these regions are called the Fhyumees. A place that will become the willing servants of the emperors. Among these cities are the Potentate Phirul, the bureaucratic Vismitcher, the Royals, the Maladroit legatee, and the Potentate Phirul Inamorata. These are the top of the society, they are the pedigree and applaud of the Fhyumees, but they are not the richest or most powerful. Above them are the seniors, the Holoky, the Lutimet of Serluvis, and the Hierocracy Hierarches—these are the businessmen of the era, the most active and most powerful members within the collection schemes.

CHAPTER 9

The Attack of the Heart

The beings of the systems are the idols of the Dieu. Prestige and glory are part of the culture of the beings. The duty and obligation to the care and health of the system is the perfume that brightens their world. These humans are the stars and are revered as lords and gods in the face of who cannot do as they do. The status and splendor of their worlds are given to the humans' guardians as they are those who guide and teach the men as they live. The royals and the emperors are the elites who control the fields. Stories are told about the lives of men, the greatness of their accomplishments, the magnificence of their victories on earth. Upon their deaths, they all cheered and decorated their shrines, crafting gifts, singing songs of their glory and exhibiting gestures of acceptance until their arrival in the Dieu.

The Battle of Troy was where Achilles was adorned by the gods. To humans, his life was a holy scripture of his military achievements, but to these beings, his life on earth was a piece of art. It was a moment in time and history where the abilities of a man was celebrated as he rose over others. His death was an extravaganza as he was to cross over into the Dieu. His arrival in their world was the birth of royalty. Achilles was a star. He was given many gifts and many servants; he was adorned with never-ending pleasure. The crowds of reincarnated dead all admired and respected his life and accomplishment, which was inherited by his bloodline. They are respected and beloved; many owners of the lines on earth would send their images to bed with these great men to acquire a seed of the triumphant specimen. They too can be a part of the grandeur and celebration of the accomplishments of these men.

Upon the deaths of his descendants, they became beloveds; many wished to become soul mates and marry the descendants of these great men. Many wish to pair these lines with the lines of their beloved to create a pure line of greatness. These lines have become perfect and must be protected. There is mass jealousy among the collectors of these lines, and many wish to acquire these individuals at all cost. These are the secret aristocrats within the earthy society.

Many of these people secretly live on the earth where governments and world leaders have no record of their existence. They are the participants of cults and secret orders that serve the gods of their ancient forefathers. Many of these lines can be found near eastern Poland, Belarus, and Romania. Many earthly royal societies are descendants of the beloved warriors of old. They do not engage in warfare and are always alerted by the gods when the presence of danger is near. The average citizens would never get the chance to know or be among these few elites. It is not about their power but the purity of their bloodline along the lines of their godly criteria.

The first Romanian king Septus Cothelas was never a descendant of the aristocrats of the Holy Roman Empire; his line remained pure until the death of Septus Jeulescules, who was lesser royal who was a duce to a town on the outskirts of the Black Sea. The Romanian lands were conquered by Austrian and Serbian forces, and the descendants of these unaccounted-for royals had to leave for the rural areas for safety. These lines eventually spread across the land and were mixed with the Baltic and Polish royal lines. They had no choice but to keep their identities a secret, as they lived relatively nomadic lives throughout the last 600 to 800 years. These people today are still living in the Romanian countryside, relatively unaccounted for; many still live in castles maintaining the titles as descendants of the Romanian lords.

The descendants of the remaining Pharos of what was known as Egyptos fled to the south near what is now called Ethiopia. During this invasion by the clans of Kush, the cities and its people were destroyed; many lines of the holy men were intentionally destroyed. The jealousy of the gods have caused fear among many, forcing the creation of schemes of protection. The human had to reside inside castle-like structures that accommodated their every need until the nineteenth century. The French incursion into Africa caused mass movement of the citizens of North Africa, where they moved to Chad. In fear of being discovered, they hid themselves in the far reaches of the rural countryside among the Coushavy tribe. If these people were discovered, the leading royals would legitimize many of their claims to collecting these lines through laws of intermingling and interbreeding.

The continents were filled with the lines who were the descendants of the beloveds. In the ancient kingdoms, the gods would often go to war with each other. Their human devotees went to war as hate for the devotees of the enemy of their gods filled their minds. Many nations waged war for years in the same way the Roman royal cities went to war with the Danish court of Rivals. Many of the lines of the human victors were destroyed in later battles because of squabbles that originated within the Dieu.

The collection of these lines and the value and purity were the pertinent issues. The latter triumphs in law was achieved by the holder of the best combination, for which they became the dictators of the terms and conditions. The loser had no choice but to abide, and this caused the hunting and eradication of many lines. Many people had no choice but to exile themselves and become nomadic nations, moving through the regions as simple wanderers of the African continent.

Many of the gods became bitter; the bantering and chanting of their rivals got to them and caused many wars within the Dieu, where many gods were destroyed and the humans were left to wander across the continents. Many cities adopted the godless people, and illegitimate collection eventually took light in law and they were unofficially the property of the collection cities in charge. The law surrounding the lines could not have been easily erased. The lines of the northern African peninsula were walked along the Northern African plane by a city that was not responsible for that tribe. They broke many laws of handling and coloring for war infatuation. This led to the salvaging of law. He was charged, and the people were left to wander the planes.

North Africa at that time was covered in forest with desertification spreading southwest from the Middle East through Egypt; this period began near 3900 BC. The cities of operation did not want that line in existence. They went to war with the people, leading their tribes to war and genocide. The city of collection, the African city of Jerimeish, saw this happening and sought to go to war with all the tribes within the activity. In an attempt to banter the cities of operation into a forced escape, technique was used to remove a tribe without disrespect to the presiding faction of collection. This led to mass genocide of almost all the tribes within the North African continent.

Approximately 4,000 years of full-scale warfare resulted in the slavery of millions of people for which the Europeans of a few hundred years ago exploited this trade, naming the it Atlantic slave trade. The city of collection named Suandoller saw this and cursed the lands, for they had cursed the lands of the Middle East before. The desert spread across all the North African continent, creating the Sahara Desert, which is still spreading today.

Many of the tribes of North Africa moved southward in search of better lands and better lives. The anarchy created by the wars caused many tribes and mixed-lineage people to move to the south near the nations of Congo and to the Middle East, eventually to make their way to Northern Europe. These lines were fully consumed by the lines of the original people of these lands. Many of these people were killed and put into slavery as invaders. Many cities of the collection saw this as an opportunity to steal lines and acquire lines in an attempt to take revenge on the people of the prestigious cities for the battles they had lost. Many of the people were cursed and fell to shame and disgrace, with many curses and metaphysical beings following them. They were tormented with their minds and bodies bruised, creating psychological and physical trauma.

Eventually, many cities triumphed and degraded the stature of these lines. The descendants of their beloved warriors Boku Sarai and Couchou Shcousanchu were now the fallen and were not acceptable in prestige standing. The status quo has shifted, and many of the enthusiasts and contributors to their line's achievements have forfeited their sponsorship. Owning a fallen line can be tormenting; the status of the recently fallen can be unbearable since the prerequisite for law has to be fulfilled without waver. This was a serious issue for they can be executed in contact with some cities through acts of self-indulgence.

The Roman royals were major participants in the North African wars, for they were a clan of great agenda in collection and war. The attack on the pyramids of Garamantes and the descendants of the Pharos had to flee with a minority population of about twenty descendants; they left Whaejetu and landed in Sicilia. The people of the pyramids were killed, scattering the lines. The Roman royals' chosen line was a descendant of these scattered remains of the holy men of the African court of religious ;ractices. Many of the royal cities saw the travesty in the decimation of more than 1 billion inhabitants and sought to acquire some of these line legitimately in lower standing. Thousands of years have passed, and many of the fallen lines of the African people were purchased as slaves and sent to Rome, Greece, and the Ottounian countries. They were eventually mixed with the lines of the natives and became part of the populace. This became a battle for strength; the prestige of the lines were not degraded but seasoned, and their popularity and favor in law had risen to new heights through the wars of Europe and the Middle East.

Many of the gods sought to acquire the line and legitimacy to land since many of the African people had the right to indemnify the gods of the human beings. They took these lines through slavery with the Arabian nations, acquiring the bulk of slaves to participate in the teachings about God, for which many are the descendants of these human gods. African slaves were bought by the Holy Roman Empire—Curonians, Polotsk, Novgorod-Serversk, Keiv, Raska, Bulgaria, Argon, France, Georgia, Erzurum, Mosul, and Jazira, just to name a few. This trend continued throughout the latter side of the last millennium until the end of slavery by the British in 1834. Many of the people of the worlds today including the southern Nazi of Germany are descendants of these beloved African bloodlines.

Many collection cities saw problems with these dominating moves by the Roman royals. Arab sultan cities and the Danish Court of Royals sought to keep their lines pure, meaning, keeping the people more than three hundred generations from the original African lines. They chose to hide their lines in the rural areas of Europe until the exploration of the New World. Many of these lines belonging to the collection cities moved to the rural areas, of the New World and were very protective of their lines. The lines of the cities would eventually be incorporated to the mass populace for the benefits of the favorable lines from the African continents.

Many royals and their cities sought to accept the African lines, but this would lead to the drowning of the cities with the lineage and associated laws to the European and Lithuanian lines. This was not a good idea for the Dacia royals, who were largely in the collection of pairs by marriage and not by lineage. They are the original collectors of some of the Bohemians through Cotini and not through Lugii. The law prohibits the discussion of forced acquisition at the border territories between two disputing cities during land negotiations. The Danish council and the Darcian governor sector's lines were not of the original Egyptian or Ethiopian line but through those in Congo and Togo, which were originally from Osroenia. These lines were drowned in a similar position by the Swhaleem lines of Arabia, and the laws of polygamy stifled the collection schemes. This was catastrophic and resulted in the sharing of the young and wives with collectors from servants and worker cities.

Many of the men who were married to multiple women did not love all of their wives and wished not to be forever obligated to them in the afterlife. This created many problems in the Dieu, as this was an issue that had to be addressed on the earthly plane. Many Islamic laws were set by their god, stating that the treatment of wives must be fair and equal and must be embraced. In fact, the laws in some regions had reached to punishment for the ill treatment of their wives. This issue in

Dieu led to many wars for which many women were destroyed and the treatment of women on earth worsened. Many beings from these cities sought to curse the women of the earth with temptation and defilement of laws, leading to their execution and poverty.

The women were helped by many who saw the cruelty in their situation and advised their humbleness; this led to their men implementing the laws of covering their entire body. Some of those cities who hated the women made them specially beautiful and put lust in the hearts of their men, creating wars and hatred for the love of their women. They further worsened the situation by cursing the women with beauty so that their flesh will always be desirable to the point of shame. If they were to display their beauty, the men had no choice but to choose to go to war.

When the wars of the Middle East were gory, a Jew, the father of their lines, found an answer to the curse. They would reclaim the lines of the Islamic people and return them to the honor of their forefathers. They specifically worked on the lines who needed the most help, breeding them carefully with the lines of the northern tribes and initiating laws to the holders of land and tragedy to release their minds. Initiating prayer and mead to help pacify their minds, they must pray at least five times a day to stay in the presence of God, for they could fall into the traps of the scorn of women. Finally, when all women could not be hurt anymore, they cursed their hair to be the most beautiful part of the body.

The hair of a woman in the Persian lines had to be covered from a man of those lines because he was powerless before her. Her hair became just as with nakedness, which could lead to her execution. This caused another problem in the Dieu since these people were to be remade in the Dieu. The reincarnated men would seek to spend their eternity in the presence of these women. Many sought out these women as soul mates, for their beauty transcends boundaries of the Dieu; many of the men that looked onto the women on earth were looking for the beauty of the Persian curse. This beauty is known as the Beauty of the Shallows, for the wars within Darcia led to the reincarnation of many of the executed women to more humane cities and confiscation of excess wives who were unhappy or ill treated by the citizens of the Darcian cities. Many complications befell, and the laws of collection of the beloved had to be revamped and later repealed.

The Incipit was the beginning of the change for women of that region; the cities of collection that cursed the women had to leave through a deal with the Jewish fathers in exchange for the collection of the women and the people of Somalia. The humans needed to fully understand what this meant and had to physically conform to laws of diet, housing, and marriage. This was a long and arduous journey the people must endure, but they were surely not alone for the laws of collection of the Jew were in favor of the creators and were of ancient laws of power and jurisdiction. The Surah chapter 24 states that if a man is unfaithful to his woman, he is to be issued many lashes, for this meant the human had to be physically coerced into doing what was right for his own sake. If they were unfaithful, they would now come under the jurisdiction of the Darcia and would have to be collected by them.

One such woman was Salaoime, a very beautiful woman who was pursued by many men in her society during the time before the covering of the heads of women in the Arabian/Persian Empire. One day while she was talking to a merchant in the market, her husband accused her of heresy. She was the friend of this merchant for some time, and she was dragged out of the markets and taken to the Raddirscria or the place of execution and was stoned to death. The laws of Darcia states that if a regional corporation collects a woman that was unfaithful to her husband, it is decided upon by a court if she and her husband would live together in the cities of celibacy noncheating.

Salaoime was displeased in her afterlife with her husband for the mistrust had transcended the grave; he eventually renounced her partnership and had to become a lesser being in the city of the royals. She could not be remarried or could not seek another mate. Displeased with her social position, she fled to another city and was killed. Her components were put into a container, which was placed in a tomb of disgraceful things. During the war, combatants raided the cities and confiscated all the valuables of that city, including the condemned. She was eventually saved by the Court of Women and placed in the

Council of Reconciliation. She now sought to collect all women within the systems, disbanding the cities' rightful claim to free use of their collected beings. They are now the supporters of philosophy and laws surrounding women's rights. Women in the system suffer under the rule of men, and the grandiloquence of the royals afford worse faiths upon females within the Dieu.

Women have caused many wars throughout the history of the Dieu. The curses that befell women are carried to the Shangri-las in haste and hate as they transcend through the ranks of reincarnation. Women in battle were scorned until after the war of Scarcellies; this ended after the Greek dynasty, where the women of the Dieu fought for the lines of their descendants. They were given the judgment of extinction because of their position in the physical world coupled with their jurisprudence and tariff in the laws. Many lines of the North African cities were to be ended as they had the advantage to cleanness and intelligence in the ways of mind control. This would mean that the alternative to acceptability of law regime had to change, where the laws of Zakabhuke could now no longer dominate since it has reached an obstruction in applicability.

The women were not of the position or opinion to breed a human with a being from the latter verses of the universal Fhyumees. Especially like the virgin births of the stories of old, which meant the humans would gain supernatural powers for some time. The Zakabhuke were in favor of these lines since they could use these lines to eradicate the lines of their foes, forcing them to accept their lines as dominant and superior in ability and legal standing. The Zakabhuke were not easily giving up their scepter of superiority to struggle with the bitter wars of the laws of army distribution military might.

Lines of the Spartans and the Philogeons were of the gods of Dieu and had the ability to physically and legally destroy the armies and cities of their enemies. Many of these lines eventually return to mere human strength but were revered as golden lines legally by the citizens of the collection cities. These lines are afforded all the rights of God within the system, for which only a god can kill another god. The Jews hasve been one major line that has been and still is practicing these laws, followed by the Hindus of India and the Africans of North and Central Africa. Many of these lines today still practice various forms of witchcraft as a remembrance of their ancestors' abilities.

The Darcian royals cannot afford such stance in law since their claims of collection are tied and cannot be resolved until the issues regarding polygamy are unhinged in stance from military operational laws. The Zakabhukians pleaded with Darcians to accept the motion to vote for the induction of demigods within the systems, which quashes both military operational laws and eventually reinstates monogamous laws. This was literally nonsense to the Darcians since most military operations depended on polygamy for soldiers and coupled with the presence of the Spartan Principle. The creation of a demigod can only strengthen an army and the polygamous practice. This was an insult to the Darcians, and they chose to withdraw themselves from the meeting.

The Darcians wrote a letter to the court of issues regarding the takeover of their lines by the Holy Roman Empire. They openly stated that they had no intention of engaging in war at this time and had moved their lines to Alani across the Black Sea. Upon reaching Alani, they were met by the Mongolian Courts of Revenge, which were in the operation of capturing the lesser city's tribes within their kingdom. The Mongolordian armies were in the practice of capturing the smaller tribes of their foes via military force and used them as slaves. The Mongolordians openly replied; in this era, the allotted timeframe for slaves was a thousand years without legal consequence.

The Darcians replied that those lines were in remediation from previous applications of law for which the regrowth of the line and legal standing must be regenerated to acceptable standing. The Mongolordian Court replied "agreed" for the line will not be enslaved for no more than two generations, for which the court would abscond the claim. Upon such date, they left the region; the Mongolordians added the lines that were crossed that will now belong to the Darcians and all titles and obligations have been removed. The title of embellishment shall be put into effect where the lines are to be revered as brand new from the date of handover.

They replied thank you and sought to move those descendants to a remote concealed area. Many of the lesser cities deployed spies to see where she could have marched those lines. There are many cities who hold license to freely capture in low standing among the courts of appeal. If the Darcians openly allowed these lines to become entangled; they could topple the practices of interbreeding, delaying the processes of the Court of Liberalism of the third emperor, a move that could shift the balance of collection for eleven eras. The Darcians immediately shifted and spoke through a self-projected avatar of the Courami.

The Dacian royals had no interest in war during this period since they had many enemies who were ready to invade and sack their cities. They simultaneously motioned for the humble disillusion of separation of the lesser acceptance of law from the African courts since they too were advocates of polygamy. The struggle with the laws of collection were challenging enough to maneuver within the legal framework of the Court of Women. Uprising in their cities caused resentment for the Roman royals and the emperors, which drew attention to their schemes and debauched their cause.

The Danish Court of Royals asked the Darcia to join their fight for the removal of the Roman royals' hold on the illegitimately intertwined lines of the European nations. The Darcia humbly replied no for they cannot take a royal stance against the Roman royals. The royal stance could not be fostered because their lines and laws are intermingled. These intermingling lines could result in a devastating reshuffle of affairs. The Darcians in a measure of good graces sent a small court of influencers to join their cause until the situation arises where the Roman royals release their lines to the Egyptian councils or to a military court of appeals.

The Darcians were advised to seek help from a willing clan, but many were scorched by the affairs of collection within the society. The leader of the Darcia was sent to the Odedi, a very ancient clan that was made by the kingdom of Peroidus during the era of Faltashou. During this era, the systems were far different, and the earth had not been in existence. Clans that were this old were rare to find since the wars take their toll on the lives of the patrons of collection. The Odedi were born of the era of space travel for which the devout beings were allowed to travel within their domain as gods without boundaries for physical ambient needs and dependencies.

They were given the abilities needed to roam space for millennia, moving from planet to planet, creating life, and interacting with the beings of the distant systems of Pearlfieltheous. They were allowed to travel the different alluvials, interacting with their alter selves and alternate version of their own reality. They called the upper and lower versions of earths the Saltuschian and the Norshechethien. These were the dimensions that were used by the wizards and witches of old. There are many other dimensions and alluvials that were created by many other beings of the collection schemes. The Jewish cities have many for which there are four main realms men can access. They are the Atziluth, Beri'ah, Yetzirah, and the Assiah. The Jewish concepts are broad and are assigned in an order of ascendance. These were old practices that were banned during the eras of Olieishaaurha, where the Odedi, along with the help of the Jews, were one of the first to reinstate its functionality within the collection schemes. The Odedi were responsible for giving man the ability to do such things.

They were a clan of justice and advocated for the balance of life, allowing all beings the ability to enjoy their life, removing discrimination and misplaced hatred from the lives of the downtrodden and the underprivileged.

They were the warrior clans of revenge, teaching the science of defense, and the recognition for the growth in technique; they were the start of all precise strikes. These were the teachings of old that were lost to the last era. These ideas left the collection schemes in shambles, directly causing the Raija to take over. The new leaders including the Raija implemented laws of sectioning and endorsing the appointment of the emperors. The Odedi's mode of psychology is one of the symbolizing of ideas in a stanza of downward lettering and syntax, which is displayed in their writings, where tacit and fatwas are impossible. The minds of their beings are especially designed in the old systems of the Kajwaisha, where the syntax in recognition of ideas are the lettering for the collection of associated factors in assimilation and synthesis.

The queen of the Darcia opted for an alliance since there was no war between the Darcian royals and the Odedi. The Mongolian royals who were under the Odedi emperor Galthrones welcomed the Darcians and their cities. They were presented with parcels of land where she could safely and quietly rebuild a city of a monogamatic culture. The Roman royals were severely jealous and attempted to go west with their armies but met stiff battles in Scythae, where they absolutely lost. They could not have reached the center of the Mongolordian Empire for their population at the time was 3.5 billion with the Chinese and East Indian cities at bay. Many nations could not have physically defeated this army since they were as fierce and skilled in war as they were accomplished warriors.

The inner Mongolian autonomous regions were controlled by Shenshuas, the royals in charge of all affairs within the society. The ideas surrounding the building of castles, martial arts, war strategies, conquering of cities, execution of rivals, and the pillaging of allies were all managed by Shenshuas. The laws of Completion of Succession states that if a tribe has been the breaker of rules, his claim to laws shall be in violation and accounted for by the number of their trespasses to their foe. This law dictates all laws of behavior toward the system, including stance that can never be broken. All individuals must participate with a clean tongue and speak with specific words without tarnish.

The laws of capturing the minds of the men cannot be utilized because of absolute noninfraction against the court of arbitration. Their strength is unmatched for their only major rival was China, who had no choice but to build a wall against their armies. The Romans were greatly afraid of this army, and their cities were impenetrable. The Roman royals looked to the Odedi for advice in conquering this adversary. The advice and guidance of the Odedi was of ancient wisdom of long-standing opulence within the succession schemes. This was not the style of the Roman royals who could not afford these schemes even though they accommodated long-term invincibility in war. For honor, loyalty, and intelligence are their mode for survival, a hard task if one does not accept the realities of his life as a soldier. This is especially true for the beings that live in the Dieu.

The desires and drive for gain and change has led to the destruction of countless clans. This was accounted for in law but was ignored by the emperors as they had great need for collection because of the need for defense and safety from the ancients who partake in constant war. Almost all the ancient clans participate in the collection schemes, viciously exerting their will upon the citizens of the various cities in an attempt to acquire increased numbers of souls. This led to the abandonment of many laws. One such city was the city of Furuchett, who was an enemy of Feltheiade. The Furuchett's example to the system was one of long-standing survival in good standing as the laws of the system evolve along the lines of increased need for predominance in collection.

This has afforded the situation of frequent destruction of many. Many of the citizens of the Dieu have never seen the change of the Galealo, the change of the guards of a thousand eras. The guards of a thousand eras were the guards of an ancient queen who ruled the collection schemes of the previous terms set by the bankers. This was new knowledge to many of the royals, but the African court knew of this forgotten history. The African courts warned against speaking of this story because of the Purger of Hearts, the broken heart that closed its door to those that operated on the systems, the destroyers of men. The Purger of Hearts was an ancient woman named Torube, who dominated the systems. She and her people were the architects of law and the anatomy of the beings, designing the systems along the lines of beauty and decadence, lavishing the cities around.

The cities were successful, and as the cities grew, so did the importance for collection. As the cities became full and the schemes became productive, the desired became harder to acquire, resulting in the silent choking that would become strife among the collectors. The Feltheiade had no choice but to implement a scheme that would avoid the laws of reward and adornment of the beings, leading to the implementation of the right to merely ask for compliance. In an attempt to gain concordance with the law, they chose to implement the act of tutorship as the devout could accept the position of student. The laws were changed to accommodate this new popular scheme as it would afford more beings that were willing to learn. This resulted in the abundance of art and engineering minds within the society.

This became a problem since the acceptance of a soul mate became the best practice in asking for their hand in marriage. One awful day during the festival for the Convivial of the Royals, a powerful god asked a young human mage for her hand in marriage. She denied his voice and said no, for which he was angered at his humiliation and cursed the woman to a malformed shape into the conjuncture of animals. This became a pet-tie in their law for pleasing the Gods, which caused many Gods to do the same to beautiful women in fear of not gaining their hand in marriage. This caused all the gods of these cities to be killed for cruelty. As a result, they destroyed the cities and the lives of the villagers with plagues and disasters then killing the young of their rival and those of allied tribes.

They willfully created many psychological trauma on the human beings; the Torube cried, showing their disgust for their actions. They reminded their leaders and cast plagues upon the lands of the cities and destroyed her beloved people. Upon confirmation that she saw them kill themselves, cursing her name as they died. She wondered why and how this could have happened.

An enemy said to her, "Your love and the love within their cities become their pride, for they were ashamed to become low ranking. Their beloved self-images that you congratulated became their pride. Their self-inflated egos drove them to madness that went undetected under your reign, which became the evil you have despised so much. They have become dirty murderers just like the rest of our soldiers. The only difference is they destroyed entire cities because of a girl."

She chose not to love a god, and they killed many for it. Their shame became their tears, for the tears of a few warrants the murder of many. This was the beginning of a war, for which the Torube people attacked and destroyed the Furuchett's cities and left none standing because of his words to their queen. She was saddened by their behavior, and her heart was broken. Shame grew upon her and her people; they have resorted to violent action because of the denial of affection.

She silently left the collection schemes and locked away herself. The cities under her were in great shame and assembled around their queen. The shame that was upon them caused even more wars to the destruction of the remaining pieces of her celestial heart. She created a new race to protect her cities, the guards of the Galbulcheuzri meaning the guards of those who were once made of blood. The Torube and her people were never seen by many again. What was seen was the presence of the guards and their swords. The people vanished into the blackness of nonexistence as the times changed. Many have tested their strength against the guards, but none has survived to talk of their experience.

The Darcians were afraid of what could happen next; the idea of deception from foreign allies dawned upon their cities once more because of the knowledge concealed by the Odedi. They were very old and witnessed these massacres firsthand. The Odedi surely knew who were the individuals involved and who were the clans responsible for the slaughter of millions of cities. They had no choice but to stay with the Odedi until such time where they would leave indefinitely. The court of Danish royals wondered where was the system the Torube built. The Odedi pointed to the lesser Fhyumees and to the southernmost regions of the earth, places that were now covered by water.

The Danish royals sought a partnership with the Odedi, but they no longer operated in a physical capacity. Many of the older clans don't. They simply advised the Danish royal to extend an invitation for the Odedi to be an official adviser to their court. The Odedi humbly accepted. There was only one stipulation; they must swear an oath of secrecy—they agreed for the African royals were reluctant to court with the Odedi. The Odedi knew that Ashuni was aboard the African court of councils. The Africans laughed, and Ashuni asked the Odedi if they were afraid. The Odedi said the wars were not theirs. It was not the war of their forefathers, and if their eyes did not deceive them, they were the very last being of their civilization.

Ashuni laughed, but her voice sounded of the hurt from old tears, they said in an ancient African language to be careful, for the blades of the Okahi never dulled. She replied, "I was the last because of my beauty." The old man among Odedi replied, "We have never seen your beauty but heard of tales of something beautiful among you." She said in Skeddiesh, an old stone language of the created beings, "You have many tricks to learn." The Odedi said, "If such rumors were true, you Ashuni should have the power of the Conguari, and only the Mysarrios and their descendants could conceive its unconceivable power. The court asked Ashuni, "How can you use this power if you do not think of the way they do?" She said, "The Feltheiade." The old man of the Odedi said, "Fear not, child. I feel for your loss, but that age is over." Ashuni replied, "The allies of your creators will die." They all replied, "That was never our fight."

CHAPTER 10

The Control of the Lives of Men: The Death of the Heart

A young city within the Arabic court interjected and asked who was the most beautiful woman they had ever seen.

The Odedi master sighed and replied, "There is a myth of an ancient type of people borne of the systems during a time when all components of a being could have actually been collected. A time when the laws of collection and design was not dictated by numbers and productivity. Collection was because of art and beauty, the concept of perfection was the passion of the architects of the system. The woman's named Cheiruel Nierufrios of Sansamata. It is said that she stood 500 feet tall and her body was strictly designed along the lines of feminine sculpture.

"Her voice sounds of the resonating motion of a G as the bow caresses the dead strings of a violin as it creates beautiful echo across the atmosphere. Her eyes were of the colors of the rain. Her hair was like the waves of the ocean flowing all the way to the base of her back. Her skin was the color of metal with no blemishes, annealed to the point of accenting her smooth curves. She had no cracks or marks on her body. She was perfectly proportioned by divine incriminations. Her hair was as white as snow and shimmering like a golden sunset on the flowing surface of water.

"Those people of old were not created in haste and legal ramification, there was no distraction to the cause and no effect on the designs of anatomy. They were created in wisdom and aesthetic during a period of freedom many eras ago. These stories are very old, and no one knows where these people are. You should not concern yourself with beauty for beauty leads to the destruction of many."

The African cities concurred. Ashuni replied, "How is it that I have never heard of that race?" He replied, "I am sure you have heard of the tribes with metallic skin."

She said yes, but they are now of folk law. First you must try to find Sansamata, and just as she tried to look into the old man, he said, "No, Ashuni, you cannot see inside of me." She cried and shifted.

A member of the Arabic court asked, "Has anyone ever seen Ashuni?" The African councils replied, "Of course." The young macer asked, "Was she beautiful?" They said, no she resembled a toad, and they all laughed. One man asked, "How could she be saved because of her beauty?"

The African court replied, "It was true one of the soldiers in the exercise saw Ashuni hiding in her quarters and hid her in a purse. The battalion thought all of that race was dead and left. She found a way out of the parse and was found wandering the barren planets by the Oyabami, where she got her training. She was just an insignificant mage. Don't be too taken by her aggressive attitudes, she is just preoccupied with gaining power." Mainly because of fear for what might become her reality, they asked, "Is she powerful?" They all replied yes.

The Odedi replied, "Yes, she is too powerful for her temperament. She is not to be toyed with, and she has made extinct millions of races after leaving the Oyabami. She can be a toad of a monster if one does not know which buttons to push."

The Odedi stated she is far too young for her power; she will die when she meets the leader of her enemies. The African court said, Why don't you train her?"

They all replied, "She needs to be humble to learn the ways of Shinousamara. That is what she needs to defeat Goutouka. The African worriers laughed saying Ashuni has no chance of defeating Goutouka. If he knows she is hateful toward him, the battalions would surely return to finish her off and us as well."

The Danish court scorned the topic, saying, "Let's take the gesture of the Arabic cities and create beauty in the world." They decided to implement a competition where all the women of the world would be judged to be acclaimed the most beautiful woman of her time. The Miss World competition was created in 1951 from an earlier bikini competition, where Kiki Hakansson was the winner. Almost instantly, all the owners of the beloved lines vouched to be a part of the line where the most beautiful woman of all the world was crowned. This meant the resolve to many clams and conflicts surrounding beauty and structure of the lines. For the first time in years, many of these issues in lines applicability of beauty could be weighed.

Almost all the collection cities agreed this could be good resolve. There was always the age-old adage of the most beautiful women on the earth coming from southern Europe; the African and Asian courts all laughed. The Roman royals were furious and inspired the pope to bless the pageant and announced the removal of bikinis in the proceedings, making it a professional competition of beauty, poise, affluence, and insight. In 1952, it was won by Sweden then followed by France; the Arabic courts laughed when in 1964, Egypt won the title. They claimed the women of their lines were always a high standard of beauty.

The Roman royals scoffed at the year France won, but the Arabs laughed and said those lines were partly that of the Danish royals. In fact, the physical shape of the women are not of the original Italian type. The Roman royals realized they have lost, for it was true the shape and colors of their women are of the Iberian types from the northern Roman Empire. To their delight, the Danish court claimed if they accept the fact that the lines do not have the shape of the Italian lineage, then the line must be absconded from the legal royal registry because of the laws of dissimilarity from origin; the Roman royal cursed the pageant.

The Arabic cities' courts asked for a motion to keep the pageant fair and allow the world to judge the most beautiful woman. From the beginning of the competition to present time, it seems the Italian people have never won the Miss World competition. The Roman royals attempted to cheat and changed the human record where in 1953 to 1969, Italy won the Miss World competition. They inserted a win to remove their shame. The humans would never truly know the truth about the competition. In 2015, the Asian gods attempted to cheat to win the Miss Universe pageant over the Spanish lines of Columbia. The host made a mistake and read the wrong name; in the alluvials, there is the existence where Columbia was recorded as the winner of the pageant in 2015.

It was said that this happened in Estonia where the host of the pageant read the wrong name. The Roman royals were not always a clan to play fair. The Roman royals are the laughingstock of the Dieu; they were given the title of ugliest women of the world. This was just a jeering gesture to the Roman royals court; they seemingly took it seriously and sought to release their claims to soul mate collections with no legal titles to collecting wives from foreign bloodlines. A stake to the heart of the Bleudals cities, for they collected the beloved through the lines of Millan.

CHAPTER 11

The Animal's Right to Priesthood

An era in time used to be a dimension of a timeless place. The Wimzghraes were the inhibitors of these eras; they are the beloved beings who were revelated. They were a cherished being and commensurated because of their profound knowledge and perspective. They were made from the remaining components of the exculpated dead, mainly from confiscated tormented and tortured beings. This led to their beloved stance, and they were cherished like the women of the earth. Kings adorned the Wimzghraes and all in their presence. For this, they were widely sought after as companions. They were the preferred helpers of the emperors and then their descendants were adopted as the children of the Salashouires. These were the collected animals of the human kingdoms. The emperors and royals pay homage and salutations to their direct descendants for power.

Their creator is still in contact with the elite ruling societies of these dimensions. No one knows for sure how old their lines of succession are. It is now an issue in the lower courts to search for a general to lead in the wars against the Algurador. The generals Einestshlund, Jaeiphesys, and Gourmey were borne of these clans. The courts are always in search of soldiers to continue the wars against the Algurador. Many soldiers and generals abandoned the battles because the courts simply wished to coerce and pressure the Alguradorians into signing an agreement for alliance. The generals looked to themselves to find a way out of their obligations to the courts. They abandoned the wars during the Faltashou era, where the wars were of heightening intensity and power. The generals were untouched by the wars of the collected beings because they are from the dendritics of Oushghnour, a place only few men can visit.

The first Wimzghraes was made from the remains of the very first cursed and thrown-away woman of the old-lover societies. The women were collected by the god of the Feltheiade as they forced the women into servitude in attempts to gain the rights to their soul. The women were tortured and killed as the laws evolved away from the favor of the gods of that city. The gods cursed and tortured the women in the usual fashion as the law would permit in the seasons. It was thought they were secretly moved to another dimension far away from the collections schemes, forgetting the pains of living a human life. In fact, they were moved to a secret location to assist in elevating the position of the women of the world were in. Looking onto the world, they would secretly help the people find their way back into nobility and honor. In this, they could not be seen or accede to the laws of collection; their operation was illegal and has caused immense damage to the cities' surrounding systems. The emperors and Schougnars are vile and egotistical men, driven by power and greed. They have always respected the Wimzghraes, but value the efficiency of the systems more than their relationships with the Wimzghraes.

The Wimzghraes took what little unwanted components of the humans they could and slowly reconstructed the facets of men and women as the wars persisted. They brought an existence of an honored civilized society of people from the collected systems. The wars for collected beings were too vicious and outlandish where the workers and volunteers were scarce. This is largely due to the violence and genocide that was committed by the emperors and the royals of the schemes. During the era of Miluescious, a woman was cursed under the laws for the appreciation of precious things where she was given seven years to live. The God malformed a plant to show her the doom of her choice.

She cursed the god and spirit of his vicious gesture that he called kindness, for which he proceeded to torment and traumatize her.

The beings of Wimzghraes saw this but could not intervene, so they used a cat that was given the power to comprehend human ideas and the power of speech to change her existence. Upon the hour of her death the woman was not devoured into multiple parts but was kept whole and crossed over into an unknown dimension with the cat. This was done for all to witness, and the awe of the gods was their shame. This caused many wars for the woman could not be found and the wielder of this power was not in their registry.

The sentiment of the gods were of the thoughts that a woman cursed on earth for the denial of the birthrights of the gods led to the shame and disgust for many of their counterparts. The mistake to ask for her soul and despite her answer of no, the god chose to curse the woman and proceeded to execute her in so-called correct standing, to collect the soul in the legal procurement as though the answer by the bearer was yes. The legal practice of accepting a soul as if it was in the right of being answered in the assured decision of yes, and proceeding to continue, informing the woman of her demise in kind stance, as if she was waiting for her time with him in the Dieu.

When the woman proceeded to insult the god, cursing him for his actions, the god simply left, accepting legal position for a caveat and initiating taunting the woman. This was under the subsection of law associated with soul collection, where the soul can be acquired if the bearer agrees and allows the asker to take the soul. If the reincarnated being is in the event under dispute for the legitimacy of the actual ownership of the soul, that being must love the asker and agree to be with the asker absolutely. Those laws are associated with his statement of "I did not and could not have heard that," which was a disrespect to the woman and a show of lack of care for her ideas and feelings, which is breaking of the laws of care and guardship associated with the god of benevolence.

The assistants to the holder of the law proceeded to torture and maliciously gestured the woman in the attempt of taming and gaining her trust and acceptance of his hand in marriage among other invitations to affiliation. He was advised that he could not keep her mind and was gestured or advised to change her temperament and disgust toward him. The god simultaneously attempted many factions of law consecutively and simultaneously created beings to convince the woman into trusting them. This was also an infraction of the laws of procurement.

The woman knows that acceding to the gestures and offerings would lead to her absolute death. The law of accepting a soul in the denial of an answer has to be protected by the holders and beneficiaries because of its stance in lineage and land applicability. The presence and acceptance of the god over the line was ignored. In the event that the god was of an observer, their stance in law was of they had more rights than the God over the line. They asked the woman for her soul without permission to speak to the woman from the god of the line. They openly acceded to the laws of lineage Durilthieans, which states that a god can do what he or she pleases to their lines. They also acceded to the law that any God can ask for the souls of any devotee. Implementing the law of Apelaintes control, where the woman must not be allowed to say some things to offend the judges of the applicability of their laws.

Among these, the judges are very protective of the laws and the compliance for laws in an apparent stance of preponderance. These judges do not acknowledge the acceptance of the souls by the God of the lines since they are not in the stance of feud or in direct agreement. There are many violations of presiding laws of the lines of the system, for example, the laws of birth, where the month and conception of the being contribute to the being's existence and endemic energies. The length of time the God of the lines is presiding over, whether monotheistic or polytheistic acceptance of God and gift of knowledge to teaching to another God or entity.

If they proceeded, they can erode the laws of lineage, land, God presence, and knowledge about the origin of the devotee. This resulted in many wars for which they still did not accept the idea that the devotee does not appear on their own but must be reared by a school of a god. They have neglected the fact that a God takes care of them, and they cannot just come to a place and ask for a soul, get the answer of no from the devout, and simply take an article in law and claim the right as though it was yes. For which lies are a part of their law and is endorsed by the emperor in charge of their city. For if they claim one correct stance in law, the God must leave the field, and they can torture and collet the beings of that city.

They have not known where they have evolved to for in the alluvials of the upper court, their laws are in line with what is insane and madness. For the god cannot state the detail of the incursion due to the effects on the events on the future. That statement could warrant the confiscation of his devout by those of lesser abilities than a god, for a god does not create law in effects of standing on the future. They have proven to be lesser beings for which they can be executed for the excessiveness in law.

The animals of collection are all under one city; any other city of collection wishing to collect animals must accede to the laws of the cities of the Wimzghraes where cruelty to animals is forbidden. Animals are not allowed to be devotees. Animals are not to be a part of the sanctions of Sukuniesha and Ascureuda where animals are not to be put in front of idols or statues to serve the gods. They are not to be cupped for the sake of praying in particular stances and influenced in the sequencing of being degraded in the presence of a god. These are scenarios in law where a god must be in domination of the devout at all times.

Animals are not allowed to take part in mortification rituals and male sodomy. Human beings are not allowed to have sexual intercourse with animals. Men and gods nurtured the idea that they could do as they pleased with the animals of the systems. This was partially true with some distinctions; the allowable domination over the animals was described as domination and uses, ideally for food. This soon led to philosophies of men having the rights over all animals, which resulted in cruelty of animals by man and the gods. It was said that man was given dominion over the animals, and the gods were not given authority over the animals. The gods were given authority of the lines of men, for which the gods claim they have dominion over the animals, which is a perversion of the rights of men.

Many rituals have sprung up through time where the torturing of animals, by knives and by fire, was accepted by the gods. The gods endowed the men with feelings of joy and superiority over all things and life. This became the savor, a desirable type of mind within their schemes. These type of minds pleasured the judges of the courts as they joyously inflicted pain and suffering on the disobedient and the beloved who have fallen. These practices both on the system and in the cities of collection soon became law. Men had to commit the act of self-mortification and animal suffering to remove their sins and gain favor of their gods. In some cases, they were barred from the divine regions of the cities. The gods delegated cities to punish their devotees who were displeasing and disobedient to their word; these are the places humans call hell.

Throughout all religions, there were many gods who had their own versions of hell, where they cast the souls of the disgusting and hateful or simply their enemies. The collection schemes soon favored the schemes of torture and self-inflicted pain where the gods would worsen the pains of the devout to display their presence and pleasure. Many of these reincarnated beings became gods themselves, for which it was required for men to emaciate themselves to gain wishes and favor of their gods. These men eventually grew hateful personalities as they were required to perform these rituals from birth. They grew insensitive and inflicted pain on their wives and children as a gift to their gods. They had to suffer their wives and newborn children by various means as a pleasing gesture. One such ritual was they had to tie the neck of a three-month-old baby to the feet of a goat and watched as the baby was dragged along through the dirt. The god would fill their hearts with joy and abundance as the baby cried and eventually died.

This culture remained until it reached the Court of Kings, where the kings of the countries would torture, kill, and slaughter many of their people as a sacrifice to their god. Naturally, the population of the people of the kingdoms of men would be depleted and the rituals had to become of season. The sectioning and breeding of particular casts and levels of societies were chosen and bred for these rituals. Animals were used in place of humans when there weren't enough humans to offer, to the disdain of the collection schemes. Many cities sought to use the devout of their enemies as their willful Durghametis, the being who is suffered or sacrificed in pain. The sacrifice of enemies became a festival throughout the worlds for which laws of collection were altered to endow these new delicacies in collection and sport among the gods. This led to the building of centers and colosseums for the impalement and sacrifice of human beings.

The same practices were adopted in the cities of collection, where for their sins on earth, men were killed, burned, and sacrificed repeatedly with their bodies regenerated as they diminished; they were tortured and suffered for eternities. The laws of collection became tricks to put the devout and loved ones of foes in the pits of torture and doomism. The tears of the gods soon reached the earth, for which their participation and unsuccessful position soon led to the desire or want to remove the torturing of the beings on earth. They could not because of its popularity and their stance of being unsuccessful, so they quietly and slowly sought to quash the effects or feelings of the men who commit these acts.

They simply added small mental gestures and signs to the dead or suffering Durghametis to reduce the signs of joy and abundance. This was done silently as not to offend the god that was the successor of the ritual. These signs were disgusting to the sacrificer and was low-lying beneath mindful presence within the scenario. Torture continued to flourish among the systems where it became enshrined in the culture and languages of building affluence. It was the guideline for how one should behave, ideas of actual self and aught self, for which behaviors of contemporary human being would be considered madness, especially those of humane concepts.

A festival or evening gala entertainment would be the observance of the emotion, pain, and affliction of the tortured and suffering beings within the Dieu. Virgins of the earth were chosen then groomed and sacrificed to become these beings in Dieu who were to be displayed. They were the evening entertainment; it was an honor on earth to become one of these virgins to be sacrificed to the gods. They knew not what befell them, and in heaven, they lived until their time came and was tortured on display and then burned and destroyed in a beneficent poise. In some cases, they were applauded for the way they were seen surrendering to their demise.

These soon became favorites among the populace and were reenacted and reembellished to commemorate the scene and its triumph over the scenarios of law where the legal parameters could not have allowed a victory to secure an article of interest. The member of the courts became astute, beloved, and famed for sacrifices. The name of the rituals were given popularity and notice. Many of the cities recreated these scenarios of suffering a devotee as a form of celebration and commemoration of their national victories.

These meetings were given gesture and was becoming a speech in artistic articulation of compassion in speech. Multiple effects of torture were committed in an open dialogue. It became a complex language, where affluence and poise became a sort of discrimination of those in society. The acts on the system were already enacted in law and was now the articulation of the affiliate suffering cities. They soon became even more desensitized toward the systems, destroying major landmasses and even entire systems.

The sacrifice of entire civilizations became a necessity; soldiers would go under the instruction of their god and murder and slaughter millions of people to the pleasure of their gods. This offended the opposing gods; they resorted to using fire and brimstone to destroy enemy cities. The appeasement of the gods would usually require the sacrifice of a virgin of pure line in appeasement for their crimes done and to avoid the destruction of one's people. Many humans throughout history had to pay the toll of sacrifice to an opposing foreign god for which they did not know in an attempt to save their lives.

This homogenized the laws of collection and was considered a law for inviting a foreign god into one's city of collection. They incorporated gods of hatred into their schemes of collection, where among the children of the head god one is of vile nature; this was an attempt to cover these loopholes in the collection schemes. The popularity of these schemes led to an intervention within the system by the Jews and an unknown being in the upper reaches of their society. His agenda was that the lives of the humans had to change; he understood the inner workings of the society and knew that an in-the-face approach to changing the worlds would lead to more destruction and torment for the human beings. So they used what was available; they used the laws of the systems of torture and spoke the languages of the Durghametis of suffering.

The Jewish cities all engaged in war and acts of violence until the major cities of collection among the Durghametis nations had lost and saw that they were no longer prestigious. Their failures and shame forced their articulation, skills, and proficiency to be channeled in alternate directions, allowing them victories in the directions of health and well-being for humans. This was a slow change, and it took many years, but they eventually reduced human torture to isolated cases and human sacrifice to near zero. The Jew did do all of the above atrocities, but the father of the Jew was wise and knew how to change both of the worlds without violence and wars among the courts. He was never brought to a motion or had a case against him, for many did not know where he was from. He eventually left, leaving the world to what we know today. The last sacrifice for man was the Lord Jesus Christ; from that point onward, there is to be no more human sacrifice on the earth. Jesus Christ himself knew this, and the ritual of communion was no longer associated with cannibalism, and the bread and wine are symbols for the end of consumption of human flesh, which is a ritual known as Vargraasi.

Looking back at the changes within the systems, many hypothesized it was the popularity of the schemes that afforded this permanent change. Many of the then-powerful gods of collection have fallen to mere daemons in the eyes of the human beings. Many humans today would not engage in such activities openly, and in many cases, they were possessed to commit such acts. Many frowned upon the exercises, and because of the popularity of more peaceful scheme, they can no longer be employed. More than one-third of beings of the Dieu cursed the humans of these days for practicing such rituals. Many of the old gods hid themselves and silently operated in the shadows, influencing men to commit heinous acts while rewarding feelings of hate and love for dominance. These feelings can only be administered in moderation as stipulated within the framework for themes of the society. Eventually, many alliances were broken, and regions were split, creating even more facets and pockets of societies.

Among these split societies, animal cities were formed; many animals within this society's schemes sought to collect components of other animals to be reincarnated. These cities were not of the schemes or of the clans relating to the Raija; the emperors were once very jealous of their power and stature and sought to erode their noble standing. He tried to shame the clans in collection by belittling their animal stock within the worlds of collection. Cows were once revered as god in ancient Egypt, Rome, and India, and now they are heavily farmed by the global commerce.

This means the stance of the God belonging to the cow was to be erased, but this was prescribed by daemons of the falcon. They have broken many laws simply by prescribing this, for if the adornment of a god was awarded, it cannot be erased. The bird's application asking for the removal of the cow's embellishment as a God because they were not collected by them. Some say it was jealousy because the bird has committed many sins in the eyes of the Gods, and has fallen many times over.

The sheep was also a God in ancient Mesopotamia and Egypt, but have also become livestock. The God Aset turned into a bird during the period of the dynastic period to suckle her children of the earth. Fools trembled the earth with scorn and hatred; demons among men and honor creating Jews caused them to instill jealousy and beguile, resulting in wars that engulfed all the earth's societies while creating malevolent hearts within men. This was the beginning of the fall of all of earth's inhabitants as the gravity toward war and destruction created scorn for those that are not of the same as theirs. She moved to the mountains and hid there. On returning to Dieu, Ra in kindness gave Aset her own kingdom. The gods were jealous and sought to destroy her. She was never found, and the bird was a thief of Aset's build of herself and was used to capture the hearts and later the minds of men.

Eventually, this led to the destruction of the gods that were in charge of the birds by the Jew, for which the animals fell to the ground, becoming the fowls, the flightless birds we know today. Since then, the bird's status has fallen and its mind obliterated, for which chicken is a common source of food and the chicken is synonymous with stupidity, with stigmas attached to its name. In the Dieu, the chicken is a scorn as it is used in many rituals by some religious sectors and daemons of Carmensia.

The animals upon reincarnation would go through a number of processes to enhance their cognitive functions; they are put through a process known as growth of cognitive expedience, where they are taught through life experiences the ways and values of the Dieu. They are practiced in a dimension that does not actually exist but is a singularity of minds in a parallelism of connections, creating an infinity of systems in a band of information trajectory, which creates a learning environment that accounts for all the mistakes and challenges any being can encounter.

The beings inside are slowly drawn to the point of cognition as their physical body is modified to accommodate these changes. This was an ingenious system created by the insects, mainly the bugs, as they possessed the largest capable minds of the animal kingdom. Many of the lesser cities copied and made variations of these systems, resulting in a number of physical modifications that are available to many beings of the systems. It is thought that the animal cities are the first to actively modify themselves for cognition. This has evolved uniquely for pack animals for they have strict laws surrounding abilities and modes of perception, which results in exacting codes of conduct and segregation along mind types and behavior.

They have grown to be skilled modifiers, and through their proficiency, they have become solidary and reclusive. Many wars have befallen the animal cities, both from human cities and independent animal cities. Humans have created animal cities in an attempt to deceive and hurt the Wimzghraes animal cities. They were taught and instructed to instigate and wage wars against all known clans and become bounty hunters within the human and other cities of the Dieu. This created mass discrimination for the reincarnated animals because they were lesser beings on the systems and should be lesser beings in the collection cities. Many of the emperors passed laws, banning animals from being within city limits; and in some cases, speaking to an animal would result in death. The laws surrounding women as a lesser being was propagated, and women too were discriminated against. Many laws surrounding women were repealed, leading to the reinstatement of old laws that states women were not allowed to be unmarried in the city unless advised or recommended by an official. They could not be found without a partner or ruler to vouch for their existence.

The animal cities have also caused a lot of chaos within the systems. The laws governing their worlds have caused many malformed head modification practices. This resulted in minds that behave and cognize in many seemingly uncivilized and barbaric behaviors. These beings shaped the norms of the way they treat each other—a mass presence of jealousy, callousness, gall, and envy with little respect for anyone, especially the reincarnated humans of the system.

As a result, the royals of the system sometimes instill hate, discrimination, and torture on these independent rouge animal cities, conveying the message of respect. They should remember they were from animals, especially bugs and spiders. These result in torturous hate wars, protests of laws, and general city riots. The courts of cities that preside over the rights of animal remediation stipulates that animals should always be subordinate to humans and are to be removed if they become disaffected.

In scorn and education to the animal cities of the systems, the royals would change the bodies of animals and the minds to a design that spells what is wrong with the animal cities of Dieu. In turn, the animal cities would seek to destroy the humans of both planes; the humans would use the animals of the world to instill plagues and diseases, resulting in the need for extermination of animals and some insects. This is what the royals of the courts would like to tell the animal cities, but many of the patrician animals are out of reach to the royals, the various emperors. The royals have hatred for the animal cities, creating laws for limits to their upgrade and annihilating the disobedient and runner ways from their court workers and soldiers. Many of the animal cities feel shame and pity for those who cannot escape the wrath of the royal court and mostly seek to reduce this by limiting their reaches in collection schemes.

The animal cities are often of the position of hate for the royals because of the collection of souls; it is said that animals do not have souls, and if an animal does have a soul, it belongs to its master. If an animal that has a soul has no master, the souls of the animal goes to the highest-ranking official. Wild animals that do have souls usual have an origin of a human existence through shape shifting or from breeding with the beings of the other Nefectries. Animals usually do not have souls, but the Plotolemy is like a soul. It is an energy that comes from the earth that possesses their Arakeishna that acts like their kundalini, creating an unbreakable bond to the spheres of nature. This is a place where man needs help from the gods to experience. Through their interaction with the gods and man, they became apart from these spheres and thus needs help in their minds' operations; thus, a soul scale is used to form a soul in the being.

Animals with soul are more willing to accept ideas from foreign beings or races. Their mind is dominated by opportunity rather than nurture. They are readily becoming the subordinates of what is termed a superior being. Ideally, all animals in the wild with their Arakeishna intact are similar in behavior to a cat, for they do not wish interaction and cannot be persuaded to be the friend of a human or any other type of animal. The royals through their use of the applications within the system teach animals to assist in the system, playing stipulated roles. A dog is the best friend of a man, for it is his guide when he is disabled or handicapped, his soldier tracker when he is hunting, and his best friend at home. All dogs have a soul; dogs were given a lot so they can understand and successfully survive the worlds of men.

This is true for all animals in use by men; horses are especially mindful of their riders and instantly know where and when to allow the rider to take control. All mammals are animals that were designed to assist the human being in its endeavors. The issue with mammals is that the ancestor of the mammal was controlled mentally by the royals of Sauheidlgher and was taught and shaped to assist the human through their lives. All mammals can become food for human beings; many humans would accept eating a mammal before accepting the idea of eating a reptile. Fishes were created by the Jewish cities of destruction and punishment when they purged the earth by flooding, spewing water from the skies.

Many royals have no quarrel with the Jews since they are one of the oldest and most powerful clans in their civilizations. A fish has no soul and by law is required to be free; the laws of human affiliations are relaxed when it comes to the collection fishes. For the Jew has and will destroy entire cities for illegal collection of fish because of the gluttony afforded by the collection schemes. It has been proven that the schemes afford pain and insensitivity to the lives of the beings that are collected. The god only cares for their issues and the idea of his own society. The ideas that is of the humans as the devout does not matter to the god, for they claim the humans do not know better. This is the consensus within the cities, for which the Jews openly stated their repugnance and disagreement of the collection of fish in the court when the matter came to the courts surrounding the issues of collection of sea creatures.

The gods are seemingly worshippers of intelligence, not the intelligence of design or understanding of concepts, but rather intelligence of persuasion. One's point of view is intelligence and acceding to another's point is a sign that intelligence is within the man because he understands. Intelligence to them is the correctness of one's point of view, for which the winning of an argument is the dominance through intelligence. This, to many, is a sign of what we can call convoluted or egotistical, which is rooted in opportunistic thinking coupled with poise and beauty in self-benefit. The Jew and the Ottoman royals understand this, for which they sought to remain unnoticed but remain wise as to not accept foreign law and maintain the application of their laws. In an attempt to save face and state their elaborate right to collect anything on the system, the royals built minds out of components of the Fresnoured and created spirits. The spirit replicates the behaviors of the beings, and when the being is transformed into energy and agglomerated with matter, it would seem as though it was the being that was collected.

The royals infused two partial blended dendritics and created a doorway for which these creations would originate, claiming the laws were reconstituted from fishes and other sea creatures. In that a mock scheme was created, emulating the oceans of the system, which was controlled by the emperor's chosen officials. It was heavily inflated by the premise of the most productive facet of the system. Mass amounts of jealousy arose. Many vouched for tickets of collection to the being components, but they can only be collected by the emperor proprietors. These tickets were given to the businessmen to distribute. Upon hearing this, the Jews vowed secrecy, for it was a sort of lunacy on the behalf of the emperor.

If this word got out, the emperor could lose his standing and stature in the courts. The emperor was given exponential praise for his accomplishment and the wealth he acquired. This collection scheme created may wars for which the emperor miraculously won, most usually ending in a deal and the handing over of the collected sea creatures. These schemes increased the demand for animal in the collection states and increased desire for specific angles of belief. This resulted in many engaging in animal torture, revamping the torture schemes, which was quashed by laws of implementation of wicked acts upon the earth.

Animal pain in coercion was mostly what was allowed. Emotions of rage, anger, indignation, umbrage, disgust, and sloth are some of the emotions they instilled in animals in an attempt to control them while simultaneously refamiliarizing the cities of the latter schemes. They diverted from their previous schemes completely for these were the schemes of yesterday, and they neglected the animals after being made. Many strays and rouge clans were formed and became popular in the lesser cities. This eventually resulted in the installation of rage and ill-faithed emotions in the animals of the Dieu.

These animals fell to the lowest of lows and became vile and vicious creatures of hate and destruction. Disturbing these components to the cities, the courts of judges and the baroness of the worlds caused even more conflict. This was a sign that something had to be done about the discrimination of the animals among the collectors. The solution was found in the education of the animals, where it was prescribed that the animals should be raised in the light of beauty and articulation. They can now traverse the upper reaches of the system. Many rouge animal clans were adopted by the baroness for which their beauty became unmatched.

The beauty of animals transcends the worlds because of the wars that began through their discrimination. At one point, beauty was the panacea for the ills and detriment to all mental states. It was considered that art and appreciation was the cure. Beauty was found in all things, for beauty was translated into all forms. It was the general consensus of their world, a language for which everyone can speak. The beauty of women was the peak of these cycles for which the beauty of a man was made in jealousy, creating vile and up roaring ecstasies among the patrons. The washing with the handsome has proven to be insanity in the reputation of the members among the courts.

The handsomeness of a woman always cyclically followed the discussion of application of beauty of a man. Some of the collected dead men have a taste for beautiful women, which leads to the separation of women from some cities. To many, the issuing of spawning license for which none can be of a reproductive kind forms an excitement for flagrant essence of rare events. The availability of this cavort, as it is described, is a game of adhesion where the application of delightful amusements in legal legitimacy thwarts sedition, concomitantly circumventing carnal vehemence, abdicating the laws surrounding these modification schemes. The language is recited cyclically in an alluring charismatic eloquent doggerel.

His name was Anipostumous, born and built in excess of beauty and magnificence. He was murdered at the birth of the tenth cycles for which their world was based on the beauty and cycles of his apparent instincts of innate behaviors. His behaviors replenished the vicissitudes of life through the coherence with his cicisbeo. His idea was eventually seen as a form of cruelty to his kingdom for the national cultural sequence was based on the rhythms of his minds and relationship with others. They were seen as drunk on love, beauty, and joyousness to the point of impracticability. They were destroyed by the Wanghalrian, a vicious animal city. It was observed that his philosophies affected the world of thinking associated with the distasteful attitudes toward animals, advocating the use of his techniques as a way to control the lesser cities. He was seen as a wicked man in the eyes of the animals. They could not have put up a fight for they simply could not recognize when they were being observed or targeted in a military stance.

Many of the animal cities thought that after the destruction of many high-ranking officials like Anipostumous, they would be able to collect human beings. The soul of the human being could not be collected by animals as stipulated by the laws of the Raija. They knew they could not openly engage in war directly with the Raija so they had no choice but to collect the record of lives from the human and make it into a being. They would make these into human gods and silently insert them into the schemes and legitimately collect human souls, unnoticed by the officials. At the end of an era, they would remove the cities and share the collected souls along the lines of similarity of temperament.

The shaping of humans became what the animals considered beautiful and not what was necessary; the birth of animal gods was flooded. Many gods due to the severity of the situation and the violence of the kingdoms had no choice but to create animal kingdoms to collect without the blame of doing something wrong. Many openly broke the minor laws of the courts in attempts to desensitize the royals from sympathy. This caused them to commit violent acts in situations of control of the populace, which were social mistakes resulting in mutiny and war. They tried to hide their intention with the laws of coercion associated with the Frestution.

The royals did not understand and sought to destroy the colonies; the animal cities claimed that the perception of the royals are skewed along the lines of their own selfish favor and lawful perception of what is acceptable behavior. They even went further to state if the royals would consider their point of view in technique and position. They were met with discussion of dishonesty and beguilement. The ideas of perception associated with the situation were skewed; the animals only saw the collection side and not the well-being of the citizens. The animals stewed and tried to figure out a way where the royals could see their point of view. The animals concocted a mock collection city where they were allowed to collect human records under the license of ramification of species. The royals saw what could come of this and allowed their example of exterminating the animal cities.

The animals usually saw themselves as superior to the royals because of the extensive modification and education schemes their long-standing culture and origin has afforded. They can adequately and peacefully maneuver the alluvials of the situations better than the royals; they simply did not get into as many conflicts. The royals were disgusted by these ideas festering in the lower cities. They sought to destroy these animals but were told to wait by other courts of interests because of the gain in their collection scheme. The animals of the Resituce were scared of what the royals would do, so they silently made gestures of gifts to clans of neutral positions and enemy factions to the emperors. They would shift positions of collection schemes to clans of Omeiaja and Carthula who were under the African cities of collection. The animals and the insects' cities applied pressure of evidence for the implementation of gods on the cities. They instituted witchcraft and other facets of metaphysical power to the humans of the system.

The bat was a beloved and was a god of great wisdom and knowledge that spoke to man and helped him in his time of need. The owl was the protector of man while he roamed the forest and jungles as he moved. These were gods that sought to help man along his journey; they could not help man directly so they sought to help man underhandedly and gave him powers, which would result in his ultimate survival. Many of these animal cities were cities of scorn and had to use the arts of torture to give man his gifts. They could not shine, and the royals destroyed their images doing bad and wicked things in their name. The vampire was instituted to help the Romanian people survive the Holy Roman Empire's hate for commoners. For their people were of God, and they were the only people God seemingly loved for the Roman god did not love commoners. The bat came to Albia Ramnuscia, giving him the ability to turn himself into a bat and travel to distant places.

During the invasion of Hungary in the 1500s, Albia was confronted by a band of Roman soldiers and was about to be murdered by a spear and instantly turned into a bat. This was to a surprise to the Roman court of royals for these practices were outlawed during the period. But the Wanghalrian animals were smart, and the discussion on the table was the fight against the Danish Court of Royals. The Odedi knew what to do with the stance of the Roman royals, for the ban of these practices was of the royal court of servants for which Cercaverous was a member. The Roman court stewed for this was to be the new reign for the kings of Romania.

This dawned a new age for the common men of the world for in the Holy Roman Empire's high-ranking members of the church were the only ones allowed to dabble with what was called the dark arts. Witchcraft was not allowed to some clans of commoners and nobles. The royals and their gods both fought for the abolishment of witchcraft and human-given powers on the system, giving their human kings an absolute edge of dominance and absolute control of the world. The Jews and the courts of the royals were already on this agenda within the Roman Catholic churches and later to the Austrian aristocrats. This was to be the new age way of war as time continued. The Danish Court of Royals needed the support of the Romanian countries because technology alone could not ensure the safety of their humans. They were unsatisfied at the way the courts handled these situations and left the issue in the hands of the court, claiming the stance of Aventis Adendeium until it was fixed.

The animal cities knew that they were in trouble and sought to continue their gifts to man. The Roman royals grew angrier and displayed their disgust for the animal cities. They proceeded to implement rituals that would denounce the Christian ways and the Roman religions as a whole. This war lasted until the 1930s with the death of the Romanian religious fighters. The Whulusgulares had no intention of waging war with the royals under the emperors since they had very little allies and abilities. They simply sought to help the enemies of the emperors. The Danish court realized this and thought of the repercussions for helping an animal city in insolence.

They were a very tricky clan; they continued the war of Austria-Hungary in 1890 where the Roman royals launched another attack on the Budapest Castle in Hungary. The Roman royals were maddened at the methods they used and sought to destroy that animal city, but they looked forward and saw something they could not understand. All they knew was it was something immensely powerful and very unrecognizable. All the animal cities could have said was this was called the Maralaio Radiants. The African courts were interesting in this new radiant and asked around then searched for what this could have been. Finally, they asked the ancients what it was. The ancients replied it is called the Maralaio radiant. The animal Whulusgulares city used the Maralaio radiants as a message to the Roman royals. The Roman royals tried to destroy the animal cities immediately after realizing the energy could not be deciphered.

The African courts realized that the animal city could be an insurgent for which the entire city could be a message in the same way. This was a blinding light in our world; the question was who could be so ingenious. The Danish courts looked at the city and asked why would they think that it was. The African royals said, "Look at the beings and look into their minds." The Danish royals realized that their minds worked like clockwork to avoid detection and not to draw attention to themselves from the aggressive leaders of the cities. The courts said, "Look closer to what was happening to the system. Their minds worked in clockwork in correlation to what was on the system. A man falls asleep, and a being senses the opportunity to change the factors of the system that relates to the laws of collection in the Dieu."

The factor that changes in the Dieu associated with the laws of collection affords man the possibilities within his decisions that associates with the laws of collections of a particular god or city. The god or city in Dieu decides that if he will accept the stance in law to collect the souls of the man, those who sees the opportunity and accepts the stance influences the man to decide along the criteria that affords the claim. The animal city maneuvers these situations and laws to their advantage. Their advantage is immediately looked upon by the courts of appeal and the courts of arbitration among some others. The minds of the animals would cognize the correct answers without actively looking at the courts. The animals would then issue statements to various cities.

This would relate to each of the individuals in the situation, and they would react to the animal courts as correct.

Synchronizing of nonrelating ideas and schemes triggers the courts of appeal divisions of investigation, where the laws of speculative observation for intent becomes primer for all substantial law. This division of investigation would then be investigated by the internal affairs, for which the city of Guiold of collection would appeal the court's decision to revamp the bond on the law of perpetration. The collection of beings under false religion would now go to the operator and not to the religious body in charge. This would lead to the revoking of the band on the application of impersonation of gods. The impersonation of gods will be allowed within the schemes of collecting and the shaming of gods where the tarnishing of their name is required to efficiently operate in this type of environment.

The environment can be highly competitive as many gods can have access to the same devotee. This will lead to a war among the Anouskha and the Gerald Injunchiel, for which the Injunchiel think they can win with ad hoc methods of defense. This is what the radiant message could have stood for. The Danish court realized that this could be true for many cities of collection, and we are not sure of who is the architect of this clockwork. To them, their world has just became more dangerous.

The animal city simply looked at the Danish court and said, "That is not the answer. We hope that this situation does not lead to unfriendly meetings between us." The Danish said they hoped not, as they touched one man on the system and instructed him to drink a beer. This man would be enticed to drink even more beers and go to his home drunk. He would physically abuse his wife and then make love to her. As the animals touched the man's mind and induced his appetite for beer, the Roman courts and Danish courts called the cities for collection. The court of religious teachings touched the head of a woman telling her not to go home. The Roman court touched the head of an officer, telling him to patrol fifteen streets that night. The courts of appeal called the Roman courts, initiating laws for conduct over the humans. The Lithuanian court of religious teachings levied the law of Frestution into a resolve for implementation. The Roman collector of the city of

Appalling rejected claims of negligence of the Roman court and claimed illegitimate collection.

The law of Frestution was no longer applicable for their stance was tarnished by wanton claim. The law of beloved matrimony was denied by the court of religious teachings and the Roman general court because of its applicability for long-standing union within the cities of the Dieu. They further discussed the laws where the applicability of archaic laws could be utilized. Laws of promiscuous procreation and male jealousy was to be implemented. However, another law took prevalence where in the event a man is jealous of another man's wife the married man will fall. Another woman can take the fallen man; the law was repealed based on application inflexibility.

This led to the discussion of the law of unknowing collection of the sire, where if the god cannot tell who is the father of the being. The line is marked as from the mother, for which the child has no sire of lineage or father. The Danish court asked what they were implying. They simply said the interactions of the humans are along the lines of Malodorous; all the alluvials and degrees of distance in between are too far apart. The Roman royals tried again to destroy the animal court, but couldn't because of a strange unaccounted-for presence.

The Romans desisted and admitted that their plan was to assassinate the animal cities and the royals of the Danish councils. The Danish could not understand why they would openly state this and thought they were surely backed by the Raija and the emperors. The Danish royals said, "In this hour, your aggression is ill received, but there are many tricks for which you are a part of." The animals said the humans will never reach an imaginary point due to the minutes of angle between their thoughts and ideas, their understanding. They were simultaneously talking about both the humans within the systems and the humans of the collected cities. They kindly responded with a ditto to the interactions between the Roman and Danish royal cities. Many simply agreed the same goes for their cities of reincarnation within the Shangri-la.

The Danish court disagreed, but the African court agreed. The animal city went on to say, "We are the same in clockwork. As we influence the minds of the humans, the things that must happen will happen, resulting in psychological behaviors that causes the interaction among many. Some things are inevitable. The effects of our conversations spiral through the Dieu, affecting the laws as the court behave to your demeanor. Just as what was said, the judges of the Court of Appeals, Court of Litigation, and Court of Acknowledgment changed their stance for many laws, which were put to rest and pegged to laws of standing and acculturation. The laws of understanding and application of negotiation theories were acceptable once more."

The animals said the simple induction of alcohol to the scenario of the beating of a man's wife would change the laws of abortion and runaway collection. The court of religious teachings of both the Danish and Roman royals noticed that no laws of collection were changed, and they simply said the child was not born. In a timeless scenario, the child was born. The court realized that the larger courts were deceived and was being robbed of souls from the court of the Liencheistiene, where the law of series sequence collection proved the laws of dominion remediation, for separate minds are the same beings in variant sequences. These could belong to the variants of fathers and mothers within the combination. The court has lost during the period of Eurestuian to Gerinethesh for this led to the changing of the priests of Olreich during the restructure of the churches of Oleriantheon.

The Danish court realized what was it about, and the Roman royals simply said, "It was us." The Jew and the animals said, "No, it is not you. You are just another puppet to the schemes." The African court cloaked and shifted; the Danish royals did not know what to do. They asked the animals what was there to do. The animals said, "Learn to read the environment. Look at the humans and learn from the patterns of what they do. The Danish thought this was preposterous; the animal city said, "Look at the animals and understand what they do to their environment." Everyone looked and realized that there was someone talking within all animals. They watched and saw that the influence was channeled through their bonds with the earth. They thought it was guiding them, but they realized it displayed a lot of violence. It spoke a language for the more intelligent among us to understand.

The Danish was in awe, and the Roman royals tried to destroy the Danish royals. The African court shifted, and all the Danish royals said to them was to please be more careful. The animals were the killers of Anipostumous, and his sin was the philosophy that drives these actions in the world. The Danish court moved to the abode of an ancient being; they met the African court there, which said there was a Cusnustriea on the system. This is a being that speaks with the actions or behavior of other beings. It is not the idea of touching the beings to accomplish its goals, but it touches the atmosphere to coagulate relationships to vector mental trajectories. Many know where it comes from, but it is a widely kept secret for it seeks to destroy our systems; it seeks to destroy lives of the collected. They asked the ancients, "Does the Roman royals know what is within the systems?" They said no, for they were too young when the war began, and many of the ancients were not born when this came about.

They were said to look at the systems, and all animals of scales and four legs moved simultaneously, illustrating a pattern; the pattern is a swirl like an eye. They stopped and thought this could be morbid. The African court said, "It means I see you." Many of the cities of collection simultaneously raged, as the law of collection took avail over the laws of stance." The judge gained the favor of the emperors' will, winning the heart of the Deuceshes. The Danish royals thought that was not it, that could not be the reaction to its intention. The animals said it was and they should look at the cities and measure the distances of reactions within alluvials. The Danish thought how, and the Danish queen saw that the laws were of collection.

She looked deeper into the field and saw that the reaction to emotions spelled the sequence of a quarrel between two people because of vengeance from love. She thought how could this be, these could not be the links to its speech. The animals said it was angry, and many would think its actions was simply coincidental. The queen attempted to speak within the system and spelled, "Who are you?" Instantly, the laws of engagement with application in an affluent port city aligned with the regulations of an evolving cherished city of the inamorata. The wider laws fused instantly with many reactions of violence and reclamation of beings. The confiscation of souls and other mind components led to the death of many, creating new laws for instincts and emotions within the reincarnation sectors.

The recollection of many created large-scale violence among the citizens of Carailvier and Burschurdvilde in the stance of regret. The Danish queen wondered, "How can this be, where can we hide?" They said it cannot cross over, for there was the legend of a curse. Ashuni immediately appeared, causing mass uproar, saying, "Where is this legend?" The ancient said the legend is the Cusnustriea of Congyaba, which was cursed to remain in a void for the chance of creation has taken a toll on trust, creating missions for regret. The lives of the beings of collection can be a rotting fruit because of the application of law. This has become the intentions of the aristocrats within the cities. They intentionally created unknowingness with compassion among the winners of the greatest achievers, who inculcated a culture that has afforded the obliviousness to true danger. The death of Anipostumous was not a mistake, for his mother knew their faiths if the Kurtanuran was allowed to cross. Ashuni did not know what this meant because she never heard of a legend of this type. The Odedi said, "Yes, they know, and we should not babble for the Crakihenga was never banished. We should be silent and not take a stance in fear or misaction in doubt."

CHAPTER 12

The Phases of Matter

An old man named Amario calling himself the guardian of the Ashieres came to the place of the discussion. He said, "They have seen, and the war had already begun for the latter dimensions have taken to war and the Foresters have already started killing the strains of Ascharmiara. Those who have taken up the asquires are the enemies of many of the cities, and we should be very careful of where we are seen." He said he knew who could have shown the animals the Maralaio radiants and how they could have used it against the Roman royals.

They did not know what the Maralaio radiants was. He said, "I am the creator of the Maralaio radiants for it is an alphabet where the elements of the radiants or particulates of energy are letters. When combined, they can form matter and alternate realities unperceivable by any other realities." They still could not understand. The radiants of Maralaio the animal clans possess was a few letters put together to form a word. When put in a sequence, make a rhythm but not a full song. The rhythm acts like matter reacting to the regime associated with many realities. The matter is pushed and pulled to the constituents of the vowels within the rhythm, restructuring the components as the decentralizing stability of the matter, destroying all in its radius. The full alphabet is constructed of 159 components or letters, for which all those who speak the language have many dimensions and abilities across the various spectrums.

The Jews are very proficient in this language but do not know all the letters within its alphabet. In this, the words of the languages could mean the same things, but the spelling is different. The same can be said for the letters of English and Spanish; languages can be decoded because of this similarity. Only the writer can know the entirety of the language written. They still did not understand there are many languages out there, and many of these languages are based on the uniqueness of the creator's minds. These are remnants from a period of the creation of minds and other things. A place that is inconceivable is new; what the mind does not perceive does not exist. The animal speaker is from an old civilization speaking a language that is partly lost. The speaker of the animal clan is far more powerful than many of us for his power is mostly inconceivable by us.

"The language was constructed by a constituent of the universe in a lesser description of a particle. The particle was specific in its movement with very precise angles through time Endreghtics and Furgeresh, where they would form a lattice structure at 19.5 degrees to each other at very specifically equidistant to their incidents. They would specifically coagulate repeatedly in a series of bonding relationships for which they can now be used to create a new form of matter and energy regime. This was the birth of one letter in the alphabet, the *M* for which all letters are combinations of. The *M* that Amario created developed 159 perfect consonants of this alphabet, for which many others created vowels. Vowels are violent versions of letters creating vigorous actions around the particle's Flavarantuing effects on time and alluvial dynamics. This results in the being's perception being angled along vile and selfish motives with appetites for destruction.

"The Parlestual can be one from my inventions from many years ago. After the war of the Furegursh and the Heailentine, the Parlestual destroyed the gates to these dimensions, losing all contact with the Fugerush and starving the cities of particle and radiants knowledge. Many before me tried to replenish these gates but could not and eventually gave up and disbanded their efforts. We the younger clans sought to create new dimensions and created beings. Within our reality, we saw the use and beauty of these combinations creating new forms of dimensions and experimental beings. We eventually thought we had perfected our formula and created the dimensions of Bangurhamairirs. Within, we created Eshulthies. They grew smart and pleased us, but their rhythm of matter changed like seasons. Their minds became destructive and sought to destroy us because of simple concepts they eventually could not understand. Many were slaughtered, and we had no choice but to close the dimensions with them inside. They had a lot of knowledge and could create dimensions within."

It was proposed that the Eshulthies is the Cusnustriea of Congyaba. The animal speakers disagreed and stated that the Cusnustriea of Congyaba is one that mostly speaks violence. The other is that it is from one that has fallen from another dimension, seeking us for use since it mostly speaks near the systems of collections. It is a vile creature creating wars in specific tone to control the ambient to the detriment of all within our alluvial. The Jew theorized that it is the Bhagdesh, a race banished from our alluvial many eras ago because of their crimes against the Eseishxer clans of old who lived near the fluvter systems. The African tribe said, "Maybe not for they have been in peace for many seasons and no one sought war with them." The Jews said, "Maybe you are wrong. If the spelling is correct, another war could be upon the season." They all saellicise and saw no wars, but the Jew said, "If you look forward near the sun's zenith to Assereight, you would see the war."

The African tribe said, "It is the people of the third sun, for they prophesized the return of their king, the dead Afesshuer, for which he will be born of the death of a dwindling sun. The Jews saw the children of the sun and said maybe it is not our time to participate. We should seek council with the westward dimensions of the Wollorodian. The African court agreed, and the Jewish council left. They proceeded to the dimension of Anghuschkas, where upon the gate they were met with warnings of deceiving enemies and this fight could be fierce." They asked, "Could we see the queen?" She instantly messaged, "Not at this time for they were from the collection systems before the wars of the Raija." One member of the Arab court said, "But you were from the collected systems?" She replied, "Yes, and that is the reason why you were banished from within our city's walls. They are all followed by war."

They left saddened by her reply, the Danish court said, "We can only return to our thrones of collection and quietly observe what the Cusnustriea of Congyaba has to say."

"We must stay safe," the African court replied. "We have no choice for our time is upon us. We can do nothing but do what is in our reach." Upon their return, the Roman royal tried to destroy the African courts, saying, "How can you abandon the city, allowing the animal cities to take over the Courts of Appeal and the Courts of Reverence, a move that afforded much power in their worlds of deliverance of law?" The African court said, "It is just the seasons and the Romans' defenses were easily shattered." They said, "We would have given it to you, but you would not give those back."

The Roman royals, angered, modified some of the beings within their city, thinking the court of issues were plotting against them. They asked, "How many of us here is willing to work toward a unified system?" The court said, "We can all lead the systems." The Danish asked, "What about the Ottomans and those that were accounted for?" The Romans jeered and wondered what was to be done. By this time, they were focused on the earth, which was in the 1960s where it was the height of the cold war. Tensions between Russia and the United States were now about to simmer with wars flaring between the Ukraine or then Reichskommissarait and other Soviet fallen states. The Roman royals had no choice but to continue what they were doing. They could not openly attack the court of the Danish royals so they went to Asia, invading Vietnam, Korea, and other small East Asian nations. The problem was this was not done through lineage and was done via the then president of the United States. There were no laws that could account for this legally within the courts of the Roman royals.

The Danish royals realized they had very little footing in the world, saying, "You have truly lost your grip using the United States of America." The Italian people were somewhat lazy during the 1960s and were in a state of presidential reform. The Roman royals asked the

Court of Technology and used the Italian country to attack the African court's human cities, invading North Africa then Algeria and Libya. Showing the Danish court they could still make a footprint into this world. The Danish court said the world of men has changed and we should try to teach morality rather than war. They replied by saying, "We and them should stay strong."

The Roman royals further sent their troops to invade Sudan and the middle of North Africa. The Danish court jeered, and in 1983, they attacked the US Embassy in Beirut, Herzegovina, and Istanbul, saying, "Strong is not flagrant." They immediately attacked the African country with Italian forces destroying its plains, resulting in the deaths of millions. This ended during the discussion of the Russian and American peace talks, with the Danish court saying then take your forces and attack Russia. The Italians said, "No fear with the president Sandro Pertini threatening the Russian people." The Danish court laughed and said, "This era is different. In fact, you will release your grip of western Germany. The Berlin wall will fall, making it one nation again or we will go to war, settling this the old ways. All or nothing, the Roman court took the challenge, and the spread of the nuclear weapons began. Many courts over the countries of the world took this opportunity to arm themselves. Ranging from Far Eastern Asia to the Middle East, saying we the Roman Courts are never afraid.

By the 1990s, the tensions in Dieu took its wages on the worlds with the restarting of the Gulf War, where a lot of the descendants of the Holy Roman Empire went to war with the Middle East. The court of Arabs said their people has been constantly at war for the past three hundred years. The Roman royals said the Holy Roman Empire has been at war for four thousand years. The Arabs were not too accepting of this statement since the law for the Roman royals' operation was illegal and had to be dissolved. The Roman royals were in operation in the angle of cultural evolution. Their legal system of governance allow for such laws as the tenaciousness of their leader and could not be implemented since all leaders had a specific time in office. They made reference to the Holy Roman Empire not to be responsible for the aggressive nature of the world. This led to many wars in the systems since the Roman royals were to be held accountable, and they were to be charged for breaking the many laws of collection. The appearance of their ill in war had to be demonstrated.

In the ten-year period from 1992 to 2002, many wars were forced upon the men of the worlds; the technology of the day made these wars worse. The Roman royals moved for a motion to absolutely allow the men to choose for themselves because their technology allows for the destruction of many. The court's laws account for the incursion of an army with swords and bows, which does significant damage to the people but not in a ratio that exceeds ten persons to one soldier. The human's lethal potential has grown beyond the count of law.

In 1991, the war named Operation Traira was launched by Brazil to Colombia where they both fought for gold over the border territory between the two nations. This was a sign from the Roman courts and the court of religious teachings, saying the fight for gold is not worth the incursion of men. The Romans agreed but stated the world is not yet festered. The Danish court of appeals openly stated they were going to play this game the way the Roman royals intend it to be. They instituted the Ossetia war Croatian war for independence, the Transnistra war, Abkhazia war, Tajikistan civil war, Chechen war, and Karabakh war, restructuring the East European continent.

The Roman royals were always dominators of the human courts of democracy; they instituted border lines and underhanded techniques to win votes. The African court knew what this meant and started many conflicts to gain entrance into the human courts of the worlds. One such court is the League of Nations, which led to Benito Mussolini invading the sovereign nation of Ethiopia. The Italians claimed that they could rehabilitate the cities of Ethiopia because of the many wars waged on the territory by Italy, Spain, and France. The Roman royals' success in democracy was the angle of misdirection and secrecy.

Many stories of the situation were dispensed hiding the truth but were specifically misleading to gain public support. This was not the truth, and in the event that many were to say otherwise, they would be hushed by violence. This was the trademark of the Roman royals; this led to many conspiracies, hidden truths, and agendas, degrading the very pillars of the principles of democracy. Benito Mussolini went into Ethiopia to conquer the Ethiopian nations to claim them under his empire. Among many other benefits like ancient artifacts of power date back to 32,000 years. The African court knew of these traps in civilization, which leads to the fall of many nations.

Forced creation of the need for survival through decisions in civilized standing and court processes has caused the people to abandon the democratic process of the league through bias thinking and discrimination. This was a detriment to many honest and upstanding people since honesty and fairness is not the values that causes the rise of decision, but through practicality and safety. The African court knew that many honest and upstanding people would eventually have no choice but to use these underhanded techniques to keep the peace and endeavor to success. A channel that would lead to the concepts of necessary evils eventually lead to true evil. The minds of men would become angled to the worlds of violence through doing evil for good.

This is deemed not good for doing evil for good results in doing evil for evil. Killing a man is evil, and killing other men because of that man is the evils of staying good. The war that is fought is evil so the question is, is the man that wages war in evil for good evil? These situations lead to the values of men becoming skewed toward evil for which men no longer see the lines of good and evil but see their own intentions and survival as good. This was terrible, and the African court had no choice but to gain standing in these courts, to help the world of men. They silently engaged in wars for civil rights and independence from beneath the remains of the Roman empires and from the influence of the rulers of their tribes.

Many wars were fought: the Tuareg rebellion, Djiboutian civil war, wars of Sierra Leone, Algerian civil war, Somalian civil wars, Burundi civil war, Gabon civil war, Nagaland war, Bophuthatswana war, and the War of Congo. The Roman royals saw change and the growth of democracy outside of their favor and fought hard and illegally to stop the Democratic Republic of Congo. They had few installments into waging war against the Democratic Republic of Congo. They illegally used Namibia, Angola, Chad, Uganda, Burundi, and many other to stop the rise of the Democratic state of Congo. They could not, for that region had an immense population, which the Roman royals could not see.

This was the beginning of the psychological wars among the beings of the Dieu. The end of this war could not be seen; the Jews noticed, and for fear of what could not be seen, they were willing to absolutely wage war on all clans. The paranoia within the atmosphere was apparent, and they could not alleviate their situation. The Roman royal said their armies never fully made it into central Africa, and it was mostly uncharted territory with many diseases and ailments that can occur. The African courts said to the Roman royals that this was something they will pay for. The lines of the African people were not of the Roman or European lines; your actions were more than illegal during this period of injunction.

The Roman royals shrugged, saying, "There is nothing that cannot be paid for." The African royals said, "Look at the cities and the changes in law. Your cities now moved toward free assemblage of law to go to the motion of immediate control of the law for Returucion Insembell." The laws of collection for the African people were now impartial to that of the Roman lines. This give the rights to collection in war to the judge of subordinate for Ghurnes. Only he can collect during an incursion of the territory. The laws of a judge's Ghurnes state, the occurrence of an injunction on the forced application of a lesser law could be an infringement resulting in the restitution from a motion of degrading the wellness of the courts.

The cities said, "This is a repercussion we are willing to accept." The Roman royals stated out widely what they wanted to do and that the Ugandan people now belongs to them. The transition should take three hundred years. The African court simply said that the laws of Carneish cannot be applied since that was implemented after the birth of Streigheigher. The first of his kind after the wars a Lamdheir Embaldhier. The African people are not of his bloodline and moved for a motion of renouncement of the Roman royals under the premise of malobjection. The Roman royals immediately shifted and sought to adjourn, destroying their cities of motion and revision of laws. This was a move to appease the courts.

The court simply stated that the people of Uganda and Angola were never of the Streighigher line, and those that were cannot exactly fall in the right of forced capturing. If they can find a man of the Streighigher line, he must be of absolute rulership so that he can legally lead an incursion into the Central African continent. He cannot dominate his allies since the laws of the rulers are of the ancient of tribes of men from the periods before. The monarchs who are of the strengths of the Roman courts in these eras are relatively inapplicable because of the principle where a tribe can become a kingdom.

The laws of their forefathers cannot be weaker than that of the descendant. The laws of the blade agreed. The Roman royals saw this as an opportunity to have a footing on the African continent against the Democratic Republic of Congo. They were a small group of royals over a nonsovereign that was in transition to lead the operation but was nearly not enough. The Roman royals, angered, had no choice but to use the lines of the Iberian conquerors and conquistadors, but these lines were in dispute since the Roman royals were not in good standing with the courts of the Spanish Empire. The British were under the courts of religious teachings, the Roman royals were not allowed to completely dominate the British lines with their own endeavors. They simply wished to inspire the lines to reach for control over the lands of the African nations. These cities were not of the statues to be governed by mere citizens.

The Roman royals realized they had an uphill climb to conquer the Democratic Republic of Congo. They had little options and did what they could do—they instilled racism and discrimination among the people, causing a cultural trajectory for war and hate for women. In an attempt to destabilize the region, the Roman royals gave their forces reason to invade the country on the basis of human right. They left the region with a set plan for they were skilled influencers and were of the ability to implement their plans legally in a few decades. The African court looked at the people of that region and wondered if that was best for the people and saw that the Roman royals would not stop. Their values and ideas are of the indulgence for the loathness of monarchy. They spread chaos across the planet, leaving a trail of underprivileged and discriminated against people in its wake.

The Danish court and African court grew weary with the lives of men for they saellicised and saw even greater weapons of mass destruction. Many wars were propagated across the planet, causing millions of deaths annually. The Roman royals only sought to benefit from these wars, and without our stand in court, the world could slip back into the dark ages under the rule of the Roman royals' empire. The Danish court wondered, "What is the faith of the world, and with all the wars occurring concurrently, what was to be the true outcome?" Something had to be done soon because the world could not end in such a haste of destruction.

Amario called upon the court with words from another dimension. "The wars are coming to our alluvials, the Askhurier are mobilizing troops to invade many dimensions." The Danish court asked, "Was this army related to a member of the Cusnustriea of Congyaba, the speaker of the system." They replied no for that speaker was an unknown being presumed to be from an age that has long been forgotten. Amario said, "Take this. It is a sequencing radiant that creates a tunnel between dendritics. It is invisible to many, and you will be safe within it. It can take you to many places, but be careful of what you may find on the other sides." They all agreed to keep this knowledge a secret for many of our rivals can use this to our disadvantage.

The first thing they did was create a dimension of new spellings based on what they have learned about the Maralaio radiants, a place where they can exist without trouble and the existence of their enemies, a place where they can be safe. They filled it with soldiers and traps to keep out any intruders; the presence of a being from the usual constant dimensions would restructure their matter into destructive forms, creating events of radian-charged storms that destroyed their matter upon entry. The Maralaio tunnel was the only way into this dimension. They wiped their memory of how it was created and stored it in a shard inside the dendritics in a secret place. Hoping the alluvial cannot be destroyed, they soon sent their loved ones into the dimension and silently went back to the systems to endure the task of surviving what was to come.

The Roman royal knew something was about but could not figure what. So they asked the Danish royals if they had war jitters. The Danish laughed and said that the Romans are all dead. The Romans naturally tried to strike them down and failed, saying, "Your African friends have proven worthy." The African courts said, "Your ally, the animal courts, have proven useful." The Roman royals said, "They are not my friends but vermin that are to be destroyed." The African court looked at the animal cities, saying, "Equality is a far dream under the rule of a Roman." The Roman royals cursed at the African courts, saying, "How dare you incite a riot against us!" The African court asked, "You are my king, is it not?" The Roman royals simmered and said, "No, and you are being disrespectful." The African court said, "No, I am being truthful."

The Roman royals shrugged, saying, "You will get your turn under my blade." The African courts said, "You are not the one that is capable of doing this. I am not the one to keep you at bay, and the African royal captured the young Roman royal, making him a slave." The African royals said to them, "I am the creator of slaves for you have none, but all was given, and you were my patron and don't ever forget this young royal." He immediately called out to the Roman courts, stating the right to his capture under the law of captures within the Dieu, reciting legal philosophy from a past elective under the judges of the Roman courts. The Roman court openly stated that they cannot appeal such decisions in this era. The head of the African queen's councils stated to her subordinates, "This is a fine specimen. We will keep him in our Cadourary." The Roman royals saw this and realized that there were many laws they could not pacify in these times for their position in the systems would not allow it.

The African courts said, "You are young and do not know what the actions of your behavior allow. You do as you see fit, but seeing as right or justified is the same as what you have learned." They grudged, and the African court stated, "Allow me to continue. You do and teach other to react to what was done. This teaches others to react in repercussions for justice and fairness from violence, for which you have taught all men to do as you do. The world has become a basket of repercussions and vengeance in the light of incursion. This is now the right or justified way of dealing with the issues of life. In the science of men, there is the law of every action has a reaction—the singularity of things, for in every one observed action, there are multiple reactions for which is observed. You have created the singularity of thinking of men and of Gods for which they have become what is now called narrow minded. You, the Roman royals, are the cause of the detriment of all earth and the Dieu."

The Roman royals laughed for all the earth is well and the earth is going through the natural cycles of life and replenishment. The courts watched and wondered what was the Roman royals thinking. The world of men is filled with wars and disease, a palette for suffering. They asked, "Is this usual for your courts?" They said, "For many cycles, the worlds of men has been based on the mind types of the Raija and the requirements of the schemes. This is the preferred design recommended for the human being. This is what is best; these are the most beautiful beings and the most capable among those from the systems." The African courts stated, "These are the most resentful, conceited, and temperamental beings of all the systems. They smell like the bowels of a carnivore."

The Danish royals, saddened, moved to adjourn, allowing the courts to travel to their home worlds. They discussed the wars and the hate of their enemies that was cast upon them throughout the interactions with the cities of the system. The speed of escalation of the situations, coupled with the egos of the royals and the ways in which they would wrap the cities around their fingers, all contribute to the escalation of violence and hatred spreading among citizens throughout the Shangri-la. The laws of entrapment and the obligation of the cities to do their duties within the timeframe to permit the evolutions of the laws. They all pondered what was the solution; they proposed to attack the laws of the emperors. Specifically, the laws of unification and generalizations of the terms within the collection context. If they were to control the collective agreements of the cities, the fall of the emperor's laws for unification could be achieved. They stirred and wondered,

"What if we could use the Maralaio radiants to control the Roman royals in secrecy." They went to an old abandoned dimension where the wars had destroyed everything and left none alive, an abandoned city for more than ninety eras.

They practiced the use of the Maralaio radiants, thinking of the consonants like letters writing songs and poems creating beautiful art and partial structures of beings. They thought, *How can we defeat the Roman royals?* They all came together and created Ithecia, who are old and terrifying royals who hated the mother of their queen Heghater. They tried their best to emulate her fabric but could not; they envisioned her and retailed they could create replicas of otherworld matters. They created matter that emulated the reactions within social interactions. This was achieved through the creation of responsive matter that emits radiants that were constative of various responses when radiant intrusion structures are induced.

They put these types of matter together and created a version of Ithecia. She was calmer than the original and would usually forget a lot of things she did. She had some mental ability issues where she would spend large amounts of time and energy in attempts to remember minor incidents. They thought of ways to control her, and she instantly realized this and begged. She said, "I have done you no wrong, why do you wish to possess my body?" He said, "We need your help." She cried and thought of her life. Heilgurth said, "We should start over." He erased her memories and asked her, "How are you, my lord?" She replied, "Fine, and how did I get here?" He replied, "You have died many years ago, and we have only just rebuilt you."

She cried, sobbing for her family, and wondered where could they have been. Heilgurth replied, "We will find their remaining components." She asked, "Who else is alive?" And they said, "None, the entire consulate was destroyed by the Arvertians." She was angered then calmed herself and then asked, "Where can I stay?" They said, "Here. If the cities knew we were reincarnating the Roman consulate, they will execute us because of the dangers it could bring." She looked around and realized she was in a ruined city, asking, "What city is this?"

"The Alventians of old." She said, "It looks very ancient. I guess I have no choice but to make this my abode."

She began to build a new home. Heilgurth said, "I need to teach you more about the particle structure in these ancient dimensions." He showed her a lot and thought her a bit of Maralaio radiant; she immediately started building structures of a palace and immediately moved in, calling them inside. She clearly did not understand she was a replica, and she did not recognize who they were. They sat and talked for a long time, speaking about the history of the Roman court and how they fought and struggled to survive as Emperor Kaihielga took over their city; they were given the option to be executed or serve absolutely. It was a terrible time for them; the Schougnar would call upon them and execute an official just as a reminder of their superiority. They discussed the intricate stratifications of the Schougnar regime and the absolute rule of the emperor. Any rumor of disobedience could lead to the destruction of the entire city without redress.

The Danish royals knew of this and was glad to not be under the rule of an emperor. The Danish royals looked at her deeply and thought how could this have been avoided for them and asked her, "How do you think your freedom could be achieved?" She said, "You need to control the Huthtetiaed. He was the adviser to the Schougnar. He can be used to sway the culture of the cities away from the violent strife of survival." They said they will return; they left her alone and promised to return with more of her loved ones. Upon their arrival to the systems, they realized that there was another war on earth, the Nigerian delta war, where the new Nigerian ruler could be controlled by the Roman royals; this was the indication that this war was to be terrible.

The Roman royals were about to initiate a plan to go to war with Cameroon when the Danish royals asked, "Don't you think it's enough?" They said no and continued another incursion into Cameroon. Their main intention was to push the Cameroon forces south, causing political disruption and creating opportunities for new leadership, eventually making way for new influences and cultural practices within the region. The African courts were nowhere near worried since wars in the region would bring aid and new lines. This can be used in the advantage of the

African courts; the same lines can be used to the effect of law, bringing prosecution upon the Roman royals' legitimacy to claim.

The Danish court realized and pushed for the African court to have more leaders in the global setting. This caused the implementation of many African descendant leaders, who mostly advocated for peace. The Romans were not pleased and said they were not in the business of growing man boys. The African court replied in scorn, "A war will befall you, and all of your cities will become mine. You, Matteia, will become my slave." He grew afraid because he knew the African courts had power and were very old. They had many rights to many lengths of scripts of law.

For the first time, the Roman royals seemed afraid; they were afraid of slavery. They knew their existence could become unkind for all time. The Roman royals stewed, and some moved from their current position. Looking at the African cities, they raged and instigated more war. The African cities said to them, "Only when the Roman royals could collect the African dead I would take those gestures seriously." The Roman courts shrugged, changing laws and vouchers, setting traps in law but eventually to no avail. The Roman royals immediately asked for a truce, and the African court replied, "A trick in the sight of a hunter makes a man a monkey."

Heilgurth and some other Danish royals left the court, going to the old cities of Reuitleigher and Fesutidhegher that were destroyed more than 130 eras ago. They looked at the dimension's structure and how it was built. They looked mainly at what were the constituent parts, where it came from, and how it was used. It was an old design that was not very complex and was very stable but not seemingly very precise. It was not a mystery, but the creation of a brand-new dimension that was an esoteric idea. They compared the energy particles of cities and the Maralaio radiants, and they found they were vastly different mathematically.

The dimensions that we are in has a number of rooms for which this dendritics is not a regular pattern of dendritic dimensions. It is a spelling within another spelling; they wondered how many spellings this room was built on and how we can access them. Upon entering a dimension, we are taken to the point of interest and not to the structure of build.

They wondered where were the other navigable points. They went back to the city where Ithecia was and met with her, telling her what they found; she was glad for them and volunteered herself to help. They immediately created a dimension with limited consonants. They asked her to help them figure out how to build within these parameters. They instantly realized the relationship to the possibilities that can constitute a build that can accommodate a living capacity. The question arose, "What were the consonants of our home dimension?" They thought, *Maybe it is not that kind of build, for the Lexicurviur is not based on the principle of the Frosvestornode.* Within this, creating a polynomial structure cannot be physically accomplished. They wondered how was the Cusnustriea of Congyaba could be trapped in that dimension. They pondered on dimension where it was near impossible to escape. They looked at the particles and the effects of foreign radiants on its ability to affect the latter dimensions. They looked at the particle structure and interaction and wondered what were the circumstances that afforded this situations. They concurred that was what everyone would like to know.

The Princess Heghater asked, "What about the first beings of our universe? What about the stories about the creation of our universe and the things that cannot enter our universe, like the being that have fallen from other places? The beings that were of the creators of our universe, what about the way they were built and the way our world is built to prevent their entry into our worlds? What if the Cusnustriea of Congyaba is one of those? There are too many rumors surrounding our origins, and those stories are very old and could not be proven because there is no evidence. How can we find the people who know where these beings are. Finding the oldest being in existence could lead to our deaths. Just asking about it, your city could be destroyed. They might even be very hostile because living in the Dieu means they must have fought a lot of battles and must be very proficient fighters."

Heghater said she had heard of a race of fallen beings from outside our universe that seeks to collect souls, spirits, and other components from the collected dead. Some say they even eat the parts of the dead. They wondered, *How could we find such beings?* She said, "All that was rumored was that they are very intelligent and sought the most intelligent among us to aid in their endeavors. They give a lot of love to citizens of the systems in return for their services. I have also heard that many have died pursuing the endeavors of impostors of these mysterious beings so we should be careful."

"Yes, but how can we contact these beings?"

"I guess they are smart and love intelligence, so we should display our intelligence." They both laughed and thought, "That's a plan, but how can we implement or achieve this?"

They agreed, saying, "We should start a vault. These fallen love souls and other collected things, we have a lot of souls and other components we can give to them. We can hide the vault near Isdeiasha."

"That would be a good idea, but we need to simply keep those souls off the record. How do we get the souls past the Roman courts? They usually account for all the souls coming to the Dieu?"

"Esthereighter of Malouauog, she could help us with the Roman record keepers, but how can we keep her silent? I guess the only thing we can do is help her get back in the system—that might be the war of our lives. If we are to do this, we need to keep it silent. Oughneshina, son of the emperor of Gashneighard, would want us dead, and we cannot afford a war with any of the emperor's beloved." Heghater said, "We should at least visit her in her dimension."

They went back to Ithecia's palace and talked about the love some got from fallen beings and what were the circumstances of their fall. How kind were these fallen, and would they readily accept a plight from a lesser clan? They came to the decision that they should sit and wait for an opportunity that would swing some power their way, maybe the favor of a king or an emperor.

"These are beings outside of the universe, so we should think of what we can help them with and how we can win their favor. If they collect souls, we should build a city for them where they could reap as many souls as they would like. It must be that the men and women of this city are of the best quality and must be absolutely loyal to them. If they do love humans and their souls, they must have remade many beings to live in their dimensions.

This city should focus on the love they give for the souls of women and men. We should try to focus on the love and appreciation of their presence. We should not extravagantly display what they are willing to offer. We should earnestly consider the fact that they eat spirits and the souls of the collected dead. These are some types of being that eats the components of our body types. They should be treated with great respects and a lot of precaution for the roles of individuals in their society could be counterproductive toward our survival. Unknowing to us our ally could be deceptively dangerous and we could become dinner. Even though the rumors state they are very civil and their societies are great givers. We should be very careful when engaging with powerful beings of the Dieu and should show a lot of respect.

CHAPTER 13

The Cruelty Within

The cities of these fallen could be filled with trauma induced by those of higher positions for their own selfish reasons. Their world could also be filled with disdain and hate like ours and their reasons could be of having wealth, stature, and acceptance by the upper sectors of their hierarchy. The prices of souls within their cities could be very expensive, and they probably are willing to pay very little for them since they can afford it. Their food is your souls and could be their prize. They could be proud to the point they laugh and scandalize your failures and discard your presence as we have been useless as failures. They could be of the law where the hierarchy should remain the same way and should not be reconstituted. The methods employed should be of a specific legislation to keep the status quo in a specific way. Maybe we should send one of the animal cities to make first contact; it seems more likely they could be more deadly than friendly. This could be an even bigger issue since we have very few animal cities at our disposals. The wars among the dog, deer, and cat families under human laws make things worse; this will result in even more war.

Creating a new animal city could draw unwanted attention to our city, and many of the ancient animal cities are very powerful. The Agamourose would fight fiercely to destroy the allies of the deer so we can count on them, but the graousingher would fight to the end with them. The king of the deer have saved their cities many times from the asgouresh during the invasion from the emperors of the human cities of Garnendilea and Furlendia. The deer would attack under any circumstances, creating a war without remorse for all repercussions. The asuneighers will destroy all deer if given the chance; they are the monkey clans of east that are great allies temporarily but will destroy us if given the chance. The Danish is allied with the human cities of Melandhears and Avendhers, which are their enemies and which could truly be dangerous. The Haluthchers, the Gureouthers, and the Chouldhiers would all go to war against the deer but could never ally with each other. The deer seemed to be a dangerous adversary; they have enough enemies to keep all the Danish occupied.

The severity of their coldness and their resentment toward humans and other created beings is a destructive trait that their King Ameiheilder loves, for they were of the times when animals were used as soldiers to the then gods. The death of their soldiers resulted in the torture of priests and goodly people. Priestesses were forced to sacrifice families to their kings and queens. Many people were forced to accept this way, and when they were spared by the generals, they all committed suicide because of the living conditions they forced upon the people. Many moved to collect people as workers to the animals, and this collection was adored by their king. Their king was a human from the royal families of Imeilaretian and Kestambeul, whose notions were that these humans were of very low standing and his animal cities were better. Many objected, but the king won this war and later the deer family had to give back those humans to the cities of the Amerities. This was the beginning of the war for Armelliean control.

King Vergurled issued the dog clans to exterminate the cities of Valekeerian, Vhemerikeran, and Fredhieghan during the retake of the systems of Hespetutian and Veliterighn during the Suetherian era. The dog clans were vicious, and many did not know they were that dangerous. They moved swiftly and deadly with accuracy and efficiency. The Armada of Dephepherion did not have much choice to do what they needed to do. They lost their cities and lost their king;

the Dephepherion of the throne was the prize of the gods for his head became a statue. The lives of his subjects became the sight of plays for Altheuriehgh where they were all used to be the tribunal of the rulers of Osmengher and Jusherourgh and were eventually condemned to be stoned.

The wars with the dog families are still ongoing in the Efengush systems, where they are still at war with the human king Furthemustian. Their King Vergurled still want to destroy the cities of Ogmesh and Onmeushe, for which the emperors do not care. The dog clans are not of the Raija, but the dog clans are destroying the Sheleikada who were loyal to the emperor. This faith fell on them with no acknowledgment by the emperor. This could be a key to something the emperor was hiding. This could be used to topple the rule of the emperor. Survival became the theme of those cities; they became irritated at the sounds of the emperor's name. The Schougnars did not even consider an invasion under the laws of disrespect. It seemed as though they were afraid, or there was a secret that resulted in their action.

This is why they socially disinherited the situations of the cities and renounced the titles of the courts to the jurisdiction of law. These cities and the implications of hate wars within the territory spawned mass espionage, sabotage, and terrorism within the region. The Schougnars once implemented spies to that region; they were seemingly afraid of the dog clans, and the question became who is funding the dog clans. It was presumed to be the Raija or someone near their inherent royals or the king. Either way, the Danish royals needed to get their hands on that information of who could be behind the attacks of the dog clans. There was a rumor of the eyes of Thelgreas, a weapon they used in their defense, and it is the single reason the war has lasted this long. This could be the reason why the emperor could be afraid of the dog clans. They could be at war with the Jeriunis secretly through the Aphelthies clans.

The cat family is the largest clan among the animal cities. The Danish royals all agreed they should seek out the cat clans. That may be a dangerous journey because the cat family has the ability to create life in the cities as they create life within the systems. One cannot defeat the cat clans unless they can rewind the signs of the times. To many, attempting to meet with the cat clan can be like suicide; the cat is of his own knowledge of the earth and in the Dieu. This may not be the right place to look for knowledge of Jeriunis and the eyes of a Thelgreas.

The cats are easy to find if you can find a collector of a cat. The illegal collectors are killed at the change of every season. We should endeavor to follow the trails of finding the cat of Collegheters who was the stone of the Schougnaries who killed the Herounepis of Alvernadeir. The cat of Collegheters was not actually a cat, but a man who was given an extraordinary power by cat upon his death on earth. The Danish royals thought their endeavor was getting more dangerous as they planned. If they were to implement this plan, the questions they needed to ask was enough to warrant execution. They wondered how they could get started.

It is said there is a place for those who seek the cat countries, but most reach a simulated Durescatchure of radiants and the aboschoture of the radiants makes up the body and the mind in resonance of their original signals. The sun and the holy vessels of life are responsible for these radiants; those who possess these radiants raise the suspicions of the Raija who seek these radiants and resonances as the vessels for power. These radiants allow for transcendence of creation, nobody ever truly dies in this there is existence and assimilation of character along the lines of the alluvials. Who should we seek to find these relics, and where could they be? What is the relationship to King Vergurled of the dog clan. The dog clan is seemingly thinking like the Fevestulerian who was the human counterpart of the Gureouthers from the cities of Ferlendia. The designs of the dogs are like the love and magnificence of the animal cities near the transcended cities of the Wimzghraes era. Their aggressive nature is of the inclination for torture and dominance from the position of admiration and not from the position of absolute victory over their opponent. This is not the usual way they design and build a being near the cities' centers. They are more designed like the gods of Dillerithius during the miluescious era. The Dillerithius citizens were almost out of term for qualification for collection.

The wars of the dog clans were vast and was mainly because of the eyes they sought after. They attacked the owners of these relics, killing everyone in the dimensions, fervently looking for the forge that built the relics. Who are these clans that are the keepers of these relics? And since we are not the highest of the states within the systems, we need to be careful as to who we ask for information. The cities of the systems are almost never the wealthiest or the strongest in all the dimensions. The Danish wondered who are the nobles that own the most relics of power, and how can they be found. The Danish royals asked their courts for a list of possible royals who might have relics. The dog clan heard of this and instantly attacked the abandoned city. Heilgurth and the others had no choice but to run to their Maralaio hideout.

Upon reaching there, they immediately made another dimension and left their hideout, unknowing if they were being followed. The dog clan did not know what that was and could not follow, but knew they went somewhere. On completion of that dimension, they returned to the Danish council that was start of the Danish war with the dog clans. Heilgurth told them the story, and they realized what was happening. They asked the dog clan to stop, and the dog clan openly refused, saying, "We are the destroyers of the of Vergurled, and all of your spoils will become ours." Immediately, Heilgurth left for his new hideout and made a tunnel to the palace of the dog king. He covered himself with a hardened matter type of Maralaio and shifted behind the king, taking his head into his hands with a swift motion. He looked at the king's head in his hands and wondered if the Maralaio radiant would be enough to keep his identity a secret.

He immediately left the palace with the head and returned with the head to the Danish council. They looked at him and smiled. The queen walked to the balcony and showed the head to the dog clan's generals, saying, "Your king is dead, and you are to be next." The general screamed and ran for the city's hills. The Danish court ordered their men to hunt down the dog clans and destroy them. The king of the Lisetiakiluras clans saw this and was astonished as to how quickly it was done. The Lisetiakiluras tried to look for Heilgurth but could not see him, and they realized that the dead king was killed by an unperceivable assassin. He called the others to look and could not tell what it was, but they only knew it was a type of radiant from the old cities of Wangblisdheis.

They immediately looked at those cities and issued soldiers to attack some of those cities and to find anyone who knew anything about these radiants. The Roman royals saw this and looked at the dead king and saw something that looked like beings of the animal cities near Wangaries or somewhere else. The Roman royals looked at the Danish royals and said, "War is in the air." All the African royals instantly covered themselves in an unknown armor, saying, "We like Roman royals." The Roman royals saw this and hid, saying they were sorry. The African courts said, "Not today boy," and invaded the Roman royal cities, destroying everything in their components—animals, humans, inamorata, judges, and courts men.

The Schougnars ran and cried at the sheer destruction of the cities and the speed of which it was destroyed. The emperor cried as the other cities turned a blind eye, stating the laws of Remediation Carnage for this was the ways of our world. They immediately made alterations for the laws, giving the rights to smaller cities the first preference to take the Roman cities to the African courts. They immediately took all the Roman royal cities, claiming the right of cities that were sacked. The African court took all the dead from the Roman royals and cities and remade them as a ghostlike structure, claiming the right of council to the Roman royals as a slave to knowledge in the stance of partial existence, not allowing the laws of freedom of beings in courts. The other cities bowed their heads in shame, for this was the right of the ancient royals and the remains of the Roman royals were now entirely the property of the African courts.

A mirror image was created of the Roman royals, a poltergeist that was an arbitrator to make people believe that roaming spirits could have been freed. This was a clone of a spirit to settle the minds of the other cities to readjust without fear of destruction through the execrations of war. They are encouraged to use different methods of resolve to the issues experienced in the courts surrounding the collection tables. They were also encouraged to use the Calavary as a means of a vacation or sabbatical from the stresses of the courts. The African courts also described this as how spirits and beings can become evil, how people can become overstressed to favor demonic characteristic of essence and fragrance.

Many saw this as a scene of major disrespect from the African courts, for the laws should have protected the Roman royals. They left the courts in a storm and uttering disgusting words, saying, "This is not over, and the proper authorities must hear of this." A cousin to the prince of the fourth city of Ohareigha, Shealthurial, immediately shifted and left for Machesdonia. Many of the allies of the Roman royals pledged their alliance to the African courts in kind stance. They gave gifts of land and application of laws, giving them the rights of control and gifts of the stance of abominator, whose law is absolute. This was adorned as the prosperous gain in production from the royals of the African courts.

CHAPTER 14

The Clans of Ziauddin

The destruction of the Roman royals alerted the Ziauddin collection rackets, and they could no longer be a part of what was happening. They saellicise at the destruction of the Roman royals and saw their cousins killed and made into slaves. At that point, the Ziauddin cannot afford to go to war with such strength, and the leader cannot afford to be identified. What they can do is disguise themselves to collect souls and continue their agenda as a poor village that can hardly support itself. We should make the move to pay half the price for misused souls as the law or usual clauses is now in the hands of the Danish royals and African courts. What they can do was to discomfort the relationships of the African and Danish royals, but this could be dangerous if they knew who they were. We should be wise in this era. This could be an era of change; the era of soul collection could be better since the Danish royals were a clan of fairness and honesty. We could get cheaper prices for souls and more accessibility to the system.

They thought they could implement the old laws of the latter systems, which advocates the laws that states that the sale of a component is allowed to the recipient if he can afford to pay. If the recipient cannot afford to pay, he is legally allowed a payment plan that allows payment over time for which he is allowed a noninterest rate. The sale of partial credit is deemed not good because of habit of the law for nonpayment. The partial sale is defended by those seemingly supported by the giving of souls for free or the legal conversion of souls. The issue is one should release the souls no matter what, especially in the light of brotherhood. The law even accommodates the system in the light of collection through brotherhood, where personal gain should not be an issue. Others think it is downright dishonest and deceitful, like a thief that uses the law to pry the souls from their hands. The souls are not for free; the boatmen has to be paid. The collectors, businessmen, royals, and other rulers must be paid.

The wars have taken their toll on the worlds, making economies advantageous. Someone has to teach about economy and the way the industry turns during these kinds of events. It is not comradery and the way soul collection works. So he in the clan asked, "Why not get the boatman and the others to do it for free?" Comradery is not enough for all the workers to engage in these activities. One other says, "When it is time for us to receive souls, how much do we get?" Another clan asked, "What type of souls do we get for those types of services?" The Ziauddin reached the conclusion that their only strength was the Roman royals, and now that they are slaves, we should be wise and lie low.

The dangers of the cities for the Ziauddin was of the way the Roman royals ruled. They caused a lot of fear and hate for their cities, and they destroyed many of the people's homes. One clan where all of their enemies were destroyed was the clans of Oeicheirer where they denied the people the right to serve their own god. They prevented the sacrifice and offerings to their god and were met with murder and genocide. This clan has not forgotten the Roman royals for that. Even if they vouch for peace among the Oeicheirer, the Ziauddin could still be in trouble. They would have to give back the souls of many because they were taken in dominative stance; the Roman royals were now slaves.

The Ziauddin clans warned about the events to come, saying they cannot afford to befall the same fate for the laws of Ahechemeed state that if you kill your enemy for their god, the souls of the enemy go to their god. They wish to take over the entire world so that all the souls will belong to their clan. These articles in law can no longer be accepted in the Dieu since the regime has changed, and those laws were of the worlds of the systems and should not be accepted. If they wish to change or reshape the minds of collected beings, they should remove the laws of the discrimination of old. These laws are to be changed to a way that is more appeasing to today's rulers, which will align the sectors, making a superior system. This is part of a large war among the royals and castaways. The Ziauddin was the clan that is responsible for many murders and wars in the Dieu. They sought to change the laws in order to collect the souls of men. It is the change in laws that causes the breakdown of the system and large-scale shifts in psychological mind types accommodating unfair distribution of souls.

The Ziauddins are the clans of the Churolindheras, who caused frequent law upgrades and changes in collection schemes that caused many clans to result in using animals for workers. The fall of the deer and dog clans was based on Ziauddin clan's wars between the Danish royals and the vicious way of the generals of the dog clans. This caused a lot of wars over the rulership of the systems and the control of the minds of the cities. The Cheiresuel clan is a cast-out clan with the links within the inner circles of the royal court, for which they can help push the tides in specific favors. They are the stirrers of the inner cities. They would be the winners if it was not for the Bravustradias. The Ziauddin had the power and the use of mind control through the relics for which they believe none can match their abilities. They would use the relic of Hurequloris and badger their ways into the power circles of the royals. They used their newfound abilities in court, and no one knew how this was truly done or on what scale.

The Ziauddin is putting its plans into action; they are secretly using mind control techniques to add pressure to the existing families. This has a hefty price for many of the royals who have the ability to know when their minds were tampered with. The Ziauddin afforded many larger cities the ability to gain a lot of wealth. In return, they afforded the ability of the mask of their hands. With the mask of Pantheaoleon where no one can see their faces and their intentions, no one has the ability to see their thoughts. It is a powerful artifact stolen from the

Archealeon of Ameiraha; it is a powerful weapon for only the prince knew how to use it.

The prince of the Ziauddin clans use this to order the Schougnars to do his bidding. The wars with Alverchieria has taken its toll on the clans of Ieasalseie, causing the Schougnar to have ordered the removal or sale of many souls. This measure was implemented in a lot of the cities under his lower kingdom, affording the ability to gain position of judge of equity in the higher court. This afforded their ability to make a change in the laws surrounding the rules of excavation and exfoliation of free-held souls from city's clans, a powerful move shifting the votes of the royals in the favor of the queens of Bouqartheis.

The courts are unaware and unsuspecting, but many royals already know. However, the leader of the Ziauddin clan is still unknown, for it is a royal from a powerful and dishonored family. He is an unscrupulous being born not of earth but another system, a system born in war and forged in flames and death. His way is the way of strife, for this way is the way of beauty. Evil is nothing more than excess to his kind for surgery in execution is the path forward. These have secretly crippled the lower houses of assembly while pipetting the courts, increasing wealth in cities that would topple the balance of power. They cannot turn the power in their favor, for that would awaken the clans of the Chreighen. The judge of the Chreighen's allied courts were banished because of issues surrounding decorum for beauty and honor, which only goes so far; poise and affluence is the pinnacle of their way.

Princess Kamadahara, the enemy of the Ziauddin clans, the Court of Person in the case of Jhungeskhes for the Ziauddin, wanted all the souls via the laws of Schumirg. This law states that all souls go to the central vault of the Shrmeishures arm school in the remembrance of the removal of the counteracting guidance school. This happened simultaneously as the schools were destroyed during the shift of alluvial of the Suetherian era, where person alluvial stitching caused the reclaiming of souls, forcing collection from many cities within the Shangri-la.

This was to be a great shift in a number of collected souls from the collected systems, with the teachers of the humans' collection earning more than 30 percent of all souls within Derelict state system for an undefined period of time. This was coupled with the favors of the judges, resulting in a wavers for remuneration. The fallout of Jhungeskhes was immense, with the Roman royals and the Ziauddin controlling the minds of the judges and in the courts. The Ziauddin was vicious and controlled the minds of the beings, making them forget and tying their ideas to other ideas. They mixed their explanations as they cannot describe their thoughts, an issue the Ziauddin clans wished to appeal.

The Ziauddin has powerful methods for mind control and induced persuasion, even total possession. Mind control is allowed within the courts, except in demonstrative and convincing circumstances when a subordinate of lesser eternity is present. This is not allowed during law appraisal, the ability to give and remove thoughts from others in the same way they can in themselves. The law accommodates for deep learning memory, predictive analytics, translation speech, text speech classification, clustering relationships, and information linking extraction. The Ziauddin goes a bit further to incorporate image recognition and misappreciation of techniques used in blindsiding the laws.

The Ziauddin in secrecy desperately initiated these ailments in an attempt to garner the rights to collect more souls for their wars. They were used in lawsuits to indict the judges and persecutors of the courts. After their court cases, the courts of appeal were all banned and resulted in the throwing out of the major courts. The situation became further aggressive and worse where they attempted memory loss, illusion implant, idea inversion, emotional tagging, and mental breakdowns on the trial members for all the cases brought against them. The Ziauddin clans for many years before their removal forced their way of life on others, expressing loudly that they should be respected as a part of the governing.

The princess Kamadahara has a touch on the judges of Coughlingnour, who had the courts of avail accede to the rights to claim of the Ziauddin over the cities' collection of females on the systems. The Ziauddin sought to input ideas within the princess's head, but she had a special veil on her head for which the hands of the royals cannot touch. They would need a special technique from a hidden clan of the first beings to access this type of matter. The princess and her family noticed that as the charm of the relic caused the fabric to vibrate, making a ringing sound. The family of the princess saw the charm follow its source to the abandoned city of the Ziauddin. This made the Ziauddin choose Lavingheighs as their ally, leaving the Levestutude unprotected.

The councilor who made the attack instantly covered himself with an unpercolated matter from the upper reaches of the alluvials that were difficult to access. He vanished and their clan lost a lot of respect in this dimension. They had no choice but to renounce their claims to the Keys of Sidnhely to collect alongside the Lelweish. They had no choice but to publicly execute their own ombudsman for infringements on the collection of souls under the laws for duration of reprisal of appeal, the respect of the law that would allow absolute stance for collection in honor.

This would shift the strokes of feats for the Graveyish clans as they attempted to keep the peace among the speakers of the Greveyih courts, but the execution was done in a blatant display of showboating and style. In this display, they tainted the observer's image and respect of the ombudsman. He was executed via Lavorris, which is the hands of the Frussion, the Schougnar's helper as a display of power, but a show of association to the emperors, a measure for the intention of the clan for their position as a fallen and dishonored royal. This was a sign for war and deceivership.

The princess Kamadahara and others watched this execution, discussing the factors for the dismissal of the Ziauddin clans and the possible allies to their ascension. This brought the idea of mass insurgence into the city and the courts via military force. The Ziauddin had already been tried for mental psychic crimes against the courts and governing members. Thinking of the Ziauddin clans, they would enslave the courts and the emperors to do their will; they would treat all the wider society's members as though they were the devotees of the fields as though they were to be influenced in the ways of the banished emperors.

They suggested that the official language of the courts should be the tongue of the first royals; this was a sign that they favored the old ways of the system and would most likely have allies from that era. The old ways of the system was near slavery for free beings of the Dieu. Possession to the point of simulating one's personality is an atrocity. The legal implant of ideas of perception, no matter how beautiful or pleasing or good, is a vile misconduct. It is always to the point of no self-control, which is the benefit of the clans as our physical anatomy diminishes. It is a travesty of the laws, the hearing loss of the court, the cold, sad, angry, irritated sonnets of the clan.

The verbal abuse from the courts and the use of irrational words that describe the issues faced by the lawmakers of the society reduced national thinking among the masses and manipulated learning dynamics among the populace. Neural languages were tampered with; clustering predictive manipulation were a hidden part of the judicial language of the proceedings. There was little left for the clans that acceded to do for the courts banned almost all the uses of mental abilities in the courts. What happened that day was never to be forgotten by the citizens during that period, for this day is the day Judeiah will get his revenge.

The Ziauddin should be executed for what they did in the court during the meetings in public and in secret. Their supporters should be put before the emperors and their judges for creating riots and separation among the people, breeding disgust for the emperors and their regimes. They controlled the minds of the public officials to change the laws in their favor and conspire to make war and separation among the other groups and cities, playing the wars in their favor.

They sought to control the schools of thought or schools that were used to dominate the modification schemes and methods. In an attempt to hide this knowledge, they destroyed the places and recorded diagrams about modification and physical advancement. This is used to control the markers and builders within the cities, keeping the power of the people low. They controlled the masses while in the cover of darkness in attempts to maintain the peace until the courts accepted the idea that they were all dead. They cannot be perceived as returning, for which the Ziauddin would secretly prey on the cities of their enemies who knew of the existence. They became the silent rulers of the royals of Alphurgher in attempts to hide their identity as they needed the cover of their deaths to be fully accomplished.

The cities of Yechezkel were aware of this and stirred as they got information from the courts that were designated for the higher families of the lower cities of the families loyal to the ideas of the Ziauddin clans. The upper leaders and officials were not allowed to be in public office because of the circumstances of their dismissal. They hid in the remains of what was an old remade human church city and emulated the gods of Jurengurish, finding allies among the dishonored remade. Wanting to rule the systems and display their system of rulership and laws over the conventional systems, they secretly displayed the productivity and beauty of precision in the mind types and kundalini of the collected dead, secretly lobbying for allies to turn the systems into mas production systems while maintaining the necessities of psychological angles of the people.

King Aliigore will not allow such a system to flourish since the beings who are collecting become evil and harmful to the beings that are to be collected. They used these beings for messages to each other while killing them and collecting their souls. They maintained their reason for being on the system, which was more than just the wrong idea, but was a wicked fate for the beings of systems. The Ziauddin was the absolute wrong clan to implement this, and their insubordination to the royals would create war if they were to take any public position of office. The clans of the Ziauddin were very powerful, and they have all the abilities of the royals but do not have the numbers and cannot transfer all of their power to the members of their cities. The kundalini is the one thing they do not have or can possess for this is a gift from the Rhixcher, one of the founding races created in the beginnings.

The Ziauddin secretly went to war with the cities of Graija and started a war in the position of recapture and confiscation. The Graija was the ruler of the Perthians, and many others were the presiding officers of the cities created by the Rhixcher. This was the first time the Ziauddin went to war with the Imonurelthus who were the cousins to the princess Kamadahara. The princess noticed the Brasissiers beginning to collect kundalini soon after the wars for collection flared and began to worsen, creating many wars between clans. Many clans allied themselves with those whom they would not normally join in battle. This was done in an attempt to release themselves from the rule of the emperors. The powerful conglomerates became dangerous, and many sought to keep the peace. The princess noticed the Danish royals and their large conglomerate, the African royal, Mongolordians, and many smaller cities and courts within those systems. She also noticed the destruction of the Roman royals and their fate of becoming slaves to the African royal courts.

The princess looked for evidence of the Ziauddin and saw even more wars between the dog clans and the Danish royals. The deer clans immediately disappeared, and the Graousingher attacked some of the smaller cities of the Danish royals. She followed the links of residual radiants to the Graousingher to find any links of where the deer clans could be hidden. She looked for any clue as to where the Ziauddin would be hiding during this season of war as this would have been useful. She and a hunting party of a few battalions went to the old cities of the Ziauddin clans to find their old stooges and snitches. Upon reaching there, they found only a few derelict half-beaten members of the Couldher clans. She asked a soldier where were the members of the Ziauddin clans; he replied they shifted into a phase they could not see.

They asked her, "Who are you?" She answered, "I am the princess of Calcuralthera. Where is your leader?" They replied, "Our king and the royals are dead. The Ziauddin invaded with strength and power, overrunning us in seconds, taking the souls of the dead and the kundalini of the females. We followed them here, but they were too strong for our armor." She looked around, and he said, "They had new powers. They wore a cloak, and they were covered in a strange form of matter that we have never been seen before in this region."

The Princess saellicise and realized that she could not fully recognize where they were. The soldier described the scene to her and realized that the recall of events was a decoy. The Ziauddin could have been anywhere since they could not be seen by the courts. She asked the soldier, "How many of you remained?" He said, "Only a few million, not enough to wage war against the Ziauddin. The leaders of our cities have made the decisions to move to the Paffarax."

She instantly looked at him and replied in an emotional tone of war, "The Paffarax?" He said, "Yes. The Usumisther has opened his door to the people of the Telepharghes." She asked, "Who is the Usumisther?" He said, "The Usumisther is a man who ran away from the systems during the era of Suetherian. He befriended a young woman who invited him to the Paffarax. The rest of the story is unknown, but he opened his doors to the people. It is also rumored that there was a letter from an old kingdom, stating the return of Aarugumheiser, the old king of the Heugoreh clans from the larger cities of Kelousiler. The destroyer of all the Avertians."

She became silent for she had no information on who these people were. The soldier himself was not sure, but all he said was they were very powerful. She looked at the cities and saw bits and fragments of destroyed beings; they thought of the Ziauddin clan's power. She asked him what were these new powers they had. He replied they could have destroyed the monument of Aurishea made from the beings of Aigheshier, which were all made from the Calalerian Mungurthery, a being from the library of the summers. She cringed for the libraries are all linked and are one of the most powerful groups of beings from the last sun's rule. Could it be they possessed the spears of the sun? she asked. He said, "No, I am not sure of the legend, but those artifacts are long lost to the ages. They had the ability of the Ashesliuphus, they can bend the mind's will and fabric, causing the matter to putrify and shape to their will." She said, "You are tired, and my men will help you to recovery."

She immediately left, heading deeper into the city. She traveled through the old ruins of the Ziauddin clans, observing evidence of their presence. She saw the remains of a child. She stopped and went toward the dead body and looked at her. She saw that the child was from an earthly system and still had many of her components intact. She rejuvenated the child's body, bringing her back to life. As the child awoke, the child screamed, and the cities echoed, "You are going to be all right." The child quieted and hugged her. She asked, "What was your name?" The child said, "Aveshneher." "Where are your parents, Aveshneher?" She replied, "I don't have parents. What's your name?" She replied, "Princess Kamadahara." The child said, "I have never seen a real princess before. I am a toy."

"Where are rest of your people, Aveshneher?" She said, "We were going to Duramesh with a group of others, and the men that were attacking our cities appeared near us. I remembered I cried and could not move." Princess said, "It's okay, don't cry. You will live with me in a palace." The child began to cry, saying, "I am not allowed in the palace." She said, "I am a princess, you can live in my palace. Did you all go to Duramesh?" The child said, "Maybe. I could not keep up with the group. I fell down."

The princess immediately sent the men to Duramesh to investigate as she and the child talked in the city. The child said, "The king ordered the men to kill the people, and the Faltheirer, our babysitter, told us we had to leave for Duramesh because they were going to take our souls away to make soldiers. She said they had already taken away many of the boys and others from the cities' playhouses." She was sorry for the little girl and took her to the palace. She gave the girl the ability to grow up because she seemed to be no more than five years old. She had little knowledge of the outside world; she told the princess a lot about her city and all the things she did and enjoyed with the friends she missed.

She talked about the playhouse and the time she spent there; she was not allowed to remember her life as a mortal and was not allowed to leave the playhouse. "We had no choice but to play with the adults when they visited. They told us we were created to entertain the adults. We were not allowed to cry in the presence of an adult. It was terrible." She said she would never choose to return. The princess looked at the cities that had funhouses. On the outside, the children seemed to be happy; but on the inside, they were screaming and afraid. Making children for the purpose of entertaining adults can be a treacherous thing. Many of the children suffer from conditions that plague the adults, and dealing with these adults add stresses to their lives in the Dieu.

She said, "You will be all right now. I will call you a princess. You are my princess Aveshneher." She asked, "Could I have my own castle?"

Princess Kamadahara said, "Of course." Immediately, she created a new purse dimension and walked inside with Aveshneher. They talked for a bit about what she can do and her life within her castle walls then began building a castle and toys for her to play with. They made together many robot-like toy men to be friends with her and small animal-like creatures for her to rule over.

Kamadahara gave her Whemsie magic, and she wondered what she could do with this. Kamadahara realized that she was reluctant to play with the creatures and asked why. She said that because of the power, they were not allowed to have magic and there was an incident where a patron gave magic to a boy. The Faltheirer scolded him and took him away; they never saw him again. Kamadahara said, "I know, but you should not be afraid because you are a princess now, and these are your new friends. I will teach you magic, and you will not need to ever be afraid of being taken away."

They continued to build more cities and towns filled with creatures, people, and animals. In this dimension, she was the ruler, and this was her special place. She immediately built things that could fly large butterflies with the prettiest wings within all of her kingdoms, giving them the best singing voices she could create. Kamadahara said to her, "This is our secret place, and do not stress yourself over things you do not fully understand yet. You will get it eventually. Only you can find the entrance to your palace. You are the only one that can change anything that exists here." She smiled and ran off to play. Kamadahara watched her play for a while and then went back to the palace.

Soon after, the men returned. She asked, "What of the news?" They said, "The Ziauddin raided many of the cities along the radiant streams of Heinduria, sacking many of the cities, taking all the people's souls and kundalini. Absolutely no one survived. The soldiers left the remains of the cognitive components, we will have them stored in the vaults." She asked, "What are the powers they now possess?" They replied, "Their powers are very strong, none of the gates to the cities could hold them back. Everyone was destroyed, they left a void directly to the dimensions of the hidden cities and towns under the alluvial structures. It seems the power is exquisite. None so far has survived their invasion.

There were rumors that the clan has invaded the Frevesturode streams within the Calavary." The princess quieted and saw soldiers entering the voids of the Calavary. They quickly equipped their troops and invaded the cities of that void, the Durcluvious fighting the Ziauddin forces.

The Ziauddin's troops were vast and strong with very heavy matter shields that were never seen before. The princess's forces swiftly flew toward the fortresses of the Ziauddin's troops, firing mass constructs of radiants, destroying their armor and combusting the flesh exposed to her radiants. They immediately opened a shield, covering many of their troops, returning fire of an unknown radiant. The princess Kamadahara shifted and concealed her soldiers, taking them to a stable position. The Ziauddin opened a mass of radiants spanning through all the mitoses, destroying everything in its path.

The princess blocked with a shield of a mixture of radiants and bitter energy, but she realized the shield was cracked and it could not take another hit. The Ziauddin clans realized that her powers were waning, and the general of the princess's Queruada forces fired a Rhsicour radiant at the fortress, destroying many of their troops. The rest covered themselves in a new form of matter. The dead lay in ash on the floor with their armor still intact, but flaking. The general launched an attack, destroying the remaining troops. The princess looked upon the fallen armies, thinking of what was done today.

They traced the origin of the troops, finding their way to the Fibonacci systems between Candura and Vercasuthia. They immediately followed, entering the city of Flourienda. Upon arrival, the general and his armies were attacked without mercy and hesitation from the inhabitant forces. The flames of the fires flew into the air, covering the cities. The aristocrats and the judges of the courts tried to flee, but were blocked at the gates and were met with radiants that disintegrated the fabrics across the streams. The people screamed and covered themselves in the same armors as the troops.

The general released heavy fire of Rhsicour radiants, disintegrating their armor, burning the people with sweltering radiants, destroying the cities. The Ziauddin saw this and ran to the outside city of Valeria for which they could stay without detection or extradition. The city of

Valeria was a neutral city for which the Princess Kamadahara would not follow. She looked at the members of the Ziauddin clans with insightful eyes, memorizing the faces. Who were they, and where could they have been from, why were they here? The soldiers collected the remains of their comrades and reincarnated them. Many of the remaining civilians of the invaded cities were collected and processed for interrogation.

On return to Calcuralthera, they immediately went to the war rooms, discussing their strategy and awaiting reports from their scouts. She asked what of the information on the identities of the leaders of the men from the invasion. They replied none yet. One of the men who went to Valeria looked as though he was from the Simoanes systems. The princess said, "Let's visit the Simoanes systems." The generals immediately called the troops and attacked the Simoanes systems. Upon entering, they instantly destroyed the parliament and their battalions.

The neighboring enemy cities entered the dimensions, attacking judges and courts men with heavy and bitter radiants, destroying the people. The armies raised and met the forces of the princess, firing bitter matter, destroying everyone in their paths. The Ziauddin's troop rushed to the dimension, firing upon the princess's forces with sweltering radiants from their new artifacts. The generals of her battalion immediately put up their shields, blocking all of their attacks, firing radiants at their troops, burning their bodies and armor to ash. The flames and ash of the Ziauddin soon filled the air, clouding the dimension.

The cities were filled with screams and terror of the civilians and soldiers. The troops immediately removed their shield as most of the Ziauddin's troops were disintegrated into smoke by the fire from the princess's forces. The scouts of her armies searched and destroyed any remaining citizens and troops that hid, leaving none alive. They instantly collected the remaining parts of the dead and carried them back to Calcuralthera. The news soon reached Valeria, where the remaining Ziauddin members immediately left, cloaking their void tunnels. She sent scouts to Valeria, and upon arrival, they were met with Valerian troops with the herald of the courts, saying there would be no war in Valeria. The princess ordered all of her scouts out of Valeria. She stated there were only three of them, and she was disgusted with the actions of their council. The Valerians sent a message to the princess, which she terminated at the beginning, saying to her soldiers, "Stand down on investigation into Valeria during this period."

The remaining members of the Ziauddin in Valeria left for Cankharoughtu, a small city in the Matishkua Kingdoms within Ashmend. The princess looked at Ashmend and only saw civilians. The Ashmend soldiers were missing; she thought they had wives and would surely need some sort of comfort, and that was where they would find them. The Valerians became frightened as all communication with Calcuralthera was cut.

The princess said, "Valeria shall stand on its own decisions, for this is not the era of diplomacy. Trust with the enemy is absolute death. For death is only for the bringer, Eghurahar Maturina Kelghier Turada, the dead will be the beauty of the mournful." She said this in anger.

The kings of Valeria knew what that meant—the princess was always a vengeful woman. "We will have no choice but to destroy her." Their advisers rallied against this decision. "Their power and strength in number are far beyond ours, we will have no choice but to seek an alliance with the Noncithier councils. In this hour, the princess and her forces are active. This means absolute war."

Valeria rallied all their troops, saying, "They are going to war, the invaders of the cities have destroyed many of the allies of Valeria." The princess watched as the kings gave their speeches, saying, "Tonight will be a fruitful night. We will kill, and we will be victorious." The Ziauddin called upon their secret councils—the kings of Barbratheos, Ingultheriat, Hemulerthar, Gurdgerytheos, and Furthelighious, claiming the war has reached Valeria. The princess Kamadahara has been on their trail since the fall of their fathers and execution of Amelgureshion. The time is near; she has destroyed the city of Simoanes, killing everyone in the city.

King Gurdeisha of Gurdgerytheos noticed that she was very vicious in this era, and of course, she was maddened for the way they killed the officials maddened her and their courts. The Hemulertharian king Jershigeon said he will go to Caskadhara and execute the council member of their persecution. The Ingultheriatians, intent on killing the princess, left for Calcuralthera. The rest agreed on a full-scale war against everyone and left the council.

King Jershigeon invaded Caskadhara, blasting an unmovable port into the dimension. The people ran in fear for the reaction was violent. The hole reflected vast violent radiants into the cities, destroying structures and buildings, creating violent winds and vast radiant fluctuations. The people scampered, and the armies assembled, firing waves of calorific radiants at the Hemulertharians. They shielded themselves, returning fire upon the buildings and populations. The people were thrown hundreds of feet into the air, with body parts thrown vigorously, as they moved toward the courts of Caskadhara. The smoke from the burning buildings blackened the air, darkening the skies to that of the night, with shimmers of light from the fires within the homes of the residents.

The armies were outmatched and were being pushed back; the courts and the remaining troops opened ports to other dimensions and radiant rifts in between dimensions to hide the officials. They knew the Hemulertharians were a vicious clan in allied forces to the Ziauddin. They immediately sent messages to their allies asking for help, stating they were overrun in a few minutes. King Jershigeon covered himself in the armor of Joeshurith and made way quickly for the court's tower, hoping to find Judge Eemuratus. He destroyed everything in his path with radiant bursts from his bracelets. The judge ordered his men to stop him; the soldiers fired thunderous bursts of digurite the strongest radiant they had. It was simply deflected off his armor, and the judge became extremely frightened and began to run into a hidden chamber within a wall. Jershigeon began to hit the base of the tower with a very powerful blast of flame, debasing the structure and toppling the tower.

The tower fell upon the building, landing in the streets. Many of the soldiers falling from the tower were crushed under its weight. Jershigeon made a large hole into the tower as it lay sideways on the street. Killing the resistance he met inside, he eventually made his way to the judge's quarters, where the judge lay damaged, crawling to safety. He looked around and saw the judge's soldiers lying on the floor; they slowly crawled toward safety. He executed them one by one as he slowly walked toward the judge. He said to him, "This day would have come because of the curiosity of the lower beings. They envisioned a brighter future without the will of the Effurtheurtide." He walked slowly toward the judge, looking at him and picking him up by the face, looking into his eyes. Jershigeon said, "You were a human once. They have always grown weak in opulence." He looked directly into his eyes and killed the remainder of his men, listening to the crush of their skulls as the radiants burned their bodies to smoke.

The judge trembled, and his eyes filled with tears. He tried to speak; his legs dangled. Jershigeon watched and saw a weak man, a fat and drunk swine loving the pleasures that were afforded by the courts. *You should not be allowed to live.* Jershigeon raised his arm, formed a Rhsicour of radiant, and evaporated his head, throwing his twitching body on the floor. He called out to his men, giving the order to execute the entire city. They followed all the survivors and destroyed them. The men pushed even harder to cover themselves in armor, but the invading forces were too much for Caskadhara. They left for the neighboring cities, destroying all in their path, leaving the cities to rubble. Their chant became "only the strong may sustain the living."

The princess heard the messages from Caskadhara and rallied her forces. At that instant, she suddenly heard a crash into her palace's Ferscound. She immediately shifted and wondered what it was. For the first time, she could not see all the facets of her palace. The Ferscound was an annex to the rooms of her palace, and she shifted through the various rooms and still could not see who or what it was. The princess covered herself in the armor of her father and lit her Fergureshures. She slowly moved toward the Ferscound; she asked who was it, and he answered the hand and grabbed her by her throat. Her armor was made of bitter matter and burned his hand; he threw out of shift into the palace walls, and she fell to the floor.

He shifted himself back in phase with the palace regime firing a blast of radiants, creating a hole in the walls. The princess was thrown thirty-three feet into the other room; he picked up the furniture and threw it at her, hitting her in the chest, throwing her across the halls. Her men called out to her and stormed the palace. He realized that her armor was tough and shifted to another matter phase. He immediately covered himself in Simunclish matter, firing a barrage of radiants, hitting the princess's men, pushing them in all directions. They could not withstand his power.

Her generals shielded as the Ingultheriatian king made his way toward the princess. The men could not remove their shield; they fired many bursts of bitter radiants, but he phased his matter in many sequential vibrations that would cause multiple phase shifts simultaneously. Making him a very difficult target, he uttered a few words in Ingultheriatian, and his army immediately shifted into phase with the Calcuraltherian matter. They immediately fired at the princess's forces, destroying parts of the cities. Her armies covered themselves in battier matter, putting up a front in seconds. They attacked the Ingultheriatians on all sides. The battle was heavy with spheres of radiants destroying the cities and the greater matter planes.

The ceiling began to fall while other parts of building began to crumble. The soldiers had no choice but to retreat. Many shifted as the large bricks fell onto the shields. The princess immediately used this opportunity to shift out of the city. The wars raged in Calcuralthera with the Ingultheriatians firing slugs of radiants at the cities. The Calcuraltherians immediately invaded Ingultheriatian, destroying the royals, killing the guards as they made their way toward the city centers. They attacked fiercely, with swift destruction slaughtering everyone in sight, creating flakes of radiants as the dead charred to dust. The queen Heilgathil's guards immediately invaded the city from the other side, and the Calcuraltherians soldiers cheered as they saw the enemy city destroyed. The Calcuraltherians swiftly pushed for the middle of the city, killing many as the Ingultheriatian citizens screamed for mercy. They continued destroying the city, filling the air with the smell of death and chaos.

The Ferthierlightious heard of the attack and immediately shifted to the cities of Calcuralthera. Upon their arrival, they met a few soldiers rehabilitating the dead; they began to execute the soldiers. Immediately, a few billion battalions shifted into the city. The battles raged and were violent speeding fierce light and sound across the cities, destroying

King Fegurtheir of Ferthierlightious forces. Kamadahara's forces were superior in radiants and was hardly damaged by his attacks but left the enemy temporarily paralyzed. The men called for reinforcements as many left their cities to attack the Ferthierlightious strongholds.

The attack on the Calcuralthera failed because of the annexed rooms within her city; this caused their soldiers to become despondent. They were a maze for their soldiers to navigate efficiently; they were soon overrun by reserved forces from the upper cities from the kingdom. The Valerians soon learned of the Ziauddin's failure in Calcuralthera, where the king Fegurtheir was killed. The Valerian higher councils immediately left for Cambaratu; the Ziauddin immediately hid, knowing the battles could get fiercer as the season progressed.

The Ziauddin knew they were in danger and hid themselves until the situation could be resolved; they had little or no options since Furthelighious was attacked and lost. The Ingultheriatians were destroyed; the court's officials stewed as the people of Cambaratu were displeased to the point of tears, saying this situation could end in the same way the last war ended. The deaths of our kings and royal societies could be our faiths, leading to our exile. The court official's conversation with the princess led to the war where their deaths were certain. They invaded all of their known allies and was victorious. It was clear they had to do something; they went to the city of Alverdury to find the forger. Their artifacts were rumored to possess the greatest strength. That was an expensive endeavor, for the forged artifacts could cost many pieces of silver, but would bring many victories. It can also reveal their plans to their enemies.

The Danish courts looked at all the destructions that was created by the princess, wondering why this could have happened. The African court added that the scouts have reported there were many invasion by the Ziauddin clans. The Danish court asked in fear and anxiety who was their leader. They said, "We all thought the royals were thought to be dead, but records state there were nine descendants that survived." They stirred, saying this was the reasons for the Roman court adopted anger and a very defensive attitude. The African court said they will get to the truth and left the councils.

The Danish stewed, and the courts discussed the wars to come. They spoke of the dog clans and their relationship to the kings the laws they used within the systems to illegally confiscate souls, claiming the rights of forced belief. They possessed the people and forced them to give up their souls, forcing them to believe what was done was their own will and intention. They made them do terrible things and told them they were wicked, killing them while they were possessed, and controlled their minds as they died. A wicked act they had to pay for, this was the reason the wars began.

The Danish court wondered and sought a meeting with the princess, but she was nowhere to be found. With all this war, we should be wise. The Danish queen called upon the armies and held a meeting and the generals. They all reported it was mass war, and many cities were attacked with some being totally destroyed. The Ziauddin was behind most of the attacks for which they were looking for power via these ancient artifacts. The dog and deer clans were after these artifacts for which they were the causes of the wars of Agamourose to revenge their forefathers. The Danish court realized that the Roman royals' attitude was to build a vast army, and their slogan of strength was to build confidence for this day. Their plans were foiled by the princess, where many of their soldiers and court officials were afraid to stop the wars.

This also caused the destruction of many cities, especially those of the lower courts within the collection schemes. Almost all the allies to the Barbratheoian royals and the Ziauddin hid themselves with many strategically appearing within the different cities scattered across the Dieu. This is especially a problem for the Danish royals since this situation could worsen into a volatile situation for all-out war among the members of the larger city states.

The Danish royals heard that the scouts of the Ziauddin were looking for the princess of Calcuralthera who was missing since the attack on her home country. This was especially a problem since the Danish royals were not sure of who among the cities would take the sides of the Ziauddin. The dog clans had already attacked their cities and fled for the hills, but the deer and queag clans were not participating in the wars. This could be a sign of an eventual ambush. She rallied the troops, saying, "We will attack the deer and queag cities within the next few days. We will not wait for them to attack us." She stated they should consort with their allies first; the courts will await the return of the African courts.

The queen of the Danish royals looked at all the cities that she could have seen. She looked at the citizens' state of mind; she looked at those at war and those that were unaware, taking stride in their daily lives. She realized that the Reguresha were building an army of rebels to march to the cause of Ziauddin. Many of the smaller city and independent courts were discussing whether to remain independent or join the cause of the Ziauddin clans.

She looked at the African clans and thought of their position within the system. Many of their citizens were of the idea that the hidden wars surrounding the being that affects the animals of the system would destroy the Dieu. She wondered if the Ziauddin clans were in alliance with these beings; the Roman royals seemingly defended the acts of the Cusnustriea of Congyaba as their own. The ideas of the artifacts came to her; she wondered of the strength and destructive capabilities of these relics. She thought of the old kingdoms and where within these kingdoms she could have these artifacts forged.

She thought they should get some artifacts of their own and summoned the armies' captains and instructed him to seek the smiths of old in an attempt to forge new artifacts, which would be capable of defeating the Ziauddin. A voice said to her, "Beware, not all artifacts are trustworthy. Some can be used to control your mind." She instantly asked who it was, but she got no reply. She immediately called together her council, asking the courts for help and their loyalty in these hours. She needed to be careful, and the acquisition of artifacts could be dangerous. Many of the courts' constituents pledged their allegiance to the Danish courts and royals as they were on the path of seeking peace within the collection systems. This time, we need to be strong and truthful to each other if we are to survive.

Many of the court panels mustered their troops, presenting artifacts that the troops would use in the invasions of the cities of the Ziauddin. Many of the lesser cities cringed as they were tied to the rule from the old cities of the system and Ziauddin's old affiliates. They had no choice but to remain in their positions among the systems, and they were too weak to fight. They eventually formed a small state called Mastheiatria and proclaimed their sovereignty. They were excluded from all military sanctions; they openly stated they had no intention of taking any sides in the wars to come. They vouched for refuge and autonomy under the African courts of justice, asking for aid in the event they are invaded by the cities' participants of these wars. The royals of the African and Danish courts thanked them for their honesty and asked them to evacuate their cities, moving to a safer dimension nearer the sanctuary of the churches in the eleven cities of the courts of Inveiliadi.

They immediately moved, and some people left for Valeria and Casberthia, cities known to be in the grip of the Ziauddin. The generals ordered the men to go to these cities as the crowds moved. They looked at the minds of the citizens as they relocated to Valeria and Casberthia and saw that they were advocating the cause of the Ziauddin. Many stood against the African courts for the enslavement of the Roman royals, but many supported remuneration for injustices done to the people over the years. The Danish courts wondered if this was the right decisions in this war. The Ziauddin has many allies and are willing to go to war in an era where the emperors and Schougnars were very advantageous and adamant of their rule.

She wondered if it would be wise to attack one of the emperors under the Raija since many of the emperors are not in alliance because of the war for conversation of the clans of Arouthicia. The emperor over the Roman royals could not have cared if the Roman royals were enslaved. The emperor had three brothers within this region under the Raija. The Danish queen saellicised at the wars when the Raija took over, analyzing the situations. The Roman royals were under a different nation to the rulers of Giazalia for which their king knew nothing of the war of Galthizura. He unknowingly accepted the position of Kheischa in the collection city of Comuredian for which he was a stooge and was ridiculed for it.

This led to his execution because of the conflicts over the lines, causing a rebellion that split the clans in two. The Raija was displeased and sought to unite the people, but they revolted and attacked the cities, killing the families under Raija. He lost his wife and children during this war as they were decimated in the palace. The Raija was already at war when this happened and destroyed many cities in the district, causing a major reshuffle of the schemes and the stances of collection. Many were displeased of his action, and he forced peace upon the nations via military rule, for which many had no choice but to obey his will or face the death penalty. The Raija was seen as an evil that was to be removed. The rebels of Carillion caused many citizens to be hunted down and killed. Many of their supporters within the cities were publicly executed in a show for the rationale of honoring the emperor's law.

The Danish royals looked at all the remaining families under the Raija and wondered how this situation could be resolved. If the Raija was to be involved with the wars with the Ziauddin, this would be mass revolt and destruction of the systems and the cities. They came to the conclusion that they should exercise precaution and first find the enemies of our cities. The courts all agreed and then decided upon the hunting of the members of the deer, queag, and gauremesh clans. The soldiers immediately assembled and headed for the outskirt systems of the Olemeish and Urgreish where the cities are abandoned and the matter is coarse and very unforgiving. The soldiers knew that the system would be treacherous and would claim many lives, killing both the soldiers and the remaining clan members.

The Deer clans realized that the wars could be coming their way and immediately reincarnated all of their soldiers. They called out to the Gauremesh who had already invaded the Danish royals and thought they were almost entirely destroyed. They looked at the Danish royals and saw very little options for survival. The king Ameiheilder immediately shifted and fled for his tunnel then disappeared. The Danish soldiers tried to follow him, but they could not follow and the entrance to the tunnel shifted. They immediately moved through the city, killing whoever they saw and collecting the parts of the dead. Very soon, after the last remaining soldiers of the deer clan were killed. The soldiers assembled the remaining civilians within the cities and executed all the citizens who were under the extermination protocol.

The soldiers of the royals immediately moved to the cities of Amerities under the king of the deer clan and began burning the buildings and disintegrating the people, killing anyone they met in the streets. They surged through the streets and destroyed everyone and everything in their paths. There were many foreigners in the cities; they were especially rich in knowledge and techniques for military designs of the destructive radiants. The Brasissers that were within the cities shifted, hoping they were not seen; they immediately returned to their city and reported what was happening in the cities of the deer clans.

The Danish soldiers moved on to the cities of Caphrpuller and Serphar for which the battle was intense; the cities near the Fregesh were fed with huge radiant circles of the Lexicurviur particle, which exacerbated their power. They immediately launched huge radiant spheres at the palace, and the princess of Caphrpuller attacked. The king Javajha was immediately killed; she cried at her father's death and raged toward the soldiers, cursing at them in a stern voice. The Danish soldiers immediately fired upon him, disintegrating his body to flakes of radiants. The people became scared and ran screaming for help. The Danish soldiers further pushed into the cities, firing at anyone they could see, causing many particle flakes to tint the atmosphere. The cities had no one left within it; the city became a tomb. The Danish councils chose to make the city a barren desert, making it a signpost for those who would stain their names.

The emperor Sahrrpuller was angry for that was one of his prized beloved cities; he immediately launched an attack on the Danish soldiers. They could not tell where the spheres of radiants came from. The emperor and his forces tried to attack the Danish forces in stealth, but they immediately were seen. They tried to rush through the Danish forces but were met with slugs of radiants in huge barrages, destroying everything in its paths. The Danish armies cloaked and shielded themselves, but their shields would degenerate faster than it should. They soon split their front, dashing for the avenues and alleyways within in city, covertly moving toward the emperor's soldiers. The emperor's soldier broke formation and began hunting the invaders.

The battle would soon become stiff with many battalions meeting each other within the bars, social clubs, and storefronts of the city. The soldiers met shooting spheres of huge radiants, chipping away at the walls, throwing fragments in all directions. They continued shooting, hitting each other. Body parts detached created a gory scene, overshadowing the city. The smoke would soon fill the city, causing energy surges creating flashes of light and deadly radiants that would traverse the clouds of smoke, killing anyone near or inside the clouds. The Danish soldiers pushed forward, using the radiants to create fires and smoke, shooting various radiants into the smoke to recreate the effect. This concentrated effect pushed the emperor's forces back.

The emperor saw this, and he and his guards covered themselves in a matter that was strange to the soldiers. He pushed to the center of the city, running through the streets and through the smoke, creating sparks from his matter and his shields. He wondered what was this and how could this be. He thought it was the matter type of the invaders and covered himself twice with different types of matter. The smoke clouds' radiants raged, throwing particles in all directions. His soldiers tried to run, but many were vaporized. The Danish soldiers realized that the smoke would help defeat the emperor's forces and made a coordinated effort to fill the clouds with Tacid radiants, causing even more violent eruptions of radiants.

Soon the air was filled with a thick black toxic smoke that rose to cover the city. Charged with energetic particles, it affected the shifting of matter and the alluvials of the dendritic in a nonfluid action. Many of the beings near the smoke could not shift. The emperor realized that the smoke was not to his advantage, and the radiants that was expelled was killing his men. He realized that the Danish forces were avoiding the smoke. He searched within the buildings to see who he could find, but almost all the soldiers were dead, some torn in half and others turned to dust.

The emperor saellicised at his guards and gave the order to move forward. They began to run and realized their armor created sparks that caused even more fires. This caused more smoke, attracting the particle and radiant movements, attracting violent expulsions of large destructive bursts that was dangerous to the men. His guards tried to speak to him, but the armor and the clouds of smoke made communication difficult. They had to result to rudimentary signals that would eventually cause the men to be scattered in the low visibility of the city. They made the decision to split up so they could not be detected.

The emperor and three of his guards moved left and then toward the direction of the fires of the dead Danish. The rest went right and then to the west along the main streets, hiding and positioning near the exits. The emperor soon reached a point where he saw a small group of soldiers ready to fire upon anything that would come out. He silently picked up a piece of body armor from a dead soldier, and just before the energy surged, he threw out the armor plating. The soldiers looked at the armor tumbling and slowly moved forward, asking who was there. He instantly climbed the side of a building reaching the top; he looked down upon the soldiers and ambushed the squad.

The men screamed in pain as the radiants disintegrated their bodies; the nearby soldiers immediately ran to their aid. They looked around calling for help. The emperor immediately rushed out from an adjacent building, knocking over the men. The other three bodyguards came from above, splitting the men in halves with the blistering radiants. The emperor soon ran out of the clouds of smoke, rushing into the battalion, lashing with lengths of radiants. The battalions turned their fire to the battle, hitting the positions of the emperor and his bodyguards. Many of the Danish forces ran for cover, as the emperor split the men and their armors into halves as they all concentrated fire upon him. Eventually, his armor began to chip away; he shielded himself, and the entire army concentrated fire upon his position.

The remainder of his guards immediately ran forward and attacked the bulk of the forces, throwing large orbs of radiants at the soldiers, scorching their bodies and flaking their armor. The captains immediately deployed shields, advancing on the emperor's guards, they changed their radiants to Tacid radiants, destroying the outer layers of their shields. The soldiers increased their rate of fire, destroying their armor, eventually reaching their bodies. The soldiers concentrated their fire on the guards, destroying the buildings, creating a crater spewing dust and shattered rock into the air. The men eventually stopped and realized the guards were killed, riddled to pieces. The emperor's armor barely held together, he lay flat on his back on the other side of town. The men immediately surrounded him and called the queen and asked if she wanted the emperor Sahrrpuller alive. She said, "No, bring me his souls, you can keep the rest."

The general said, "It is done, Your Highness." He walked over to the emperor and created a smoldering orb of Califipher radiants and looked down at the emperor. The emperor inhaled, and the general destroyed his head. His vaporized his flesh, and bones shredded into the air, leaving his body to flinch in the streets. As the general walked off, the men drained his body of all his energy, taking his soul in a captive case. The emperor's body lay lifeless in the destroyed city. The sun was setting on the clouded city as the elders opened a tunnel to their home world. The emperor of Karshingfeilt watched as the Danish troops left the dimension. He stood on a far mountain out of sight, looking at the battle. He knew he too was next as the wars continued.

Upon returning, the Danish generals went to the queen's quarters and met her having a meeting with an unknown foreigner. On seeing her general at her gates, she said, "We will be in touch." The man immediately left her chambers and headed for the exits. The general reported it was done, the cities are destroyed but there is still no word of the Ziauddin clans or the Dog clans. The leader of the Deer clan escaped through an unknown tunnel for which we cannot follow and the king Javajha of Caphrpuller was killed. She immediately sent investigators to the sight where King Armellirites escaped, hoping she would find him soon. The general added the Brasissers were in the cities investigating artifacts she immediately looked at him with intent eyes, thinking of the wars. She realized they would go to war soon with the Schougnars of the Raija; this may start the battles prematurely.

She informed her general that she got word of the brother of Altheuriehgh, and the cities of Vergurethian were rallying troops. She wondered if Altheuriehgh was in the battle of Burthemies; the dog clans were the instigators of the conspiracies before they went west to the cities of Valmediest. The dog clans were still not found; the queen asked, "How many enemies of the dog clan's enemies still live?" Her soldiers replied, "They were mostly killed by the Raija's men after the battles. She looked at the hills and watched the forests; her generals reported that the dog clan has seemingly moved to the hills of the west, through a tunnel at immense speed, we should be very cautious. She said, "We should send more scouts to monitor the leaders of their remaining allies. The brother of Altheuriehgh could know or come in contact with their leaders. She said, "I think it might be wise to eliminate them all. In this season, there could be many changes to our advantage."

She immediately ordered the generals to attack the remaining families of the dog clans. The generals immediately got to it, taking even more divisions to the cities of Vergurethian since they were rallying troops to aid in the cause of their fallen allies. On their approach to Vergurethian they were met with a strange type of radiants swirling around the cities. They immediately sent word to the queen speaking of their defense measures. The soldiers searched for a way around and through the radiants but could not. They could not see within or could see any routes in or out of the radiants' sphere. They immediately sent for reinforcements, nearly tripling their initial forces.

They called out to Altheuriehgh's brother Igeliese to come out; we know you are in there. The swirl of radiants spoke, saying you know nothing. They replied, "We are here for your head." He laughed and said, "These cities are impenetrable, for you do not know what you have done." They instantly fired at the sphere and realized that it absorbed all the radiants that were shot at it. The soldiers looked at the radiant swirls and could not fathom what to do.

Igeliese said, "I will show you what to do." Out of the sphere came billions of dogs stampeding toward the general's armies. The soldiers immediately fired at the horde, hitting the animals but only instantly knocking them down. The bulk of the group swiftly rushed to the larger groups, mauling the soldiers, springing to their necks, killing many of them.

The second and third lines of soldiers instantly covered themselves in even harder matter as the dogs attacked. The dogs were made of a seemingly indestructible metal that could penetrate the toughest armor the Danish soldiers could have mustered. The Danish soldiers' shielded and slowly stepped backward, throwing shields toward the incoming animals. The captains shouted, "Shield the dogs!" capturing them inside. Igeliese laughed, saying through the voices of the dogs, "I will show you the soldiers of terror." The swirls of radiants began to grow, and the adjacent dimensions and matter spaces began to rain the metallic matter. The field began to flood, inundating the pathways to the dimension. The matter soon flowed toward many focal points, becoming a mass of soldiers that was made of metal with spears of indestructible fibers.

The Danish soldiers soon realized they had to do something. Igeliese spoke through the dogs and the soldiers saying you have made a mistake coming here. The soldiers began to move toward the Danish soldiers and fired a barrage of radiants at the metal armies. Their attempts only swelled the matter and made the soldiers larger until they replicated themselves, multiplying their numbers. The generals called for help from the rest of their armies in the other sites, but they could not come to their aid. The captains had no idea what this metal was or how it could be stopped.

The Danish generals began firing at the ground, disintegrating the dirt, creating large craters between the metal men and their forces. The dogs were pushed into the holes, where they all melted into larger structures of men and dogs. They soon reached out of the crevices, and the Danish soldiers began to destroy the entire field, reducing the land spaces beneath the soldiers and making it brittle, falling to pieces. The general ordered some of the men to shield the substrate, holding it together. Igeliese began saying, "You do not know our true strength." The large structures began to melt, becoming a large pool of liquid metal within the crevice, seeping into the substrate. The dirt itself began to melt as the metal infiltrated into the soil.

The dirt itself became a brown metal that eventually became chrome, all of the soil toward the east and west of the crevice became part of the lake of metal. Forming a barrier bridge to the plateau to where the Danish soldiers were. The lake formed a wave that would splash onto the bridge creating billions of billions of metal soldiers which slowly marched toward the Danish soldiers. The men tried all the radiants within their arsenal, and none could damage the metal that emanated from the swirl. The general had one last idea, build a shield that would contain all of the liquid metal. The men tried, but this only weakened their defenses; the general ordered the men to take as much of this metal as they can. They shifted out of phase to an adjacent dimension, regrouping in the Furgerish alluvial.

The Danish had no choice but to retreat; the Ziauddin immediately got word of this and wanted the power of the liquid metal. Igeliese was not sharing his secrets for the Ziauddin could not be trusted, not even in a time of desperation. The Ziauddin and their allies regrouped and attacked the cities of Blulederesh, Hergurevesh, and Illifeuthia, destroying the civilians and the armies taking their components. They immediately sent a message to the Danish royals, saying, "Your time is limited, for this war is not for newcomers." They sent the heads of the kings to their kingdom gates via the sacrificial virgins of Gurmoies, which was their enemy until the treaty of Conghuhera.

This was a message to the Danish royals that their old enemies could be on the side of the Ziauddin. The queen stirred, for the battle that she had lost was an agonizing defeat that could strengthen the moral of the soldiers of the Ziauddin. She immediately summoned her generals; they reported that their casualties were minimal, but they had to find a way to defeat their liquid metal. The queen Heilgathil looked at the metal, and she could not tell what it was. She sent samples to the African councils, and they took it for analysis. They stated it looked like something they could have known, but it does not behave in similar ways. Their conclusion was it was helped by something. The queen shrugged and ordered the destruction of Valeria and Fergureties. The generals immediately sent soldiers to those cities where the Ziauddin could not have put up much of a fight.

CHAPTER 15

The Beneficiary of the Proponent

Upon reaching Valeria, the soldiers were met by the king's guard, immediately firing smoldering Chondritic radiants. The Danish soldiers immediately covered themselves in armor and began slaughtering the people of Valeria. The prince cried out for help. Within minutes, more than half of his city was on fire as the soldiers made their way to the palace halls and courtyards. The Commenshuregs from the Ziauddin in Valeria answered the prince's cries, saying, "I will help you this time, but you will repay your debts." He instantly flew into the air moving swiftly across the city skies toward the soldiers screaming and firing violent bursts of radiants as they instantly disintegrated into smoke with bright blue flashes of light. The soldiers realized they were being overrun, and many were forced back to the lines.

The general ordered a unified strike at the Commenshuregs, their attacks were deflected, and he returned fire with violent blasts of radiants. The men shielded, and the radiants soaked the shields, making it brittle. The general fired, and all the men fired in the same direction, shifting phases simultaneously. The men fired, and he deflected all; the general fired dread radiants, knocking him out of the sky. The men immediately ran to his position, but were met with the forces within the city. The men tried their best to not be hit by the Danish radiants for they were more potent than the radiants of the Valerians. The Commenshuregs immediately got up the floor and flew into the sky, heading to the edges of the city, shifting phase and exiting the dimension. The king looked upon his city and cried; he gathered his children and shifted out of the city to safety.

The ombudsmen began fighting among themselves and had nowhere to go since they thought the allies of Valeria would readily come to their aid. They called out to the Ziauddin, but the Ziauddin replied that Valeria has fallen, "you should leave for the cities of Ulmesrahs." The word quickly spread, and many of the officials left for safety. The Danish soldiers swiftly moved through the cities, killing everyone in their paths. The sounds of screams and cries filled the air; many of the children in the playhouses were killed and the prostitutes deconstructed. They salvaged the cities then destroyed the building, flattening them to the ground; this was a message to the Ziauddin clans that their way of life has come to an end. The remaining people from Valeria saw this as the final disrespect from the clans of the systems, cursing the descendants of the Raija and those of the Khazar.

The Ziauddin was not pleased with this since they were descendants of the Khazar; this could mean they could have awakened the Ascoughi, the enemy of Malghnar, the ancestor of the Khazar. The wars could grow out of proportions, and we would no longer be able to defend ourselves, falling to victims of adversity in situation where we cannot physically overcome. The Ziauddin was severely displeased with the events of the wars. They knew that no one knew their true plan for many of the cities they visited was just a mere scratch to the surface.

The Ziauddin began attacking many of the smaller independent animal cities, sacking them and taking all of their components. The queen looked for the district where the animal cities were located and saw it was in the vicinity of their old enemy, King Beilragegron. The clan swiftly moved toward the gates of the kingdom and was met by the guards of his floures. The Ziauddin tried to destroy his guards but could not even dent the armor; they immediately left. The queen watched and realized she was not as strong as she thought. Many of the peoples of the kingdoms are equipping their soldiers and guards with the finest abilities and artifacts that can be afforded.

She looked at his city and saw they were not very concerned with the war; she wondered how can she improve her odds. She asked about the liquid metal and her generals reported it can be controlled, but we do not know how to destroy it. She asked, "Can we use it?" They said, "No, we cannot trust it." She asked what of the artifacts from our allies, could they help? He said they were incompatible. How can we make artifacts from these liquid metals? We need energy or radiant types, the tools of destruction. She asked what types of artifacts do we have to deploy as weapons to our soldiers. They said they will need to run an assessment. She illustrated to her general's the importance of be able to destroy these types of matter. These types of matter fabrics are the more dangerous types among the city clans of the systems.

The African court said, "We have some ideas. We can craft some artifacts that can be used on the liquid metals, but what you should aim for is destroying these types of matter." They showed her a city she never saw before; these are the beings we need to destroy if we are to survive this era's wars. She looked at the cities, and they all looked unfamiliar; they are collected beings, but their matter types are of ancient origins. The African courts said these are the rulers of Ulescles who were responsible for the invasion of the Raija's people. The Raija acted in haste, but knew he could not defeat his enemies.

Asking the Raija for help was futile; if you look within their annex, you would see the last living daughter of the Raija. The Raija is a slave to the will of the ancients. She looked and realized there are many annexes with many beings kept in solitude. Saying there are many ancients who are the secret rulers of the systems, collecting their beings in seasons. He looked at a country in the distance, and she saw they culled the cities, collecting the dead from these created cities, collecting souls and parts on a mass scales every three eras.

She realized that we are not ready for this era's wars, the African courts agreed, for it is almost time for the wars of this era to take place. The last 390 eras there has been major military disturbances. These disturbances almost occurred exactly to date where the military city of Durridies exercises their right to kill those who break the laws of their forefathers. This military city executes and collects beings from the dead cities killed by the lesser cities under their rule. None of the officials know about it.

She realized they were pawns in a larger scheme, for this city was huge, very structured, and organized. She asked what can we do? We need to be wise for even they had their wars. He showed the past: fifty eras ago, an ancient city was attacked. The beings killed were collected and remade in an older city, but if we look closely they did not retaliate. We do not know what were the circumstances of their excavation. She was in horror and asked how we can acquire knowledge and abilities from these beings. He said we can but we need better ways of understanding their dimensions.

The queen Heilgathil, angered, ordered her smiths to make many artifacts for her, sending them on missions to remove the constituents of the Ziauddin clans. The African courts gave her a few artifacts for her soldiers as they would need strength to fight the Ziauddin. The Ziauddin had the power to hide their dimensions and their existence within the alluvial. She stewed and looked at these ancients, studying their movements and their conversations trying to learn their languages. She traced their lines of their existence to find a main ancestor, but she could not see that well.

She realized that their senses were differently designed and tried to emulate their builds. She eventually succeeded creating an ear that can be used like a sonar, which they used to see across multidimensional alluvials without incrimination of separation. They used these to simultaneously observe their neighbors more clearly the constant shifting without compromising their ability to perceive multiples of the same dimensions. The problem was they could perceive smaller increments of particles than those of her designs. She sent her design to the soldiers and the African royals for which the African royals sent her an upgraded version where she could observe severe details of her environment.

The African royals said it was time we need to dedicate some minds to the advancement of abilities, because we can all fall behind. The queen sent millions of newly trained soldiers and scholars to African courts. If they could figure out the builds of the ancients we could survive the wars. The queen ordered her own research teams to find new ways of defeating the ancients. She used her new senses to observe the ancient cities, and she realized that many of the beings kept in prison were of old designs not similar to their captors. She also noticed they possessed artifacts in the prisons. They could not have spoken to anyone because the prisons were impenetrable. She wondered how this was made. In attempting to make contact, she alerted a guard.

The guard looked right at her with a smug face and then shifted his focus to somewhere else. She tried to find where he refocused to but was unsuccessful. She wondered, *How could I become as powerful as one of these ancients.* She thought of the battles of old, can we reincarnate an ancient and learn his secrets? The African court said, "We have a few, but we need to be careful because reincarnating a being can cause vile reactions resulting in the death of many. These ancients were very dangerous and aggressive in nature and can be very unfriendly. You will need to safely restrain them. The problem is the more powerful they are the more dangerous the exercise can become. She thought it is worth many tries.

She contacted the main vaults stewards and created an appointment, she left for the vault city with a sense of safety because there can be no wars there. She looked at the guards of the vault cities and scrutinized their designs. They were all gibberish to her; she also recognized that many features and designs of many of the other guards near the systems embodied the techniques and features taken from these. She walked into the vault, meeting the steward. She looked at him and wanted to know what his build was. She thought of the decorum and practices of the vault and asked him what is his build. "If someone like me wanted to know this, where can I go?"

He said, "There is a general library attached to the vault with basic techniques of how to design and build an original being. However, the designs of beings have evolved since then." He looked at her as she despaired and said, "Not to worry for all designs are based on the principles within the libraries. All knowledge within our universe comes from the very first builder among the beings that lived within our universe. These beings learned acquired all of their knowledge from the library. These structures were built by that being. She wondered what build are you, he replied I am the original Puerugshes Moureose. There were many copies and adaptations to versions of my build but you can find that information in the library.

She made an appointment for the library and she went into the vault. She was looking at names of beings she could speak with. She realized there were many vicious criminals stored there. She thought these beings should never be freed, one such being was Curmliftuious Sergrapyuious the annihilator of the Multious systems. He destroyed billions of dimensions on the premise of praise from his master who committed suicide at the observance of his gesture. She opened the Synaptic Mental Vesicles or Psyche-emulation and began speaking with him; he was vicious and had a vile temper but she masked her features to look like his master so that he can become friendly.

She immediately pretended to become various people from the list within his memory. She asked, "How can I create a powerful artifact?" He said, "Artifacts are for those who cannot possess the Lexicurviur under the third vestitude." She instantly realized the artifacts were for those who were created in the matter space of the lower eras of the systems. She asked, "How I can possess the Lexicurviur of the third vestitude?" He said, "You must wield the Kieythiesh of the Vestitude. You must know the keys and colors to hold with your Curengesh." She was startled for she did not know what a Curengesh was. She asked, "What is a Curengesh?" He replied, "You are not a Murgurtherian?" She said no then "you cannot know for your mind will not be able to understand." She asked, "How can I understand? She said you need to find the Guromdiah of Aurothoma."

She looked for his name and realized it was not there. She looked to see if he was ever deceased and saw that his name was absent. She thought she needed to find this being; she thought there must be some information within the libraries about the various rooms of the universe. She remembered the Maralaio radiant and how it can create a room for the room of the Aurothoma could be one of the very original rooms.

She asked, "How can I be modified like you?" He tried to see her, but he was only a Psyche-emulation. She wondered and said, "Give me all the power and knowledge you have, and he asked, "Who are you?" She said, "I am from the very distant future, and you have died and is now stored in the vault for which I need your help, ideally your power."

He silenced and said, "Yes, I will help you, but you must help me find a hidden place, a place where I hid my treasure. He gave her some words to tell him upon his reincarnation because he would not trust her. She agreed and learned the words, for it was the words of a very ancient language. Hurelunture Sdcurcture Mktchure, meaning life goes without a shadow of doubt. She withdrew his components and left for the library. On reaching the library, her general called and told her of another attack by the Ziauddin in the smaller cities near the Nunlescks systems. She said, "You should hunt them down, but be prepared for invasions."

The general left and she copied all the scrolls relating to matter types and builds that were in the library. She immediately left for her city. On reaching there, she called the African councils and shared what she had gotten. She copied the documents and thought about what Curmliftuious Sergrapyuious said about helping him recover his treasure. She wondered how vast is this treasure; she became weary and decided to get to it. She began studying the books about matter and building the beings of old.

She realized that she could very well be ill prepared and would need help reaching these levels of matter and energy production. She created three helpers to accommodate her needs. She immediately left for the council halls, near the court of issues. She created a dimension where they can practice creating the matter, radiants, and energy needed to win these wars. They all went inside and closed the door; she told her generals it could be sometime before she returned. Hunt down the Ziauddin clans and do not kill the innocents of the lower systems. The general saluted and left until she returned.

The African royals looked at her as she left and realized that it would be sometime before she would return. The African looked at the soldiers and looked at the remaining Ziauddin members. They discussed the issues surrounding the eminent demise of the Ziauddin and why they were being hunted. They wondered who used the Ziauddin clans to throw the social bias in their favor. It was not a beneficiary of usual standing. None of the clans that benefitted were directly involved. They looked at the enemies of the Ziauddin and saw the Calcuralthera, who were also looking for the Ziauddin.

The African courts were not interested in war but knew that this era has become volatile, and we should try to remain safe. They also knew that the ancients were always up to collecting what was theirs rightfully. They wondered what the best course of action was. The Danish courts and the Arab courts looked at the burning cities, thinking of the death of trillions of people who have lost their souls, resulting in even more migration and fear for destruction. The riots have spawned mass purging of the systems, reshuffling of the ranks and the collection schemes, but the Ziauddin returned and no one thought they were that powerful. They wondered what the artifacts of the Ziauddin clans were. The most heavily guarded secret of this era, where did they come from.

We know they were using the dog and deer clans to acquire artifacts. The kings of the deer and the dog clans escaped and could not be found; their methods of hiding are immensely complex. There could be trillions of allies to the Ziauddin clans and how many are among the systems. The Danish alerted their forces. They said, "No, we should deploy scouts and find the pathways way into their networks." They sent their soldiers to the vault to withdraw the Ziauddin's member. Those could be of great value for exchange during negotiations and the gathering of information. They instructed them to reconstruct the beings in the cells beneath the Jurubehr for questioning.

The African courts looked around, observing everything, looking at all the animals within the system and realizing that many of the cities of the collected beings were being neglected. They immediately dispatched stewards to ensure the safety of the systems. Then all the animals simultaneously raged then dispersed. They felt empty in their stomachs. The African royals wondered how can the systems be in a state of riot. They looked at the enemies near the systems and tried to put together a plan of how they would try to invade.

We are surely in deep trouble, they said as they calculated the numbers and plans for attack. They wondered who this giant of an enemy was; they had no way to directly find out unless they tried to engage in direct combat. This was the best idea that they could fester. They looked around and asked the Roman slaves who was that, and they said the emperor's Hitoichi of the Raija. They looked at the cities and said no, it is not.

They looked at the courts and weighed their options, thinking of this era and how it could be destructive or permanently detrimental. The cities could be unforgiving, and many of them stored their parts in a hidden vault, replacing them with military grade substitutes. The citizens had to assimilate and replace their components with military upgrades, making every man and woman a soldier. They all attired in their armor and marched toward the barracks of the generals. The armies were trillions of soldiers strong; they were all given artifacts and upgraded abilities to strengthen the armada. Installing memory implants of military tactics and strike descriptions.

The African courts looked at the Raija and his emperors; they were not very concerned with the wars of the cities or with the emperors. The African court knew that the war will eventually lead to the war with the Raija and the beings that speak within the system; this being is a much bigger threat for sure. The ancients above must be destroyed or we would have to fight for the next few eras. The African courts looked at the torched skies and saellicise and saw only war but saw a means where the wars could end. This meant many people could be simply hiding their intentions from many bitter enemies who were simply just too quiet for these wars to end like that. The systems has always been a dangerous place, and the cities always found the littlest issues to invade another. They said it was wise to be guarded in this era and open their vault of reserved soldiers for reincarnation. More than a trillion soldiers strategically hid themselves in places that many of these modern enemies are not aware of.

They looked at the ancients to observe their troops and their state of affairs, looking for any signs of increased military activity. There was only the high-ranking Graija, for they were always interested in a war with the Surpurthes. This war led to many full eras of war among the two cities. They looked at the Surpurthes and saw they were deploying troops to invade the descendants of Chouthar, who were by extension the metal clans of the Soheries. He realized that within the annexing vaults, they possessed many types of liquid metals. They knew that they could gain valuable information about these metals but were not entirely sure how this can be achieved during this period of increased war.

They dispatched their soldiers to experiment building with these liquid metals. They looked on and watched the Surpurthes soldiers as they positioned themselves to invade the dimensions of the metal clans. They watched further and saw that the Graija were of the intention to take over the cities of the Surpurthes; they wondered how we could use this to our advantage. They looked at the cities and saw that the liquid metals were not very popular and were only used by the affiliates to the mental clans.

They slowly controlled the minds of the Cxulthies and forced them to attack the Durthielgres, who were affiliate to the Jslurthueriles. The Cxulthies attacked the Durthielgres on the premise that their bills were overdue and the anticipation of future perception of the war has led to their prudence and panic. This was a legitimate claim; the Durthielgres had little to pay so they gave them the liquid metal as a gift, a means to defend themselves. The African court watched as the Durthielgres taught them to use the metals. They also noticed their version was not the same type as those within the upper vaults of their cities. They looked and absorbed all that they could; they dispatched this information to the men who were working with the metals. The African courts watched as the Durthielgres maneuvered the metals, further preparing themselves for war.

They thought that surely the Surpurthes must have had this knowledge, and how could we have gotten this from them? He looked at the Danish countries and said, "We shall take a page from their queen's book." He summoned a general instructing him to send the men to secretly access the central vault and look among the dead for someone from the Surpurthes or Durthielgres clans, instructing them to look for beings with knowledge of the liquid metals, giving the men a list of things they should find.

The court members said to each other, "We should keep this a secret, for many people would frown on our underhanded method of acquiring these techniques. We should not let our allies know our intentions because we can be seen as dishonorable." Some disagreed, saying we should let them know, but at the right time. "Many of the court members of our ally's treaty council cannot defeat the illusive speaker within the system; that is, the enemy we should prepare for." They agreed but saying, "We should be more concerned with dimensional dynamics. Our enemies cannot be found, and it is near impossible to perceive all the members of the Ziauddin clans."

The African court's arbitrator looked around for more of the enemies' soldiers, observing many of the beings of the systems who were mostly interested in taking over the business sectors of the cities. The major constituents of these societies were not concerned with the wars of the emperors because these wars have only just began. They looked at the emperors and saw that they were of the intention to collect more, thinking if they caused a war between Emperor Jheuliews and Emperor Kortelieos, they could cause Emperor Cashuvieous to become greedy taking over the countries of Chane, Averosba, Marghelvea, and Brosvahaes. They looked at the royals of Eueslhaes and wondered if they could survive the invasions to their cities. They could be executed because they were simply not strong enough to wage war against the emperors.

We would have no choice but to manage the wars of the emperors. This could be a dangerous plan, but we can use it to take down the Raija and destroy the cities of the ancients. The Danish royals still do not know we are the enemies of the Comughatelli, the ancients of the third eras. She still does not know who her enemies are. She should be careful for her cities do not know the terror that could be upon them. They looked at distant cities and listened to the whispers made in panic from the Buriduos as they discussed their plans to escape the situation. The Buriduos realized they were exposing their intentions and directions.

They immediately shifted to a neighboring city. Many of the cities of the systems panicked and asked the speaker for help. They tried to appeal to the speaker, but the topics of discussion only caused the agitation of others. They tried to hide their shame and failures, but these plans only resulted in a trajectory for war and destruction. They all stood still and saellicise at all the alluvials that contained war. The African courts watched and wondered what was the solution to escape the speaker's plan. They were desperate as their cities were going to be destroyed.

The African court looked on as the smaller cities were being destroyed and the invaders took the souls and necessary components and moved to another city. One court member of a small council under the main African royal's court took a few thousand incomplete components and fabricated imitation souls out Muscularet energies, bringing them back to life. They gave them military upgrades and instructed them to collect as many remains they could find to build an army.

They immediately got to it, looking at the destruction and working silently and swiftly, collecting trillions of beings, placing them in the ruins beneath the ancient African courts of the Juombhu. The court looked at the size of the group and gave them a cloak, saying, "If many were to see the size of your army, they would instantly attack. You should keep these artifacts of Jushumba, they will give you strength and powers from the Limnec and Sormeil system's energies.

The courts looked on with despair to see the extent of the destruction as the various armies raged through the towns and countrysides, killing everyone on sight. The lower court looked at the death of trillions and wondered how this could be resolved. This was quickly becoming the largest invasion of the era. The royal courts said to them it can and will become worse as the cities became more efficient at destroying the lesser cities. It is the way of the there is a single mastermind behind this but we need to find who this was if we are to survive. They asked how, and they said we need to be quiet and observe. Doing little can make things worse; doing much can be catastrophic. We need to think and not always look for a benefactor. There are many schemes for collecting with the swing of times and shifts in the laws of possession. They replied a conundrum; they said it is worse and it is a trap. If we do not act swift enough, we would not survive.

They all looked out and saw the destroyed cities, burning dimensions that were filled with smog of corrosive energy. They looked at the cities that lay victim to the chaos. They all wondered when this could be our cities, the African court said if all of the emperors and the descendants of the Ohangra came together against us we will surely die. That is very unlikely for many are no longer part of the collection schemes and associations. They immediately began counting the enemies, and they realized the descendants of Ohangra do not need to allies to launch an invasion of this scale. Our enemies the Shurmeis only need to join this war on the side of the emperors, and the smaller tribes will join forces and will no longer accept our donations as gifts and kind gesture; we can be in a position of immense danger.

The African royals immediately counted the clans that could go against them and realized that the younger courts were right, for if the Ishurmes and the Shurmeis go to war against us, we could be in for a lot of war in this era. The Shurmeis and Ishurmes are very dormant this season. The collection schemes are not in their favor at this time; surely they would not fight for the next two seasons for the schemes would turn things in favorable collection for the Aphelthies, their allies. The African royals said, Yes it can and the Raija can use this to their advantage. The African courts saw this and realized they needed more planning.

They looked at the Danish soldiers and called one of their generals to council, saying, "I would like your men to take a small army of Augmesh soldiers on a secret mission. They would eliminate some clans that could link the wars to the Shurmeis. They both agreed and went to the Ufurleties systems, a place where the Ziauddin clans executed many civilians and took their souls and kundalinis and rebuilt them from Brashiers energy and common energies within that system. They were given the upgrades of the ancient Durlefvesh, adorning them with a replica artifacts of the Tear of Orunghah. The artifact the dog clan which was won from the Melughogite in the battles of Olundhener. They were instructed to reincarnate the dead to join their ranks and continue the fight. Upon completion, they were instructed to continue pillaging the Ufurleties and neighboring systems. They would set up a base in the abandoned kingdom of Ufurty.

The Danish soldiers immediately got to it, crafting the armies in secret; they immediately began destroying the Durlinghthies, Furtheirthies, and Simurlties, which they had no clue who they were. They worked with efficiency, destroying the links to collection states. Many cities within the region were unsure of who they were but knew that the Ziauddin were collecting souls within the region. Many turned their forces against the Ziauddin clans, deploying soldiers to cities where the Ziauddin clans would frequent.

The Danish soldiers secretly followed the masses that ran from the invasions looking for the Ziauddin and saw the Mashutuka. He was the officials of the Ziauddin clan who was responsible for many murders during the early part of this era. He was perusing the markets of Calvenghier with a strange individuals that was unknown to the Danish courts; they secretly followed them, but they realized and shifted to different dimension. The Danish soldiers tried to follow, but they had a special sequence of shifting that was new, causing their trace particles to disintegrate completely, avoiding detection.

The Danish soldiers decided to rebuild officials and citizens who died during the incursions and used many as spies. This could cause a scare giving away their positions. The Ziauddin clans realized this and sank their operations and used alternative methods. The Danish royals needed to do something quickly and captured the Emurathies who was an important official within the cities of the Ziauddin. It was assumed that he would know where the leader could be. He was the top of the Danish wish list. They ran out of options and returned to the Danish cities, looking out for any activity.

The Ziauddin was soon entirely off the radar with no one knowing their whereabouts. They broke relation with many of their allies, leaving them to the slaughter. The soldiers speculated they could have been growing weaker, but the members of the royal courts said they were gaining more power. They acquired many artifacts from their invasions led by the deer and dog clans, with many of their allies still unknown.

We should be cautious as they could be planning strikes with their allies for the old grievances of the ancients were becoming prominent, causing wars between the ancient cities. The wars with the Calcuralthera was detrimental for the Ziauddin as they lost many cities and many of their allies have gone into hiding. It is also said that Princess Kamadahara is still unaccounted for.

It is theorized that she was killed by the leader of the Ingultheriatian city, many claim she is still alive. She was in hiding because of the battle in Calcuraltheral it was that the Ingultheriatians were too fierce destroying the Royal palace and cities leaving the courts crippled. The armies were searching for the Ziauddin's members, executing them wherever they could be found. The Danish royal courts were surprised that the princess would go into hiding; she was too strong to be overrun by the king of the Ingultheriatians. The Calcuraltherians were the ones to destroy the first royals of the Ziauddin clans, pushing them into exile. They thought maybe it was a diversionary tactic since the princess was the individual who would press the issues against the Ziauddin clans. The Danish royal's court looked for the princess, but could not see where she was; there was absolutely no trace of her matter expulsions.

The battle within the castle could hardly be seen even with advanced eyes of the Fergureties; they realized that the Calcuraltherian clans were advanced to those of the systems. They wondered where she could have gone, they sent word to their soldiers, but they sadly replied they do not know. They wondered if she was kidnapped by an Ingultheriatian soldier, but this was unlikely as their king had trouble defeating her. They were still searching for her until then she was considered missing in action. The Danish Royal Courts frightened and increased palace security, saying the wars are not limited to anyone.

They all looked out at the cities and saw many going to war the society was at riot. Many feared for their lives and joined forces with rouge groups and independent nations. They were of impeccable standing in the courts and others were of collection by any means. The court officials all joined together making an army of considerable size until the refugees of the Velvulutherians came to their cities. They joined forces with the rouges, and they were angered by the actions of the Ziauddin and the opposing kingdoms, saying they are causing mass destruction and destitute people. They were all saddened, saying the wars were too destructive. The leader Vestumus said we should try to help the refugees of the fallen cities. The armies of the enemies kill many with no remorse, he too lost his wife and children to the invaders. They began to help the refugees and were instantly attacked by an invading army. He fired large bolts of unknown radiants. An onlooker saw him and tried to find who he was. He was a descendant of an ancient fallen Royal society. He did not know the extent of his royalty.

The Danish royals looked into him and saw he was saddened by the death of his children, and tried to speak to him. He looked at the royals, and they realized he could not see their palaces and everyone within. They tried to cloak and realized he could still see them. The royals became frightened and ordered the assassination of those clans; he saw this and fired bolts at the soldiers, disintegrating them into vapor. The captains saw this and launched a mass attack. He immediately shifted and then returned into an alternate matter type. He began to fire heavily into the platoons of the Danish soldiers, disintegrating them, creating smoke and ash.

The Danish royal court looked at this with fear, and one young royal covered himself in a special matter and shifted to his position and attacked. Vestumus blocked his attacks, with his hands shifting from position to position, simultaneously appearing as though he was in multiple positions all at once. He began hitting the young prince with a barrage of physical lashes to his head. The young prince, dizzied and startled, fell to the floor and immediately scrambled to his feet. He put up his fists to fight, and Vestumus shifted and came from behind with a flying kick, pitching him forward into the tables.

The prince got up and put up his fists, and Vestumus dashed forward with immense speed in a flash-like energy. Kicking him to the wall, the prince immediately fell and was unconscious. The Danish royal court looked at Vestumus and said, "You will die." He said no, and they ordered their soldiers to attack. Vestumus opened his shield and blocked the barrage of bullets with screaming hot radiants. The deflections chipped the bricks of the walls within the building. Vestumus became tired trying to catch his breath; the soldiers saw he was almost spent and attacked. He shifted and began to hit them with a heavy flash of radiants pushing the walls. He would shift and appear near them hitting them and reshift to a position of the next to the soldiers. The Danish royal court ordered more soldiers to his positions; they fired billions of bullets to the city, trying to destroy the entire city. He shielded the entire city, and they fired more bullets at the shield. The other men tried to strengthen the shields, and the Danish royal courts ordered the generals to eliminate the rogues.

Vestumus knew this was his end, and he mustered all of his strength. The Danish soldiers fired their hottest bitter radiants at Vestumus, pushing back his shield, cracking the surfaces. The men would scramble to put their shields over the cracks. The Danish courts looked at Vestumus and saw he was about to cry for this was the way he lost his family. They looked at him in shame for this was a man that would never forgive them because of their actions today. Many of the refugees stood and watched the Danish generals and their armies advanced on their positions. They fired a barrage of radiants to their positons, the casualties became immense as people were still coming to the safe haven.

The Danish commanders would soon try to surround the city with billions of soldiers, killing the citizens on the outskirts. The Danish royals became afraid of the power of Vestumus, thinking he had too much. They ordered the generals to kill him; he cannot be allowed to survive; he will be our enemy for sure. The Danish forces circled the shield, the men who supported him said they had to leave and you should leave too. He said we are tired of running; they shifted and the cracks in his shields became worse. He shifted left and shift pulse his shield's radiants, detonating the shield.

Huge flasks of hot burring fire destroyed everything in its path, the smoke filled the air, tainting the view of the city. The lightning started to flash, surging through the smoke, making thunderous sounds, shaking the grounds. Vestumus looked at the soldier, lighting his hands a fire that soon consumed his entire body. He began to scream, crying out loud, and radiants expelled from his body with violent flash, burning the eyes and bodies of all within the range. His clothes disintegrated, and his body became covered with a very old form of matter that was hard and indestructible.

They fired at him, destroying the cities, creating a crater where he once stood. The smoke cleared, and he stood there floating in the air as though nothing affected him. His head was bowed down in sadness; the generals soon attacked with everything they had. They filled the skies with bullets of radiants. Flashing the atmosphere with bright lights pulsing back and forth, with immense precision. The smoke cleared, and there was a bigger crater. He then looked up at them in wonder. He covered his head and looked into the men. The men started to glow and began to burst apart. The pieces that flew into the air caused the others to explode, causing a chain reaction, destroying all the Danish soldiers.

He immediately slowed time as he saw the Danish court began to run. They tried to shift, but they were too slow. He shifted to the Danish royals court, entering the dimension at immense speed as the dimension's walls cracked because of the radiants of his body. He entered the chambers, kicking the court master in the face with the speed of a flash of light. His head immediately came off, and he shifted to the duchess of Comwalt, punching her in the chest, cracking her chest cavity. Fluid filled her mouth, and he dislocated her jaw throwing her to the floor. He sifted to the Cumbergrde of Comwalt kneeing him to the rib, leaning him over to one side, breaking his legs. The Cumbergrde leaned over, finishing him with an elbow to his spine, fracturing his vertebra column as he fell to the floor.

The others were already trying to shift but were very slow; he shifted the princess of Gurethia. As she was partially shifted and pushed his both hands into her body, removing her entrails her eyes opened and her mouth cringed. He shifted to the Prince of Furthies, kicking him in the back shattering his spine. He began spinning out of shift while throwing him twenty feet into the air. He fell to the floor breaking many of his ribs; he shifted to the guards of the courts, who were in the process of charging toward him. He drop-kicked the left guard to the face, before he fell to the floor he shifted to the other guard falling from above, with an elbow to the back of his neck, breaking the bones inside. He shifted behind the princess of Gurthielda, grabbing her hair, kicking her back, and pulling her head and spine from her body. He used her spine and head like a bat swinging it at the face of the Duchess of Juliafesthies, cracking her skull.

He shifted to the front of her, swinging the skull at her face, cracking her cheekbones, breaking her nose. As she fell to the floor, he kicked her into the walls; he shifted too in front of the prince of Burdherels and grabbed him by the throat, tossing him into the Duchess of Lurthieal. He shifted to their position, picking up the prince and slamming him onto her, breaking her ribs. He looked at their faces and raged, becoming hard. Gaining heat, he became enraged, detonating the air around him, causing immense heat. The matter inside the palace was made of the Reschularis particles, which detonated in a radioactive explosion of radiant streams that caused a chain reaction. The entire city and its soldiers detonated, scuffing all the matter within the dimensions.

The African royals instantly looked at the Danish royals and saw the dimension exploding in reactions of radiance, resulting in total detonation of the matter type. They summoned the soldiers but frantically told them not to go into the dimension. They looked on in anger to who this could be they kept looking and realized all the dimensions and alluvials were destroyed to the point its delineations were unrecognizable. The African royals cloaked, and as the matter reshifted, resonating toward stability, they saw a very hardened type of matter that was in the shape of a man leaving the dimension in bursts of speed and light, flying toward the suns of Illughresputhies.

They looked at him and could not tell what it was; they could not see inside of him, could not see his mind. They looked at the Danish courts, looking for their remains. The matter was destroyed to the point they could not tell what the matter regime was or what the state the matter was within any of the adjacent dimension. They looked on in a combination of anger and fear, saying, "We need to find a way to destroy the Ziauddin and their allies." The African royals said, "Let us not make presumptions accusations in fear. We should try to find out who the assassin was. The remainder of the Danish courts looked upon the royal cities and cried. The annexed cities were all that remained;

they wondered where the king and the queen were. They cried, and the soldiers reported the queen was within a secret chamber near the Courts of Issues while the king was on affairs near the city centers of the ancients.

The soldiers immediately sent word to the king and queen for which they got no reply. The queen was under strict orders from the generals not to be disturbed in her private facet which they had no way to access. The allies of the courts stewed and became scared as rumors filled the societies of an assassin of the Ziauddin destroyed the Danish royals, leaving their armies in shambles. The courts stirred and tried to radiant synchronize the reflective Jegreshures in an attempt to talk with the incarnation of the Danish royals, but the disintegrated matter has strange effects on the old techniques of construction.

The courts became scared, proclaiming their loyalty to the Ziauddin, which angered the African courts, saying the Ziauddin should not be your choice for a leader under any circumstances, but they have chosen to pledge loyalty to an absent leader. This was truly tragic; the African court members entered the meetings, saying, "We are not sure if it was the Ziauddin's assassin. What we do know is there was a battle with the rogues of Velvulutherians causing the destruction of the royal cities. The Danish lower court looked around in fear, saying, "We should find this assassin and rallied the remaining soldiers, sending them to the destroyed city of Velvulutherians."

The soldiers immediately went to Velvulutherians. On reaching there, they realized there were bits of body parts and armor everywhere littering the ground. As they walked farther, they saw a large crater hundreds of thousands of meters deep with bright flames filling the air with smoke. They reported there was nothing here, but there seems to be evidence of a battle with our soldiers but there is no signs of the enemy. The African courts looked at the spot and realized the energy shifted, causing the time energy regimes to unbalance blinding the past and futures of a few dimensions. They wondered how can one being be this powerful. They had no leads as to who they were or where they went.

The African courts advised the Danish courts to send an emissary to the cities of Althemitia to find a member of the Ziauddin clans to hold a meeting. They had no choice, and they wanted peace with the Ziauddin clans. The Ziauddin replied after some time saying it was us and we will return to destroy you all. The African courts were impatient with the Danish courts because they were afraid of the Ziauddin clans. They ordered the soldiers to hunt down the representative of the Ziauddin clan to have a word in confidence. They sent many spies to Althemitia they eventually found a representative of the Ziauddin clan that was willing to speak. They arranged a meeting at the darkness of the carnage, when there was peace with the cities of Althemitia.

CHAPTER 16

The Girth of a Court

The Danish courts prepared gifts and parcels of law to present to the Ziauddin, when the African royals said to them, "What are you doing your queen is not dead; she is doing research to find a means to end this war." The court asked, "Where is the queen, the royals, and half of the soldiers are dead. How can we continue against the Ziauddin." The African royals said, "Are you absolutely sure it was the Ziauddin?" They said, "The Ziauddin confirmed it. We should seek peace." Seeking peace with the Ziauddin would cause your demise in this era for they have many enemies. You should seek counsel with the city of Calcuralthera before joining the Ziauddin because they are the destroyers of many of the Ziauddin's allies in this war. It would be wise to rally allies against the Ziauddin instead of joining them in fear. They said to them quietly, "Your queen is not dead, and joining the Ziauddin is treason, you should all be wise not to anger her when she returns."

They stewed and sadly said, "We have no choice, they would seek counsel with the city of Calcuralthera before we seek the Ziauddin." The African court further advised, "You should find alternative dimensions and alluvials to reside in. The innocent are not safe in the cities of your councils. It is where they would most likely attack." They immediately ordered many of their citizens to move to the ruins of Achiscazhar and left for Calcuralthera seeking counsel with the brother of the princess. The African courts worried and saw a major turn of events; they wondered how to rebuild the cities of the Danish, and where were their souls and the other components would their bodies. They wondered if it was destroyed; they looked intensely and could not find any remains of many known radiant signatures. They had never seen the destruction of a souls before that was thought to be very unlikely. They waited impatiently for the matter within the destroyed Danish cities to settle to investigate what really happened.

The Arab courts reported the being was speaking again this time displaying tiredness and lethargic behaviors through the systems. They looked at the messages in the worlds and saw the beings meant to be restless, the African courts grew weary and afraid and responded within the fishes of the oceans asking what is its name. The fishes began to frantically chase each other eating each other in a violent motion across multiple systems. They knew what this meant, it wanted war. They said to their ancients we need to find the source of these messages. A young court said it's an architect, we presumed so because of the way it speaks. The radiants that tie the animals to the energies to the earth were put there by the architects of old for which we do not have access to these radiants. What we need is knowledge of the architects that designed the systems thought out time. The African court presumed that the architect was banished before the change of the collectors of the systems. There were not many of designers of old within the systems today, they were banished eras ago due to unfortunate circumstances.

The African courts knew this was trouble, and we had to survive the unknown speaker. They wondered if this was an architect, and it is still alive why it would create chaos within the systems. Many of the ancients are not interested in the systems saying the systems have become trouble for anything that is living. Existing near the systems mean existence is temporary, their idea is to collect a city and leave before you are regenerated in another city. How can we defeat an architect, they replied the last known true architect was more than 500 eras ago, for which this was a rumor.

No one knew for sure who was an architect, or was it just another controller scheme? Your unknown speaker seems to have the power to control the systems, but this does not mean that they are one of the last architects. They could be a Hitoichi or Kurtanuran emperor controlling the schemes to their will. There are many ways to control beings, and this could be a being that has power over an ancient being executing his will over the animals via slavery. There was an era where the soldiers of the systems hunted and killed the being of old for their power, via an old king that possessed an artifact from the period before.

It was rumored that the kings of old were afraid of death, and they channeled their powers into statues, carvings, and articles of clothing and eventually to jewelry they gave to their descendants. A chance to defeat the ancients as their immortality was taken from them, these artifacts was passed through the ages from generation to generation. It eventually reached a standpoint of stagnation where many of them were hidden because of the removal of their immortality spawned an era of greed and hate. Time was the friend of no man and desperation spawned the warriors of the shadows.

They eventually collected all the artifacts of the era and hid them; the clan eventually went extinct. No one knows where this clan was today. There are many artifacts used to enslave the beings of old, but possessing any artifact from that era will result in one's death. The matter of the ancients are not the frail matter types of the modern forms. Many of the old soldiers of the ancient armies would come to collect these artifacts. The African courts wondered, how can we find who was responsible?

They needed to find an architect; they went back to the Ashieres and visited Amario. He said he was not sure what an architect was as the systems had a long and violent history. The people of the African courts began to cry, saying, "There is no hope if the unknown speaker is not caught. The wars will come our way, they were saying we should speak with it, but that could surely cause more war since the laws of collection prevent our dialogue freely within the system. They said it's best we prepare for war."

The African courts said it is time to take a strong approach. Instead of sitting around waiting for the wars to come to us, our plan is to invade every dimension that could be linked to the unknown speaker until we find the answers. They replied that could be our ends but what choice do we have. It could very well be the enemy of our forefathers waiting for the right time to strike. There were many generations killed based on the history between clans dating more than three thousand eras. We cannot afford to stand by and wait on an unfortunate event to deliver our ends. They stirred and reasoned, saying these kinds of actions could lead to our demise; this sort of thinking is born in panic and fear. We are stronger than this; we will wait until it strikes. They looked at the Danish dimensions, saying let us be swifter in thinking than that because their end came too swiftly.

The African courts asked for a pardon within some of the animals of the collection schemes; it was granted to some degree of freedom. They openly stated their intentions and asked many others to observe. Many cities wanted to go to war as they explained. Many cities thought they knew, but the African court explained it could be an architect of the old systems. The African courts demonstrated how you are within the fishes of the seas in various worlds. The speaker replied with violent gestures, the strong should attack the peaceful. They all watched, and the African courts calmed all the fishes and said to the animal cities, "I wonder why the fishes began to behave energetically with all simultaneously moving north. The African court wondered what this meant, and they input why within all the minds of the fish they all reacted violently, then going on their own ways.

They wondered what the idea was if it was us the speaker was talking about, the cities of collection, or the beings that were for collection. They implanted into the fishes' minds who were you referring to? All the fishes raged violently, laughing at each other, then saddened because this being was surely an enemy. They asked, "What shall I call you, it implanted in the fishes' minds The Carnage, then the fish moved around in circles.

The African courts looked at the display the fish made and realized it was a dance, a series of movements constituting a battle or fight among opponents. The African courts waited until the display was over then implanted, what of the carnage cycles? It displayed destiny within all the fishes' minds simultaneously. They stewed and said thank you and ended the messages. The fish all began to swim slowly toward the north, showing carnage on their minds. The African courts were severely displeased with this beings, calling it the Carnage Cycle; they knew the being was superior but did not know where it came from.

They looked at all the fishes and implanted into the fish, *how can we find you?* It formed a gate showing a large fish that cannot pass but the smaller fish can enter. They asked where is this gate and it created an entire solar system out of fish, which had specific markers and clockwork sequences. It also displayed a war at the gates within the system, for which many of the fishes dispersed as larger fish came to feed. They knew this was not a great sign, the African courts asked, would you kill us if we were to enter the gates? It replied, "Yes, you will all die here. It then said, "Do my bidding and destroy your friends."

The African courts sighed, saying another crazed madman on the prowl wanting to destroy all of society. They asked, "Is the Ziauddin yours?" It replied, "No, but they will do my bidding." The courts asked why; it replied the cycles of life. I was the one to rule the leveries for the Ziauddin will replace me. Instantly, we heard a noise and rumors of the Ziauddin being funded by an ancient clan from many dimensions away. The African courts left the systems wanting to find out who was this and where was this system. This is not a good idea for the ancients before the African royals knew nothing of where these dimensions could have been.

They immediately sent scouts to find the solar systems that possessed the gateway, but they reported it was very difficult to find. They immediately wondered and saw that the Ziauddin had still not shown itself. Many grew afraid of the Ziauddin and how powerful they had become. They all wondered why the cities were still so quiet; many of the smaller cities looked to the systems and asked the carnage cycle many questions. It gave viscous depictions of what it would like the systems to be. A smaller city of collect pledged its allegiance to the Carnage Cycle, and it replied, "Destroy everyone." They attempted to attack the cities upon their attack they were met with fire upon their cities.

The carnage cycle showed laughter in the fishes then showed the smaller fish devouring the larger fish. The smaller cities looked at the messages and did not despair; they then attacked their attackers, and just as they were all devoured, their bodies were remade forming an unknown type of matter. Their physical structure grew to more than 100 times their original sizes. The carnage cycle gave them immensely destructive radiants and powerful unknown matter types, instructing them to kill all the collected systems. The Carnage Cycle displayed laughter within the fish, synchronizing the designs of the swim patters in the waters, creating ancient symbols.

The cities immediately attacked the reincarnated slashers of the Carnage Cycle as they were met with fierce bolts of radiants, destroying the cities with one strike. They swiftly moved through the lesser cities and onto the cities under the emperor of Blaedherish for which they killed all the emperor's forces and the Schougnars in one blow. They moved quickly toward the quarters of the emperor, disintegrating his planets in a single strike. The other emperors immediately looked at the source of the attack and saw the inhabitants of the small city firing bolts upon any and every one within their vicinity. The emperors rallied, and they all came to council constructing a war strategy to defeat these giants. All 800 million emperors coordinated their attacks toward the giants. The matter types of the Carnage Cycle's people was strange and unaffected by the emperor's attacks; they knew what to do. They swiftly eliminated the cities and courts of the emperors within the various kingdoms. The Raija and his rivals soon looked and realized this new enemy could not be beaten easily.

The Raija and all the head of the clans joined in the battle, destroying the planet the Carnage Cycle's slashers were on. They flew out into space coordinating their attacks on all forces simultaneously. The Raija called upon his guards to attack, and they fired scorching radiants, which was simply deflected to the side. They fired spheres of clave radiants, destroying the atmosphere as they moved toward the planets of the guards. They disintegrated the guards and detonated the atmosphere, destroying everything within. The emperors could not believe their eyes—the guards of the Raija was defeated in a single blow. The Curilherel launched an attack defending their emperors; they simultaneously reincarnated their dead and redeployed them into battle with the Carnage Cycle's slashers attacking the royals of any city they could find. Destroying the rebuilders of the Curilherel, many of the clan leaders shifted, saying they would not return.

They destroyed planets filling the dimensions and space with dusts of what once was planets. The African royals looked and their jaws hung from their ears who, why, how could all of this destruction could have been done in such little time. The forces against the Carnage Cycle's people dropped to less than 2 percent of what it initially was. Almost all the planets within the alluvials were destroyed; many pieces of planets drifted into other planets and suns detonation the solar systems, causing even more chain reaction to adjacent planetary systems. The emperors were dead floating in space, with many in pieces, the Aljahara, the Culveshura, Meshughures, Vesculthies, the Jurvges: they were all dead in a matter of minutes. The biggest and most dangerous of the systems were dead.

More than 800 billion planetary systems were destroyed in a matter of seconds the fallout was catastrophic many of the smaller cities shifted abandoning their posts. Many of the smaller war ceased both sides fled to safe havens. It was not believed that so many of the most dangerous clans could have been destroyed. The African royals cried saying we should not engage wait silently until they decided to leave. The remaining forces shifted and slowly watch as they searched the systems for survivors killing any one in sight. The remaining emperors stated that they needed help eliminating this threat. They called out to the Danish and African clans they replied absolutely not, the enemy was too strong.

The emperors called out to the Raschsiers, Carvengushiers, and Gleushiers, asking for help. They shifted to the emperor's position, observing the devastation that they laid upon the cities. They thought they had a solution; they orchestrated a plan to ambush them as they glazed the matter to deal with the alluvial distortion created from the destroyed planets. The troops fired directly at them. They looked and fired at the systems where they were destroying everything in the vicinity. The emperors shifted, and their trails began to pulse shock. The particle waves created a trail; they realized they knew where the emperors were headed to. They looked and shifted to the phases of the emperor and began destroying the planets. They were shifting from phase to phase, the emperor frantically tried to shift out of synch. The soldiers all shifted to aid the emperor. They hunted them following their every move.

They began shattering the particle structure of the alluvials and caused imbalances in distribution, resulting in blindness for the emperor and his troops. The more particle structures they destroyed, the more alluvials were affected. The emperors and their men soon became slow and could not shift much longer; they shifted and began killing the soldiers and men one by one. They fired huge bursts of radiants to their bodies but to no avail; their matter type was unreactive to their weaponized radiants. The emperors, saddened, said these are our last moments. Some committed suicide, the others and the soldiers charged and were destroyed along with their planetary systems. The remaining emperors called out for help, but no one answered; there were only three emperors left. They asked, "What do you want?" They laughed. "You will die and blasted away the planets to dust."

The African royals looked on in horror of the destruction of the Carnage Cycle's henchmen; they looked at the fish within the systems and saw they were all filled with joy and were in a sequence of dance-like moves. The African royals thought we are under the will of a madman, seeking our deaths. We need to find an enemy of his. The only good lead was the gate, but finding it was a near impossible task. They looked at the ancient cities and saw some of them only watched. They looked at the Graija and the Surpurthes and saw they looked on in horror. The metal clans relocated, leaving nothing behind. They asked the Surpurthes and Graija for aid and abilities; they spilled their banks and instantly shifted.

Many of the smaller cities under the royals shifted away from the cities of collection. Eventually, all the cities near the systems would become empty with absolutely no forms of life within. The African and Danish courts looked on in horror; a strange voice said to them, "Don't make any noise, look at the system. Look at what it is saying." It was saying you are truly no match and we will destroy you all. It displayed symbols in a sequence, they drew these symbols and sent them through the information networks asking for any information about these symbols. The Danish royals said they will send scouts and personnel to the central library and will remain there on standby. It is safer there; many of the court members agreed and moved to dimensions nearer to the libraries.

Some time had passed, and the Carnage Cycle's henchmen were gone when they learned of the symbols from the psyche-emulation of an old being in the vault. He was not a friendly being, but he said it was the ancient language of the Furthildaghes and the symbols mean the death of all will come soon. He said the other symbols meant that this system was illegal or should not be in existence. He also said we would need to find a map to the gateways of Yulthies, for the dimensions of the old worlds were not the same as we know. The advent of particle alphabetization created many subdimensions that would change the shape of the maps as they populated the rooms of the universe. This meant these locations could be invisible to us in this present era.

They immediately asked for a map to the universe; they eventually gained some information but was unsuccessful for no such map exists. The official library does not account for created spectrums and dimensions, with many alluvial structures not present. They immediately sent scouts to those locations, some of the scouts reported to being fired upon by very huge beings they encountered. The matter space was very old and traversable but very durable and nearly indestructible. They fled to an abandoned city because of fear of being followed back to the main city centers. They were attacked by many troops of the Yulthies who were the keepers of the gates of Yulthies and Yulgongria.

They did not know they broke many ancient laws going to these places; the men ran to the streams of Caleradius within the Calavary, and the troops turned back. They realized they would lose against the Carnage Cycle if a solution is not reached soon. They asked for information about the Carnage Cycle. The men went to many systems and cities, asking for help and knowledge about the unknown speaker. What they found was a hidden truth about the collection systems. More than thirty eras ago, a being spoke through the system's inhabitants; this was to the delight of the then emperor, and he sought to invite the being to the festivals of the cities. The being instead spoke of violence and disgust for the systems and proceeded to fund the derelicts of the system and created chaos among the cities of collection, almost killing all the cities' inhabitants.

They said, "Look to the friendly ancients of the Lultheries systems." They looked at the Lultheries systems and saw only a few residents. The men went to the cities and asked for the help of the elders to open their doors to them, but they warned they should keep these things a secret because there are worse enemies. The men immediately realized that the being of the collected systems were created smaller as every generations passed. The ancients of eighty eras stood nearly 1.3 kilometers tall and those of 120 eras were nearly 1.6 kilometers. This was an indication of how the ancients thought of the beings on the systems. The ancients said the systems have and will always grow greedy, fighting for the luxury that is afforded. The citizens loathe in the opulence that is afforded by the success of the rulers.

For eras, the men and women were pruned by the unknowns for their behaviors against the majority. This was seemingly a tradition; there were rumors that every thirty eras the unspoken Rhuersathian, the Carnage Cycle would appear touching the systems and creating wars that caused the citizens to destroy themselves. According to the Lukgerathies, there were clans that pledged allegiance to her and do the bidding of her instruction. Many of these clans are more than two thousand eras old, for which it is said the oldest was three hundred thousand eras old. This was a clan that was sacked to mere thousands for their crimes against the systems. They pledged absolute loyalty to the unspoken Rhuersathian killing all of the beings of the systems. It is said that they patiently wait on her return every season to partake in the ritual.

The word *Rhuersathian* means "executioner" or "killer," for which she does not instruct who or how to kill. Some say it is a man seeking revenge because of its appetite for killing the successful inhabitants of the systems. Others say it is a woman for the way it loves the children of the worlds under the systems. It is said that she appears when the laws of the system take a turn for wickedness and torture of the beings that were to be collected. The Thraemfulies claimed it is a being that loves killing. Many of the clans that were touched by the Rhuersathian's blade should not be spoken to because they hold deep grudges against their peers for their decisions they made during that time. They pointed to a clan that was four thousand eras old, saying they can tell you more about the Rhuersathian. On reaching there, the soldiers realized that the matter types deteriorated immensely from that of four thousand eras ago. The beings were hundreds of kilometers tall; they had to use a projection system to speak to each other.

The beings said the Rhuersathian was something that was always there. Many thought it was a part of the wars, but it was not a being from another dimension that was trapped or exiled. We too heard the rumors during our time on the systems. No one know for sure how old the systems are and how many beings live in this universe, but what is for sure no one knows who or what the Rhuersathian was. We investigated more than two hundred thousand eras trying to find information about who this could have been. What is sure is that it comes around when the systems become selfish and destructive, killing on a whim. It appears causing little damage to the collected beings but causing mass riot and pandemonium.

The African court realized that there was no stopping this being; it was the ultimate, and it thinks it stands in justice, but it has been responsible for trillions of deaths around the systems. Many at the libraries said it was very old, dating back more than a million eras. It presents itself for the destruction of the system; many would kill for uttering its name. The idea a million eras ago was that the clan of Oultheifmeulgs was responsible, and it was the forefathers of the cities that committed the murders. It was also suspected that it could also be another loyal clan onto the Rhuersathian. Many grew tired and wondered what to do. The best advice is to leave the systems, but the wars with the old enemies will still continue. Many people asked for a room among the older clans; they were so small to those of four thousand eras ago. They could have absolutely accommodated them; many moved away, vowing never to return. The African royals stayed, saying they would observe only for a few moments. Their ancestors stated, "When the time is right, we will quit the systems and relocate to the reservation savannahs."

The African courts looked at the tarnished cities and wondered. They saw the remaining Raija and ancients looking on, wondering who was the next clan to cause the destruction of the cities. They all looked around; the African court looked closely at the ancients and saw many were still nonchalant about the wars. The African started smaller cities from the collected dead and told them to collect and build new cities from the remaining components. They showed them industry practice and made them weaker than the beings of today, for the events of the day made them sad and afraid of what they can do as the time progressed.

The African court decided to look for the Ziauddin, but remembered they could be very dangerous because the Carnage Cycle could have upgraded them. They remembered the princess was also missing. They immediately called upon the councils of the Calcuralthera and told them of what was happening. They startled and was in disbelief of the entire story. They looked at the systems and observed the bantering within the fishes of the oceans and realized that the Ziauddin could be on the path for revenge. We needed to be strong in this time. The African royals and the Calcuraltherians shared knowledge and artifacts equaling their strengths. They decided to look for the Ziauddin but did not know where to go. Many of the cities were empty and abandoned because of the destruction by the henchmen of the Carnage Cycle. They asked if they can assist in finding the princess. They replied, "Yes, we would really like to know what happened to her."

The African courts asked their networks to help in locating the whereabouts of the Princess Kamadahara. They replied, "She is safely recovering within the Zulvilian systems of Gnumzardians." They immediately went to the cities and asked the kings to see the princess. She was hidden in a palace within the Zulvilian city of Palmurthes. They were not an ally of the Calcuraltherian people, but was a dearest friend to an ally of the princess. She thought the Ziauddin would not look for her here. On seeing her, she was badly wounded with a few broken ribs and some muscle tearing. It would take some time for her to recover; she was otherwise healthy and ready to go to battle. Her guards gave her the bad news. The Carnage Cycle upgraded the Ziauddin and created henchmen from the lesser cities who emaciated the beings of the collection schemes. The wars were taking its toll on the people; the word quickly spread throughout the neighboring kingdoms. Each king ensured everyone knew about the situation since it was an extinction event.

Many of the retired cities of collection began to riot; the king saw that the long-concealed anger of the people was the sole cause. The leaders of the cities showed the killing of the emperors of the Raija, and the crowds immediately stopped rioting. They could not believe the deadly force and efficiency of the Carnage Cycle's henchmen. They all had no choice but to join forces, creating a large army that was vast and deadly. Many of the exiled cities refused, for the ways of the courts are vile and corrupt, and it was wise to keep one's sovereignty in this season. The royals stewed, and these are the reasons the Carnage Cycle awarded gifts. They replied, "We know what has been happening, and this is not the first season the Carnage Cycle appeared. We are also the descendants of ancients, and we will maintain our sovereignty."

The African court thanked them all and left for their home worlds. The Calcuraltherian forces looked at the cities and saw there could be mass war and genocide as the old issues surrounding vengeance festered and created a rotting soar, adding to the wars of the Cilicide systems. These systems are more than thirty eras old and should not be taken lightly for there are many old hateful clans residing in the wall of these dimensions. The Calcuraltherian prince decided to call a meeting with the ancients. They were to discuss what was best for the situation since dealing with the Carnage Cycle or Fcepchutu Chuar meant the death of billions. They decided to do what was always done—wait until the cleansing was over, and continue our practices while remembering the lessons of yesterday.

The Calcuraltherian prince looked at many of the vengeful ancients of the previous years, observing their patterns of intellect, depicting the directions of their decisions in the fights ahead. Many realized they were being looked at and began assembling their armies, fortifying their alluvials from the scrambling effects of particle emissions. This has been a significant handicap in the fights against the Carnage Cycle and the emperors. Many grew scared and decided to leave their homes for a safer dimension. This was soon followed by mass rioting within the cities; many could not leave for the soldiers stormed the entrances to many nation centers, causing a mass transit congestion. Many accidents occurred on a small-scale violence, causing even more riots at the gates of many cities. Many of the people were forced to remain within their homes until their situations have evolved. Many of the cities were designed in ancient ways, causing shift contamination from the presence of foreign matter regimes, blocking the exits temporarily, causing a transit trap flowing in or out of the cities.

CHAPTER 17

The Chuar's Smile

The African courts studied the Carnage Cycle, trying to predict where it would strike next. The cities of the systems near Calcuralthera and along the streams of Vestuduldia were beginning to create wars, which in that region they called the purge of the Fcepchutu Chuar or the purge from the blessing of the mold. The people began to militarize, and the kings instantly knew what to do. They upgraded their civilians to soldiers, preparing to attack the cities of the selfish royals of collection, and the prizeful court officials with the schemes. It seemed all those who were willing to go to war for the souls of the collected were their targets. They knew the purge of the Chuar was coming to them so they all joined forces creating a very large army. This army was to destroy all the patrons that would try to defend themselves against the purge of the Chuar.

The Calcuralthera would also wage war against all who would fight against the Chuar and fight for maintaining their stance in the collection schemes. This was not especially good for the ancient cities of Hilthurian and Feilthiles as they took no part in the wars but were of fierce competition for control over the collection laws. The African courts looked at the cities of the schemes and saw even more war within the systems. They looked at Calcuralthera and saw they were of the intention to destroy all participating in the wars for the systems and partially executing the will of the Chuar. They thought this could not be the way these cities would end. They looked hard and decided to call a meeting, but many replied this is a season for war. The Chuar is the instigator of the wars; it is evil, and many think its actions were pure. The slaughtering of trillions of innocents can never be right. The people of the system are of their birthrights to collect; this is the law of our society. The purge of the Chuar is something evil and must be stopped.

The African courts looked at the ancient cities examining its movements, looking for signs of their participation in the wars. The Africans became weary and asked their networks for anything that would aid in defense against this purge. The purge was of ancient traditions dating back trillions of eras ago, where the Chuar would mysteriously appear, creating chaos among the reincarnated beings. It was said it appears when greed, self-absorption, and malice grew to magnanimous proportions within the cities. It created wars that would foster the peace and bring understand of brotherhood. Many are opposed to this because they would kill and destroy many societies for collected beings. Paying homage to the Chuar can become a blessing, creating even more destruction. The patrons would continue to kill all the beings of the systems; this vastly became a tradition pruning the ranks of the collection schemes. This would eventually cause the creation of weaker and incapable beings that could not facilitate the will of the Chuar. Many sought to destroy the beings that execute the will of the Chuar, but this caused even more wars in the ancient cities, destroying many of the ancient lines.

Their scouts also reported that the origin of the Fcepchutu Chuar or Carnage Cycle was unknown. It was thought to be from an old civilization that lasted throughout the ages but was proven to be a rumor. The Chuar would reappear after the destruction of ruling peoples, teaching lessons of goodwill, but displayed its thoughts in a way as though the death of its patrons did not matter. This grew fear and many executed the will of the Chuar without question. In attempts to completely stop the madness that would occur many would instantly kill millions if they knew the Chuar would dawn upon their cities. It was also rumored that there is a place at the edges of the Verculoidisodis systems where there is an energy that speaks, the legend of a fallen being. The being speaks to the inhabitants of this universe, spreading love and giving gifts; it is said that the Chuar could be also a fallen being. It's surely not from within this universe and could be of the first-created beings that created this universe.

The African court bowed their head saying the Chuar could not be stopped, and if it was from outside of this universe, then it cannot be destroyed. They realized the Chuar cannot be bartered with and has no needs or wants in this world. It only desired to destroy the cities and people of these societies. The African court asked what is the extent of the damage it caused. They replied the largest recorded fallout was 3,900 eras ago. Where the Chuar instigated wars between the hidden puppet stringer clans and the Jurogues of the Claviestures, which caused mass sabotage and invasion of cities that were not even on the systems of collecting. They killed everyone in sight, everyone who could have been perceived. They proceeded to kill anyone who had the ability to create their own beings, killed those who can created life.

It was said that the Chuar used these newly created beings to instill its own self-actualizing ideas. This caused mass revolts for freedom resulting in violent protests and wars lasting more than 100 eras. This war quieted for some time and then restarted about 50 eras after the deaths of the Jurogues. The created beings along with many of the freed beings from the systems took to violence, moving from city to city destroying the clans. This caused the war of Mascuderia, where one of the ancestors of the Graija became a warrior clan after the wars with their descendant the Feilthiles.

Many of the African courts and ancients listened closely because their true enemy, the Oltriphians, could be a participant of this era's Chuar. They went further to explain that the wars of old were not about collection or stance but about race and hate for the things that occurred in history we do not fully understand. They did not understand why they were attacked and executed. The scouts said the Mascuderia who were the ancestors of the Culthurianals. They were one of the first and most powerful to reenter the systems more than 29 hundred eras ago.

The Filthurians created a barrier that would block many beings from reentering the cities and alluvials near the collection schemes.

The Loungegarians were created by the Uggharthians inside the barrier to execute our will on the other side of the barrier. The wars continued for many eras, and many of the ancestors of the African clans were destroyed. Many of the clans of today were descendants of twelve created clans by those outside of the barrier. Their names are largely unknown, but it was also said that there is a way to cross the barrier and reenter the larger rooms of old. The one place they cannot manipulate is the central vault and the libraries, but there is another rumor of a place from the first creation of the universe. A place where living beings are stored, called a vestuary, meaning cemetery. Its location is not on any listing within the library; all they would say is that it does exist but it opens during specific seasons.

Talk has been spreading that the Chuar has returned, many of the ancient cities began militarizing. They created quadrillions of troops; defense networks began to come to the public sphere. Officials began accessing the network gathering information about the situation and what was to be done about the large numbers that were to be culled. They immediately deployed troops to the dimensions that were the most active in the collection schemes. Immediately, large pulses of particles began to emanate from those alternate dimension. The soldiers moved quickly, destroying all the beings within. The system was entirely destroyed, many could not physically see the activities but the networks displayed these events. The countries that were invaded had no chance, and many of the citizens killed themselves and their families. The king of the struggling cities sought to destroy themselves and destroyed everything within their cities.

The African courts looked at the extent of the populations of the hidden cities and realized if they were to all go to war it would be rare for us to survive. There were quadrillions of being living in the in the shadows of the system. They asked one of the friendlier cities how many hidden cities are there, they replied more than a few thousand trillions. There were the remaining cities after the wars of 1,500 eras ago many of these are still hidden. The wars raged within these new sectors with entire sectors being destroyed. The shattered particles spread throughout the sectors like waves in the oceans affecting the matter types distorting the alluvials. The African court looked at the quieter sites as they looked on in horror at the damage that was done in rage and fear of the riots of the Chuar.

Trillions of soldiers gathered to invade the Desdurade systems for there was a rumor of an ancient king residing there who was the most powerful among us. He was of vile nature and had the intention to execute the will of the Chuar. Many said he was about to take his armies to march on the people of the Desdurade taking all of their souls and eventually taking over the hidden sectors. This was detrimental because during these periods, many were unaware of the number of cities that were present in the war exercises. They all participated to display the extent of their power. The wars of old were terrible, and they teaches one should be humble, many of the beings in our sector have permanently abandoned the collection schemes. They vowed never to create new beings from particles radiant. It was realized many times over that if one humbles and stay away from the collection cities, one can survive the Chuar's purge.

They watched the African cities and immediately shifted, saying, "Please do not return here." The African clans saddened and remembered the scorn of the ancients for the collection systems. They sat and watched all the violence and chaos that took place, thinking and understanding the issues and situations that caused the violence. They thought it was the Chuar; they thought of the name it gave itself the "Carnage Cycle," as though it is proud of its endeavor. It seems almost as if this was its purpose, its reasons for being a part of the system. They wondered why the animals and not the humans; they asked the scouts, and they replied it uses anything. It was once theorized that it used a sun to cause the riots of Caltheuide. The people of the sun was born out of this; they understood the violence that came from the wars brought by the sun and sought to create fresh new lives that understood rather than just merely reacting to situations.

It is said that the Chuar teaches newly created beings. If it uses them to purge, they disappear and never return. Their survival is dependent on their ability and knowledge. For many of the newly created beings were never found dead; it is also said that they are taken to a special place away from the systems. Many of the leaders within the systems wish to God over them because of their power and abilities, eventually killing them or condemning them to slavery. Many of the beings in the African courts realized why many of the ancient worshipped the Chuar, including the ancestors of the Calcuralthera. The African court asked the scouts how old are the ancestors of the Calcuralthera, they said that the ancestors of the Calcuralthera are more than forty thousand eras, but no one knows for sure.

They are dated back before the gates of Yulthies and the Wheurel of Comulustious. They are a heavily protected clan and should not be misunderstood, for many have tried and all have failed. Their lines of succession are preceded every three eras as their leader changes and the previous king or queen ascends into another constituent of their kingdoms. It is a living city of growing beings in the stance of knowledge and wisdom. They looked at Calcuralthera and saw that many of the officials went to secret places for long periods of time and eventually left permanently. The main court speaker usually appoints a steward until the change of the royal ministers and the redressing of the state. The new leader would then take the throne, leading the people through three eras until they have ascended.

Many believe this is an attempt to avoid corruption with the cities and among their officials; many also believe it is a remuneration scheme where the souls needed to be returned by the end of the cycles. The African courts watched and observed the city for evidence of truth to these rumors; they seemed more likely to be untrue. At that moment they were speaking, soldiers invaded the collection cities near Wesptudura. Many of the African council members cried and became scared once more. The African royals ordered everyone out of the court, precisely selecting new members of consort. They shouted at the lower members saying we will not survive if we are allowed to psychologically break down!"

The wars were becoming stressful with many court members committing suicide and storing themselves in the vaults. Many openly forced their loved ones to be reincarnated in another time, for this could be a great strategy for surviving the Chuar. One being had the great idea of storing entire cities in the main vaults and a small group would reside there until the purge was over. When the Chuar has disappeared, they would reincarnate in a hidden dimension. Many citizens acceded to this plan and sadly removed the energies from their matter then slowly died to be stored until the wars were over.

The African royals grew weary not knowing what to do, they watched as the wars with the ancients raged through the cities. It was a sight for chaos they looked at the systems and saw the Chuar was in a gleeful state as it cheered upon the wars. The African court asked why, it answered why do you exist. He said because the systems made me, it replied wrong answer. They looked at the system and wondered why that was the wrong answer, they asked who made you, and it replied you are stupid like the rest, a germ that needs to be removed. They asked why are you so hateful. It replied hate is for the weak, my fishes are strong and they began to eat each other. They watched and did not understand it was all about carnage, they asked where are you from, it replied from inside a fish.

The African courts were not amused and thought the Chuar was a child pushing them to even more anger. They stood and thought of how can this be destroyed. The Chuar said, "If you truly wish to destroy me, find the gates of Yulthies and enter." He knew this was a trap but then he suddenly felt compelled to go. He then felt that he would die an excruciating death, but then will not feel anymore. He could tell that the Chuar spoke within him and he became frightened. The fish all jeered, making laughing gestures. He thought this was something truly evil. He asked, "What is evil to you?" It said, Your mind, you are like these fish, and the fishes all began to feed. He felt ashamed for he knew it was the systems it despised.

They then asked why not kill us all. It replied in due time for your deaths are inevitable. What you chose is to die slowly and entertainingly. They were not pleased and said we should find these gates. They sent through the networks the images the Chuar sent and asked if anyone would volunteer to find the gates of Yulthies. They replied they have found it but you would need to mask yourself in three types of matter. The matter space there is very harsh, they also said it is heavily guarded by trillions of Gundger thileoths they wondered what that was, and saw images of a huge being many kilometer tall and vicious. They are very unfriendly and made of a strange ancient matter type. It is said there is a being that is locked away inside that can never be released.

They went back to the systems and asked the Chuar what is behind the gates. It said, "Your deaths, release it and all your suffering will end." The fish all looked in one direction and laughed. The African royals knew this was the end but could not leave so many innocent people to die. They asked the networks what is known about the beings behind the gate; they said it was something very dangerous and many beings killed themselves to trap it inside an unperceivable dimension. The stories were intentionally erased and the only being that know of its existence if the energy at the edges of the Verculoidisodis systems the fallen.

They said send someone; their scouts left with many soldiers heading for the speaking energy. It was a treacherous journey through many harsh dimensions of corrosive matter that deteriorated the matter of their armor. The African royals knew many wouldn't return but something had to be done. They looked at the sites and asked the Chuar, "What do you think of your success?" The Chuar replied, "I am a god. I am successful. I am not of your standards, I am you." They looked at the cities and saw the Chuar taunting with mirrors to shake our minds, to debase our belief and strengths. He asked, "How old are you?" It replied, "Time is not in numbers." He instantly thought of his origins and his mind as not the same as the first-created beings.

He said, "Show me yourself." It replied, "I am a cloud, for which you would become too." He knew this was a death chant, and his death would soon become a prize. The Chuar said, "There are no prizes here, only the flies that eat the flesh of the dead would consider you a prize." The Chuar churned the waters of the seas, pushing the dead fish to the shores of the worlds. The courts knew the stench of fish would fill the cities. He asked, "Why are you this unkind to the collected beings?" It replied, "You are their crimes. I am the lover of criminals, I am their joy, for they are my peaches." It asked, "Do you not love me?" He thought, Maybe I had it eating out my own hand." It replied, "It is the other way around, how does my finger taste?" His heart began to ache, and their minds focused on the cities, and a joyous cry filled his fabric. The fishes turned, and in their minds were images of love and destruction." It asked, "Do you not love this?" It released them, and they replied no.

They said to the Chuar, "Can we assist you?" And it said, "Destroy your friends," then the fishes laughed in a childish manner. They realized they were being duped as though they were of the systems. They wondered what else could be on its agenda, the only conclusion was our ultimate demise. They asked how I can kill you, it said by killing yourselves you will find I will disappear. They looked at the system for any hint of how they can get to it. The Chuar created an eye, and they thought staying here among the systems would only cause more harm. They looked at the wars and saw many systems turned to dust and rubble with planets partially disintegrated with pieces accelerating toward the other systems. The kings and royals went to war with many battles taking place. The smell of distrust filled the air as invasion after invasion took place, giving the citizens little chance of survival and escape.

Many of the selfish royals saw this as a chance for benefit and gain. They aided the cause of the dreaded masters of achieving their goals of capturing and enslaving the citizens and soldiers of the opposing factions. The kings of Lurventious opened a network linking the hidden cities of the Fiersmestudes systems. This exacerbated the wars; he exclaimed we will not die as our enemies are living their lives enjoying the fruits of our children as they are their slaves. Many cities added to these networks expose the hidden cities of the systems. The war crazed King immediately invaded these kingdoms, shooting fierce radiant at the systems, causing the immediate return of fire from the city guards.

Many people shifted to escape the sites, but were killed. It was an extinction event of immense proportions; the wars eventually spread to the ancient above the African royals, saying they have invaded the secret cities. The African royals immediately shifted and ordered their troops to hide, leaving the wars to rage. The hidden cities glowed with hot molten rock and burning bodies. They could not do what was needed because of the sheer numbers of the forces. The trend became one for invasion and conquering. This was spreading fast among the hidden cities; the paths to many cities were closed, resulting in the absolute destruction of the beings within. There were forces funded by the old Warghenar who was an ancient king of more than forty thousand eras. Warghenar came to the hidden cities and ordered the destruction of trillions of smaller countries. He put on his armor and called his armies to the fronts and began destroying the victorious armies of the hidden systems. He and his clans were the forgers of the eyes of Claverious and Serphemties, for which none can be hidden.

They forced their way into the cities of Querthies and Lopuquides, destroying everything. The people suffered from matter infusions, which destroyed the alluvials and the streams that caused a stable centers of the particle's agglomeration pattern. The cities cried out; a king this powerful could not have been involved in the wars. Many of the ancient more than thirty thousand eras' old were destroyed with many putting up fights, causing mass destruction of the physical fabric, creating many smaller pockets of toxic radiant that would spread to cities that were not being invaded. The people escaping these toxic cities caused the cities to be noticed by the patrons of the Chuar, leading to its destruction and the extinction of the people.

King Warghenar moved to the Manghethian cities where he met the queen of Elufieres, and she instructed him to leave her kingdom. He openly stated that he came to cleanse the cities, and she said she did her duty during the last purge. He replied, "It was your time." She immediately shifted, and her soldiers instantly attacked. The civilians of her cities immediately covered themselves in military armor and began fighting the invading forces of the Warghenarians. They immediately began disintegrating buildings and the alluvials substructures. Shattering the matter spaces of the cities, the cities began to resonate, making a humming sound, creating small voids of querked matter. The queen's forces immediately covered themselves in a matter type that would resist the deleterious effects of the voids that were created by the violent shift in matter.

The Warghenarian forces advanced with a fierce assault on the queen's people; their armor was not a match for her troops, and they became ash. The Warghenarian soldiers swiftly moved forward, heading toward the queen's castle. The queen's guards immediately shifted in front of the castle and created replicas of themselves, charging heavily toward the incoming soldiers. The Warghenarian soldiers fired a barrage of blasts at the queen's forces for which they were being turned to ash, but their numbers were too great. Soon the replicas of the soldiers reached their position, firing at the soldiers hitting the armor flaking off bits of matter until it falls apart. The first Warghenarian soldier was killed and the queens guards created even more soldiers that would cover the entire field.

The Warghenarian armies would take up formations. Shielding themselves in formations as the replicas of the queen's guards charged into them. The shields pulsed and flickered waves, causing mild fractures in the shields. The queen's guards on heights above the palace gates fired many long-ranged burst of hive-heated radiant, hitting the shields, splattering hot molten matter onto the soldiers, dripping through the shield's crevices and structures, burning the flesh of the Warghenarian soldiers. They slowly marched forward sustaining heavy fire while simultaneously firing at the incoming replica armies.

The guard's captains initiated replica support that were made of pure hive radiant. The Warghenarian generals immediately shielded the men with four layers of shields. The energy replicas came close and smashed against the shields, burning its way through the barriers, firing heated radiant at the inner layers. The soldiers immediately fired at them, and the replicas detonated, causing a blast radius that covered most of the fields. The ground and castle shook; the Warghenarian king looked at the men and began firing at the guards on the wall. Hitting the men with fervent radiants disintegrating them to ash.

The queen's guards saw this and ordered more soldiers to flood the fields with detonating replicas of soldiers. All of the queen's guards immediately started making replicas. The replicas immediately ran toward the shields of the enemies, detonating nearer to the invasion's focal point. The king ordered long-distance projectiles, hitting the replicas close to the castle walls. The guards immediately shielded them from the attacks of the Warghenarians, causing mass eruptions nearer to the soldiers.

The soldiers immediately moved backward slowly, and the general immediately gave the order to charge. The Warghenarians charged, meeting bolts of radiant destroying the armor of the soldiers and eventually their shields. The king shifted and was met by the queen's gates with an unknown shield. He shifted back, firing at the guards above the walls. They immediately fired at his position, causing him to reshift and reposition. He altered his presence and position firing with precision at all the targets above the walls.

They fired even larger blasts of radiant, destroying the grounds, causing the earths to crumble. Many of the guards shifted away from the castle walls to inside the castle, repositioning to the higher trellis of the castle. They began to slowly march forward slowly toward the castle gates. The queen's soldiers fired a barrage of radiant projectiles which only, chips away at the shields. The queen realized that she would eventually not be able to hold the castle for much longer and shifted to the kingdom of her father.

The king sensed the energy shift within but could not discern what it could have been. He tried to storm the gates but was met with fire pushing him outside of the gates; he fell to the ground and immediately covered himself in a silvery metal. He stood upright and charged into the gates, breaking down the walls, throwing the soldiers to the floor. He pulled radiant particles from the atmosphere, creating a sphere of aroral blasting away the shield of the castle. The king's men immediately shifted into the castle, firing blasts of radiant, killing the troops of the queen.

Many of her guards shifted while the soldiers created mass replicas of themselves destroying the castle walls with fierce battles. Throwing radiant in all direction, the castles began to crumble, the towers fell to the ground, crushing the soldiers beneath. The king rushed to the center courtyard where he met a general guarding a portal; he said, "I have come to purge your cities." The general said, "You will pay for this." Before he could finish what he said, the king rushed into him, pushing him into the walls above. They both fell to the floor. The general covered himself in a transparent matter type that is invisible. The king looked at him and said, "That does not matter, my eyes see all." The general said, "Your eyes sees blurs."

The general rushed the king, hitting him a large fist of radiant to his face, pushing him back into the ornaments. The king quickly recovered and returned with a flying kick dashing with hot energy kicking off the armor of the general. The armor flew to the walls destroying the plant pots. The general reconstructed new armor, saying today was your last mistake. The king fired a barrage of radiant bullets, the general shifted and the king shifted firing even more radiant bullets into the various alluvials. The king shifted into phase anticipating the general's phases hitting the general in the jaw, twisting his head toppling his entire body. The general flew into the air in a whirl wind of tumbles slamming into the walls removing the invisibility of the matter covering his body.

The general groaned and rose to his feet saying we will finish this, the king asked where does the portal lead to, he said it is a gate way to Hermerliudu. The king replied they will die too, the general said you have no idea and rushed the king throwing him onto the floor. He changed his matter covering both himself and King Warghenar resonating it creating immense heat. The general changed the matter and detonated created a large explosion that would destroy all of the king's armor. The remaining parts of the castle fell, the blast killed more than half of the king's men.

The remaining soldiers of the king's army quickly rushed to him looking at the smoke that was made of a detonating type of matter. They were cautious and the king said stand down. The smoke began to swirl together creating a circular structure, the king immediately lifted his body on fire changing his matter to a red hot annealed metal structure. The king created radiant within the atmosphere, the generals formed and stood looking at the king. The king said now you cannot shift, there will be no running. The general rushed him detonating himself and the entire dimension with him. Destroying everything in its paths the matter type instantly became destroyed and the king stood in the empty space covered in red metal thinking we will be victorious.

The king alone left the dimension, heading for Hermerliudu. As the king left, the general felt his mind and a large part of the smoke leaving for the opposite direction.

The queen immediately felt the absence of the energies from her kingdom and her men and looked at her dimension and saw it was no more. She knew what this meant; she saw the king's men were all dead, but she noticed the king leaving for Hermerliudu. She knew she had to do something and silently watched as he crossed the empty dimension of Qualtergara and San Sewishsu. She wondered if to follow him, he did not know what our true intention was. She looked at her remaining troops and said, "Let's go to Hermerliudu, they said we should be wise for he just destroyed our home. She said we should not fear, because he like his soldiers can die too. They secretly followed him, looking with the eye of Toruche Eenturielus. They could see him anywhere he went within the hidden cadastral. They followed him to the outskirts of Hermerliudu.

CHAPTER 18

The Greatest God of Death

King Warghenar looked around. A secretive voice said to him, "Where are you going?" He said, "Who are you, show yourself." She replied, "You would instantly kill me." She asked, "What are you going to do in Hermerliudu?" He said, "To purge." She said, "I urge you please do not go." "I already know, you and your father were reaping souls from the cities, like those of the systems. She said, "No, were simply facilitating a need." He laughed and said you are all dead.

"Show yourself," he said. She immediately shifted and hid herself in the deepest crevices in her father's kingdom. She ordered all of her men to seal the entrance to her hiding spot. Many of the beings of the collection schemes would destroy their entire families because of their actions. Her father knew the world had found out what was done in Hermerliudu and went to his secret chambers and disintegrated his own atoms. His last will and testament was to destroy the entire cities while waging wars on the neighboring cities. This was an attempt to hide the conspiracy that would destroy the integrity of his children. The generals knew that time has come as his master's energies disintegrated into the atmosphere. The generals rallied their soldiers and marched for Galderhalvertlia and Melfurtialeria who were their allies in the activity.

The Warghenarian king reached the gates of Hermerliudu and saw there were many soldiers guarding something deep within. He looked and saw trillions of human deep within the dimensions. They were being grown for the purpose of sale, he began firing upon the guards and the guards shifted. The captains called upon an assassin who was the head of the human military forces. The captains ordered the assassin to kill the king and shifted hiding his trail. The assassin said I am the ruler of the Pomordue, the king said your time is now. He fired upon the assassin and the assassin shifted to a pulse like phase shifting alternatively between phases.

The king released red metal radiant, slowing the shifting phases, causing the alluvials to dampen and slow in reaction to instance initiation. The assassin stopped shifting and directly attacked the king. The king was struck with a heavy burst of radiant pushing him back a few feet while stood on his feet. He immediately swung his arms releasing broad waves of flames burning the bushes and scorching holes in the walls of the Waleudliuda and armor of the assassins. His skin ruptured and the assassin began to bleed the king watched and asked what made you, why do you have blood, he replied I was never dead.

The king knew what he was and called him a Phielthide, saying, "I have never seen a being like you before. The assassin nodded and said we were experiments here, no one knew we existed. The king asked how many of you are there. He said trillions, they were building a city then an army. It seemed they wanted a private system of schemes, he looked and saw a vault but knew he could not open it. He wondered, where are the rest of the staff, the assassin said they were all in hiding. The king said tell me more about this place the assassin replied I rather die, we were free hands. We were told if they knew we were here we would all be harvested for our souls, and every being we knew would die. The king said your deaths are sure, for this was illegal. The assassin begged, "Do not kill my children, they are my joy in this world." The king asked how many, "He said my wife hid them when the royals left." The king said, "If I release you, I will be releasing a germ to live in the Dieu. You would create mass scorn and war, you all will become enslaved and a product for the torturous schemes, you will be entertainment and worse.

"Your best interest is to die here," the assassin cried, and as he began to lift his hands, the king immediately removed his head. He walked farther into the city and saw nothing. The city looked like a city of the collection systems, with water facilities, metal galvanized buildings, and mechanical structures. It was the first time the king had gotten a look of what inside a system was. He looked around saw absolutely no one. High winds blew raising dust, and he shifted further into the city and saw miles of crops as though they left yesterday.

The dimension was designed like a maze, the alluvials were not in the usual sequential order. It was designed to hide something. He called out in his native language hello; It echoed, and he shifted and explored the dendritics and then the halls. He realized that the streams that feed the dendritics bore wavelike structures that sometimes worked in reverse. He immediately tried to access the paths between the structured particles and only traveled to an unstable room filled with radioactive particles. He thought this could be a trap for escapes; their main quarters must be near.

He looked at the assassin and realized that he could only shift in a negative syncline. He immediately shifted and entered a room that was empty but could see plates and dirty dishes of a mess hall. He shifted again and entered an empty ball room; he looked around and realized they were still here. He shifted left and reached a room where human beings, they began to run frantically out of the rooms. The king began shooting bursts of radiant at the people, bursting them to pieces as they ran and screamed, trampling each other. He swiftly moved through the building killing all that he saw.

He quickly shifted moving through the rooms looking for humans to destroy, the humans with power quickly shifted through the alluvials trying to escape but the rooms of Hermerliudu were designed to prevent such a thing. The humans terrified within and screamed. King Warghenar moved strategically through the Hermerliudu hunting the humans. Many with powers went to the nurseries and collected all of the babies they could find taking them to the forested areas. They hid many of the people, they all tried to run to desolate rooms trying to escape his wrath, but they could not tell where the king was as he moved through the dimensions hunting the people.

The tears and screams haunted those that heard. One woman cried and shielded her baby, asking the other to shield her from this terror. They called out to the royals, but their voices could not reach. The kings disintegrated them all, leaving none alive. He moved to the other rooms with fervent intent as they ran for safety. They all became aware of the dangers and tried to run, but they were too many. It quickly became a stampede of trillions within the Hermerliudu, crushing many humans as they ran for safety. The king took his time traveling through the alluvials looking for the humans within. It took the king seven days to exterminate every human being within the Hermerliudu. No one was there to help them; they had absolutely no chance for survival.

The king moved on, heading to Galderhalvertlia and Melfurtialeria for which he met a band of soldiers in an empty dimension crossing the Ilufurthaides. They immediately stopped and looked at his matter and attacked instantly. They fired large bursts of radiant destroying large planets and solar systems the mass particle explosions disoriented his senses. He blindly fired back at them, destroying nearly half of their forces; they shifted, and as he shifted, they surrounded him. They all fired toward him and could not hit him because all of their radiant were deflected.

He looked around and thought it was the dynamics of the dimension he instantly fired, simultaneously killing all the soldiers. He looked outside of the dimension and did not see any enemies and began making his way to the exit of the dimension. He suddenly heard a voice saying, "King Warghenarian, I want you to come to me." He asked, "Who is this?" she said, "The Faltueorivars." He asked, "Where is this?" She showed him an image of a system not very far from his current position.

He said to her he was partaking in the purge and she should too. She said, "I will," and instantly sent soldiers to his position. Trillions of soldiers flowed into the dimension; he immediately began shooting the soldiers, and the dimension became darkened to his eyes and the disintegration of the soldiers caused a thick dense smoke of particle adhesion. The soldiers flowed like a stream of flowing men, shooting their way toward him. He fired all that he can agitating his surrounding creating particle surges around his head and body. Lightening began to strikes near his position, he had no choice but to physically move while constantly firing and killing trillions of soldiers.

The clouds became thicker, and he could no longer see his targets. He moved his position, firing into the smoke when he saw another stream of trillions of soldiers flowing toward him. He instantly began firing in their direction, destroying trillions by the seconds. He soon realized that he was not strong enough to defeat these soldiers and he could not escape. He had no choice but to keep fighting; he instantly covered himself in nine varying types of matter, which the last few coatings were very corrosive. His armor began to create a thick smoke that became a sludge-like substance surrounding him as he continued to fire a barrage of radiant.

The soldiers never stopped pouring in, and he wondered who was this enemy. He thought, *I am surely going to die here.* He immediately saw a strange silhouette appear next to him; he looked to his side and saw a soldier. Before he could think, he was punched in the face, knocking all the sludge from his body. His head spun and was disoriented for a second or two. The soldier tried to restrain him and was blasted by heavy radiant, the soldier was pushed away falling to a deserted planet.

He looked at the stream of soldiers and saw they were almost on his position, the soldiers fired trillions of radiant bullets at him; he was struck with nearly all becoming a violent burst of light shining like a sun showing the smoke of the dead. He clambered and began firing as his armor cooled. Many more soldiers shifted to his position, attacking him at all sides. He began physically kicking and head butting the soldiers, firing in all direction all at once. He shook himself and created a blast of radiant bitter and cold, a type of Galventis radiant that threw them back. Many of the soldiers regained their balance and began to assault him; he covered himself in even more matter as they beat many of the coating from his body.

He could not phase shift and thought neither could the soldiers; he immediately released a loud mental frequency from his mind, filling the dimensions with a high frequency tone clouding the tones of their mind's language. They became temporarily disoriented and could not function. He blasted them away as they were trying to recover, but they were too many. He changed his coating once more and tried to phase shift, as the matter became thicker inside the dimension.

He realized he could not sustain his defense and quickly flew to a nearby planet. The soldiers fired upon him, destroying the planets within range. Pieces of planets flew in all directions. A continent-sized piece of rock hit the king, smashing him into another planet causing the explosion of that planet throwing him to another system. He floated in space for a few seconds and shook off his dizziness. Looking for the soldiers, he saw that the soldiers were coming toward him with speed. He realized he had to do something fast.

He fired at all the planets he could see, detonating all of their cores simultaneously. The planets violently exploded, creating a violent rain of particle reactions, destroying all the stars and planets in range. The entire area became the thick clastic sludge which many of the soldiers could not traverse. The king could not have moved; he lay there thinking of what he could do. Many of the soldiers outside of the sludge tried to blast their way through the sludge, but this created molten rock, which in space does not vaporize but diffuses, creating a wider radius of hardened matter that bonded differently.

The king and the soldier were not sure what to do. The captains of the soldiers began using various types of radiant to blast away at the sludge, freeing some of the men. They all made a unified effort chipping away at the sludge, creating mass velocity gravity fields of cup-sized movements of accelerated matter. The particles of the sludge began to react simultaneously, creating a web of reactions flying vigorously, creating a zero gravity barrage of accelerated bricks. This would destroy a lot of the distant planets re-creating the chain reaction in distant places. The dimension became noisy with sludge particles moving faster than the speed of light. The king began to drift as he was hit by many incoming particles.

The king watched and wondered how to escape, he looked at the soldiers and saw they could be hit by the flying matter. He began to move left, and they tried to move but they created more violent movement of the sludge particles. Many of the soldiers bounced around as the sludge pushed them around. The king thought how can I escape this, he looked around and saw more planets to the top of the dimension. He fired Gurdesh radiants at the planets realizing that the moving sludge particles would impede the radiant he fired. He fired again hitting more planets causing more chain reactions, he continued this until all the planets were destroyed, he looked at the soldiers and realized that they could hardly be seen as there was a large field of moving sludge between them he looked at the soldiers.

He realized they had a hard time maneuvering through the particle field. The movement of the particles between the soldiers were immense and hit the soldiers with immense force. Eventually the soldier's shielded which ricocheted the particles causing more force within the fields. This rise in force increased the damage to the soldier's armor. The soldiers were hit too hard by the sludge particles and they began to become hurt. They started to retreat by the time the great number of soldiers began to make their way to the edges of the dimension. The particles had enough energy to destroy the soldiers. Many more soldiers poured into the dimension but they were met with accelerated sludge that would only do more damage as they proceeded further into the field.

They realized their vast numbers worked against them; they were destroyed by the speeding matter. The king watched and realized that the faster the movement, the more dangerous the dimension becomes. He stood still watching and observing the particle movement, devising a plan of escape. He began to move slowly when he was hit with a sludge particle. He was thrown in an alternated direction, causing him to wonder how to escape this trap. He looked at the field and thought the particles would throw off his trajectory; for sure, what he needed to do was cause a unified direction. He looked at the varying speeds of the particles and thought if he could pulse radiant away from himself in a specific pattern and timing he could create a pattern that causes a rhythmic flow of particles as he moved, causing a wavelike pattern around his body.

He began pushing radiant outward from his body and observed the reaction to the particles as they returned. The particles instantaneously

He fired large bombs of hot radiant at the city, killing the civilians and soldiers, destroying the buildings and palaces. They fired a barrage of red metal radiant as this was the only radiant that could erode his armor. He blocked many of the attacks with very few hitting his legs and hand as he would regenerate. He dropped to the floor, causing the soldiers to disperse. He began shifting into the various buildings, killing the civilians, forcing the soldiers to look for his position. He began to kill the civilians in a gruesome way, allowing them to scream as he moved toward the battalions. The people heard the screams of men and women, causing a stampede away from the battle. Many were trampled causing more screams of terror. The soldiers looked and saw the people were frantic. The king shifted near the general and put hot radiants into his chest and reshifted. Their general exploded, shattering into a thousand pieces.

The men despaired and began shifting looking for him, he shifted and taunted the men with the screams of civilians. They rushed into the building and could not see him they shifted and looked for him. He appeared and putting hot radiant into their chests, the radiant caused the men to reshift exploding as they realigned with the cities regime. The battalion shifted to his position and he began a simultaneous sequence of shifting while putting radiant into the men's chests. The generals deployed Vestuious radiants preventing shifting within the dimension. The king shrugged, and immediately shifted back to the city's regime. He walked slowly toward a counter in a building and looked around to the streets listening for the soldiers. He heard their commander speaking and began shooting the walls of the building, causing it to crumble. He swiftly moved out of the building toward the soldiers, hitting them with corrosive radiant as the building fell behind him.

The soldiers screamed in agony as their flesh peeled off and their armors fractured. The commanders ordered their men to his position. They began shooting radiant into the adjacent building, causing them to fall in specific directions, blocking the entrances to his location. The men quickly shifted to his position but could only access his location via direct route down the main street. The men tried to assemble, blocking the street but was met with heavy fire destroying their bodies and armor. The radiant the general used helped the king as it energized the atmosphere; the king knew this and used it to his advantage.

He began destroying the taller building, causing them to fall crumbling the city, the soldiers began to climb to the top of the structures surrounding him. The generals began to fire as the soldiers made their ascent. The generals fired with red metal radiant at the king causing him to dash to the rubble firing with corrosive radiant. The generals had no choice but to dive for the rubble. The king began to fire at the rubble, causing it to melt into a hot pyroclastic fluid pouring down from the melted buildings. The general's armor began to scorch, as the fluid touched his armor. They had to move cautiously away from the middle of the streets. The generals were cautious not to be seen by the king.

The king knew and sensed that they were soon going to surge on him. He charged his matter and began firing at the building, melting the matter of the rubble that surrounded him. The soldiers fell off the melting structures and were covered by the hot pyroclastic fluid. The generals attacked him, firing a barrage of detonation. The king immediately detonated himself, blasting the entire city, shattering all matter within. He looked around and saw absolutely nothing and slowly left. He realized that he was absorbing strange matter and radiant as he moved through the detreated dimension. Looking at the dimensional particles they seemed to form something that was attracted to his matter type and was absorbed. He saw it could cause his matter to shift and quickly dashed out of the dimension entering the Durgroudha dimension. On reaching there, he instantly began destroying everything in his path. He quickly moved through the streets and the alluvials killing and searing all that he could.

The soldiers of the dimensions moved to his position, causing the city to be further destroyed. The official of the Durgroudha cities went to their allies for help in defeating this enemy. The cities all looked at his efficiency of destruction and wondered how we could defeat an enemy so strong. They looked at him and saw he was very old and was very powerful; his matter type was unknown to them, and they could not have seen a way to defeat him. They looked at their allies, showing his body and the destruction that he had caused. They looked at him and could not recognize who he was or where he came from. He raged through the cities, destroying everything, killing everyone the court realized that the purge was upon them. They looked at all the cities and saw the patrons of the purge were of ancient lineage. They were huge and very powerful, destroying many of the cities of collection within minutes.

The courts surrounding the systems looked at the areas where they operated and saw they were nearing the councils of the remaining Danish and the Calcuraltherian people. They looked at the Carnage Cycle and saw it was joyous. They looked at the king and saw he was dangerously fervent in killing with proficiency and without mercy. They looked at the other patrons and thought they could cause them to attack each other. The Starvishier, a patron of the Chuar for many seasons, saw the young Arab court trying to stir even more conflict. They shifted to his position and began destroying the court of issues. Many of the citizens immediately shifted to alternate alluvials. The Starvishier stormed the dendritics and alluvials destroying everything in their paths. The citizens would try to run but the Starvishier armies would follow them to the other cities, killing everything in their path, leaving none alive.

The court member cried, leaving for the central cities near the central vault, where they would be safe. The courts cried for help, and the Couskalava and his men rushed to the cities and stood in the streets. The Couskalava said, "Let's talk about this." The Starvishier said no and fired blasts of radiant that turned them to ash, the Couskalava, and his men. The citizens of the remaining cities who were under the Raija stood in disbelief of how quickly the Couskalava was killed. The Starvishier traced the Couskalava's path to the people of the Raija they began killing all the citizens and the ancients. The cities of the collection systems looked upon the destruction of the ancients who were the superpowers of their world. They wondered, how can we survive this? They said we should put ourselves in a vault until the wars are over. Many reluctantly stood in disbelief saying we can join in the purge, they said we will not survive we are simply too weak.

CHAPTER 19

The Strong Should Live

We should move to a safer city; they called a meeting of the remaining people from the court of issues, saying there is only one solution—abandon the systems. They despaired and disagreed, many of greater reasoning said, "Look around, the dimension and alluvials are on fire. The clouds of smoke and particle radiation are toxically polluting our countries and states. We must leave this place, it is the only way." Many disagreed and decided to stay for if they were hidden, we can have a chance to survive. The others left for the central cities nearest to the vault that were severely crowded. The others watched as trillions of people overpopulated the streets and halls of the towns.

The ancients began to go to war with the Starvishier. Many of them removed their cloaks and changed the matter regime of their entire dimension. This was unseen before; the people of the systems looked on at the battle with the Starvishier. The Starvishier was well equipped to take part in the Chuar. They had many types of radiant to destroy all the known types of matter. The Oglungher were overrun in seconds; the Alverndias saw this and rallied half of their troops before the dimension became a radioactive fluid. Culgurthilion shielded themselves as they were destroyed in blasts of flame like radiant. The Curthians were killed by the very explosive force of detonation as their world was shaped to fight the wars of the old kingdoms. The Starvishiers invaded the cities through the alluvial stream partitions, detonating the streams that feed their Festitudes, killing everyone and everything within the dimensions.

The cities of collection that remained asked the Carnage Cycle, "How can you be so cruel?" It replied, "You are young, and the ways of old have been lost for you are the generation of vipers. You have become the selfish men who care only for your endeavor with determination and ruthless insensitivity. Many began to cry, the younger princes among them. Asked how can we fix this, the Carnage Cycle said you cannot for we have tried and we have failed resorting good faith and morals to you and your people, the only cure seems to be seasonal elimination of your kind. You have become the plagues of Balthalion, for he was the one who saw the use in you. A powers he used to stew the gods of the outer alluvials and change the ways of their thinking, making you the weapon of choice to destroy the heart of the creator.

They looked and wondered what this meant; they asked who are you to the creator. The Carnage Cycle replied, "A beloved for the universe was destroyed when you became its destroyer. You have become the thorn in the side of the creator." They asked, "How can we speak to the creator?" The Carnage Cycle replied, "It's your time to die." They immediately left the systems and went to the central cities. The young prince Jeshrome and his wife Hesdrapha remained. They stayed in an attempt to further understand the Carnage Cycle. They asked, "Why didn't you attack the central cities?" It replied, "It is the only place that has remained the same without violence and hate."

They watched and saw that the overcrowded cities were filled with fear. He replied, "It is only because of the guards. There is no violence there." It replied, "You have become like animals needing to be tended to in a manner that you cannot take care of your selves. The laws have become your kings or your parents, it has made you become like sucklings waiting for instruction. It is the reason you cling to your laws and abide by them, only fringing the lines that indicate where you have gone too far. This has spawned your dishonesty, this is your curse—you are truly evil." He looked at the cities and asked, "Have you not instigated evil?" It replied, "Have you not done evil? He watched and said, “Look at where you speak from.” And it said, “You looked at where I spoke from.” He asked, “What do you mean, it said your mind and its affinity toward your habits. You are not wise it is the central focal point of your world, your leaders are fixated on the collected beings.

He watched and could not comprehend: “It said you are not the sun in this light, you have done many wrongs creating slaves, discrimination, and denigration of many beings. You are the reapers of death and think you are the beauties that are the center of this universe,” he said in anger. “Look at the cities. How could you? It said, good, you are learning we will watch as they kill each other. He looked at the ancient cities and saw that they have almost been overrun by the Starvishiers. Only three main cities were standing; many of its people were killed and abandoned. He looked at the cities of the Alavenish systems and saw they were all dead, struggling for survival. They both looked around and saw only the few that were created by the African courts were still collecting. They looked at them and said, “You should leave. They replied that was not our official mandate.” He replied, “You will die here.” They said, “We will not die for our royals will protect us.” They looked at them in pity and said, “Vaosvakuania.” They replied, “Sokasonoya.” He looked at the systems and said, “let’s play a game the Carnage Cycle said we shall. The Carnage Cycle asked him how powerful are you, he became frightened saying not that kind of game. It said a game is only a game when we have more than two, if not it’s only your imagination.

He looked at the system and said, “What do you mean, it said you are the creation of a desperate need for something that was forbidden many eras ago. Look at yourselves and then observe the patrons. It said you are the creation of a false dimension, you were created out of a synthetic matter that is a replica of the first constituents of the universe. Which use was out lawed and these synthetic types of matter was created. Harnessing the energies from the system and creating a multiverse of beings that is yours. You are a weapon, used to distract and coerce the creators into changing their decisions about what is done with the lesser beings of their kingdom. He looked at the system and asked what kind of weapon are you. It said, “I am a being, and you live more like machines.”

He said it is time to do something about this. He looked at the cities and saw King Warghenar raging through many of the smaller cities along the paths to Omelsurida. He called out to the Prince of Calcuralthera, saying we need help. The prince looked at him and said it is time of the purge. We are the people who should survive the wickedness of the masters of the day. He said, how can you? The prince of Calcuralthera asked where is the Ziauddin; he replied how can I know. The Prince of Calcuralthera said they are purging; he looked at the cities of Vaculvier and Rulturier. He watched as the Ziauddin destroyed and stole everything they could. They were taking the souls of men and the artifacts from the cities. The prince looked on and said, "We too are joining the Chuar, for the hour will come where the last remainder of the wars will come to battle among themselves. The winner will find peace and will be the guardian of the new cities that grows."

He said the people need help, The prince replied, "There are many very old clans about partaking in the Chuar." She said, "You should pay attention to the Ziauddin for they have grown immensely." He asked, "How? For I cannot see where they all are." The prince of Calcuralthera said, "You need the eyes of Flermestius." The prince gave him a blueprint and he immediately built the eye; instantly he saw a lot of dimensions and a lot of people who were hiding from the patrons. They thanked the prince and watched the actions of the Ziauddin. He looked at the hidden cities in amazement, realizing many of these cities were very wealthy and very old for many did not know of their existence.

He looked at the start of many wars in the old cities and realized that the Ziauddin were only interested in acquiring wealth, but they were already powerful. It was in their interest from survival but not their real reason for the wars. Simple revenge, the Carnage Cycle would know. He asked, "What is your reason for helping the Ziauddin?" It replied, "Same reason you have for ignoring the wars above," and it laughed. He looked at the ancients and realized they were almost entirely destroyed, with only a few cities left with less than a thousand inhabitants.

He looked for the Starvishier and realized they were gone; he wondered where they are. He asked the Carnage Cycle, "Where are your soldiers?" It replied, "They were still fighting." He asked where and the Carnage Cycle said, "You need a real eye, look to the west and build an eye from the dead Cyclops of Glurthingmesh." He shrugged and replied, "Where is that? It physically turned him in a direction and opened his eyes to the dimension. He saw a trillion dimensions filled with dead beings lying on the ground with dust all over their bodies and their minds dead with no activity.

They are what the Carnage Cycle needed. He asked what happened there. It said, "Build the eye of the dead king sitting on the throne. He looked hard and long and could not find a throne, it said the throne is in the upper sevelis of the Illumpstivestudes. He looked and realized there were many strange particles within the atmosphere. He began to build the common eyes of the dead being. He began to see more of the dimension until he realized the beings were of rank and fashioned the eye of the highest general. He looked and could not see a throne, he asked how can I find the throne it said war. He looked again and realized that he could not tell the difference between the invaders and inhabitant. He looked hard and realized that it was a traitorous scene of betrayal.

"He studied the scene, watching every position of the dead bodies, looking at the uniforms, thinking of the design and distribution as the indication for rank. He was wrong, and he knew this for the eyes of the beings were not the same and was not distributed in ability but in the ability to see radiant and energy. He looked at their battle scars and realized the beings at the latter side of the dimension would have more scars than those to the opposite side. He looked at the distribution of the alluvials and thought where could they have shifted to during the battles. He wondered if this was all. He looked for civilians and saw that none were dead, he thought they could be alive somewhere. He looked for doors and streams of particles but could not pinpoint a single phase in matter.

"He wondered where would the king have been. He thought he could recreate the being but could not properly see what it was made of. He looked at the structure of the cities and thought he was stupid. His wife said to him, 'Don't despair, the throne is in a place that is above.' He looked at the structure of the alluvials and realized above is in a particle sequence, he looked at the eyes of the beings and counted the radiant they could have seen. He then figured they were assorted in alluvial and dimension, he realized he could make an eye to see the unseen. He got to it and found other empty alluvials from there, he knew he could find the rooms.

"He counted the particles and the rooms, he counted the cones of the eyes and designed an eye based on the algorithmic relationships between the eye and the particles. After 39,000 tries, he finally got it. He saw a dead king sitting on a throne. He was dead, covered with dust, with many dead soldiers on the ground before him. He looked at the king and immediately built his eyes. Upon opening the eye he saw trillions of hidden cities. They were littered with dead being of many designs that he never saw before. He looked around and saw many frozen to death or something changed the matter type, killing the beings instantly. He looked at the other beings and tried to build many of the eyes he saw. He observed all the ancient worlds of these dead beings; many were dead with shifting particles, causing a glow within the bodies. He wondered how many worlds are there and how many were still hidden.

He asked the Carnage Cycle how many worlds are there. It laughed. "An uncountable number by you." "Of these, how many are of the living," it said. "Many are soon to be dead." He looked at the many worlds looking for clues of existence and lineage. It seemed there are no descendants of these in our dimensions. He used his eyes to look for wars within the systems and saw many of the hidden cities battling with the patrons of the Chuar. He looked at many of them and built their eyes and artifacts trying to figure out their power, thinking we must do something. Jeshrome gathered as much designs as he could and stored them in a secret place. He looked at the Ziauddin clans and saw they were killing the ancients of Sulliemear. He wondered if he could engage the Ziauddin but knew he was severely outnumbered. He looked for the Starvishier, and they could not have been seen, the trails of destroyed cities ended at the walls of the Simnuclishes within the Calavary where the trail disappeared. He looked for the lone king and saw many destroyed cities. He followed the trail and saw he was settled in an abandoned city looking out toward the nations of Kirlieweil and Surlistueil. They were his new victims. He sent a silent message to the cities telling of the purge; they looked around and began to prepare. The king noticed this and got up and began his travel speeding toward their position. Prince Jeshrome looked upon the incident thinking another city was slaughtered.

He asked, "What are we to do? His wife said we should survive, for our children should remember this day." He asked, "How could we have children if we no longer have the systems?" She said, like, the first beings we could make our own. He said, "How?" Like the derelicts of the Prikestutivas, she looked at him, saying, "We should try to find peace. The Carnage Cycle has shown us that love of the systems spawn greed and hate for which he is its destroyer. This has been done for many eras, we cannot fight this." She said, "Look at the cyclopes if we could find a dimension far away that no one remembers we could live and create our own children in any way we like.

He shrugged, saying, "This is not the life we thought of, this is not the way we should live. She said life changes and we should change with it. We should be wise and keep our heads low for the rest of our existence. The systems only bring death." He said to her You should be quiet." She said okay and left for the other room. He asked the Carnage Cycle how many forgotten races are there; it said many, but you need to be tenacious because you will die. He asked how do I create life, all the fishes stopped, they replied I am not pleased. It asked what have you learned? What did you do with your life. He said he was a royal, he did his duty, it said wrong answer look out at the cities look at your creations.

He could only think of the hate the Carnage Cycle projected upon the people; he thought he should create soldiers. He looked at his stash of replicas and wondered how he can create soldiers. He began building more eyes looking at the ancient worlds learning and building soldiers. They were a few trillion strong formed from the scraps of the dead beings of the cities. He began giving them eyes and artifacts to strengthen them, teaching them to use their powers. His wife realized what he was doing and confronted him, asking him what he was doing. He replied, "We have to do something. We cannot just stand by and watch trillions of innocent people be slaughtered."

She said, "No, you are a fool, you will draw attention to us and have an ancient patron of the Chaur execute all of us and destroy our abandoned city." He shrugged and said, "We must do something." She screamed at him, saying, "The reason the city still stands is because no one is here! Look around the abandoned city, there is absolutely no activity." She cursed at him and destroyed all of his soldiers, saying, "No, for you are making a terrible decision, putting both our lives at risk." She said, You need to think about us first before anyone else.

She said to him, "Let us practice to create life." They took all of their artifacts and left for an adjacent city. She looked at him, saying, "Try to temporarily forget the troubles of the world. It is just you and I here alone together." They sat on a park bench in the middle of a lonely park and talked about what they should do, where they should travel. He said, "Try to create one being from mere dust." She said she had been trying; it is difficult, saying it lives but they fall apart. He said they are not made with souls, she said she tried to replicate the energy but it was not enough. He looked at the Cyclops and did not see soul energies or any other type of energy from the systems. She said she noticed, within that dimension there aren't any soul or kundalini he said no spirits either, maybe we should try to build something entirely knew and they wondered how.

He said in mirth, "We should ask the Carnage Cycle." She laughed and said, "That hag doesn't know anything." She looked at the systems and thought the old architects built the beings of the systems with collection as the intention. He asked, "What do you mean?"

"The beings were of multiple parts that temporarily worked together but would be separated at death to satisfy the various sectors of collection. We ourselves are built like we are put together from the many parts of the systems." He said, "I understand, we are fabricated by a smith-looking at the cyclopes they are seemingly built like one complete entity."

She said, "We should try our way." She built a small girl and began to speak to her and the girl fell to dust. He looked at the matter type of the cities, saying, "We should try a matter type that is more similar to the structure of building components." She said, "Right, and build a varying type of her original design." He said, "No, it will still fall apart." As he said that it did, she said, "You are right." He said, "It needs to be synchronized perfectly without dampening of the molecule structures, not even for a short moment." He tried and made a son out of Gurdeish energy. She looked at him and then said, "That is a weaponized energy." The boy stood for nearly a minute and evaporated to steam. She said, "Maybe you are right, the Carnage Cycle is too harsh and stood up, took a breath, and walked away." He looked at her, thinking, *What can we really do?* He sat there looking at the horizon thinking of what the world could have been.

He looked at the systems and said we need help. He returned to the old city and asked for council with the remaining Danish courts. He asked for the highest-ranking official for most of the officials went to the central cities for safety. They said the queen Heilgathil was in exile, Prince Heilgurth, and Princess Heghater were missing. He said, "Find the prince and princess, I will call a meeting with the African royals." He sent word to the African courts asking for a meeting. They immediately came to the systems with wide open eyes and dropped jaws, saying how could this have happened. The prince Joshrome said it was the Carnage Cycle, they replied I hate that thing as they look at the cities, the Ziauddin and the Calcuraltherian councils, thinking the world was destroyed.

They watched in horror, saying we have fallen. The prince Joshrome said, "It was worse, we have been annihilated. The African court watched the extent of the damage and he said there is more and they instantly looked at the ancients and saw they were all destroyed. They immediately called council with their ancients, and they said there is nothing we can do for the purge of this season has awakened the ancients of nearly fifty eras. There were many patrons of this era's purge. We are not able to win, and we will try to survive. The ancients left and

Prince Joshrome shared the eyes he acquired from the Chuar showing the dimension and the destruction by the Chuar.

The African court looked at him saying, "You are an honorary patron if the clans of the purge knew that the Chuar gave gifts to you." He said, "Keep it a secret, and it was not given in kindness." They understood and watched the many patrons destroyed the cities. The feeling of horror was immense, and the African court realized why she gave him these eyes. "Saying it means to say we have no chance," he said, among many other unpleasant things. He then said, "Look at the king near Vendhusie, the African court screamed with horror at his trail of destruction and the efficiency of his pogrom.

They said, "We must do something." He said, "I have acquired many artifacts among other things. They both exchanged components and abilities, saying this cannot go on for much longer. The prince Joshrome said, "We need to call a meeting with the Danish queen. They said no one can get into her dimension; he asked can anyone find the young Prince Heilgurth? The court did not know where he was they sent Ashuni to find him. The African court said the Danish queen may not function right after knowing her kingdom and royal family was murdered by the Ziauddin clans. Prince Joshrome agreed, and the Carnage Cycle funded the Ziauddin clan after funding the city that betrayed us.

CHAPTER 20

The Death of a Prince

The African court said, "We are truly in trouble." They all agreed we need a council with the Princess Kamadahara. The princess replied, "We will be partaking in the Chuar on the side of the Fcepchutu Chuar. It is our tradition. If you would like, we can accompany you in the rite of cleansing. The African court said, "We had no choice but to assist." They replied, "We would be honored to assist you." The young prince Joshrome said, "Are you all crazy? We are trying to stop the Chuar, and now we are assisting it. What is wrong with this world? We are naive and irrational, they said you are young and you do not understand, but every so often, men become wicked and we have to do something about it.

"The rule of the emperors have caused many violent outbreaks leading to the destruction of many cities filled with billions of innocent people. You should be careful of which side you choose for the side of the wicked in war is not the side that kills. You are young, and you are of the descendant of the Graija but the days of the emperors are over. You are one, but they are many. You should join us and defend the remaining cities from the side of the wicked. Defend us from the rule that once was the emperor's."

He said no, for we should try to stop all the fighting. The African courts said that was impossible, and you should be wise for the future for all of us is uncertain. Princess Kamadahara said to him, "Go to your wife, seek her counsel," giving him a parting gift. He looked at the gift and saw a blueprint for a design of a being, the children she dreamed of. The African courts said, "We were of the clans before the rule of the emperor, and the world was no less harsh than it was under the emperors. You should choose, but change is happening and you should anticipate your position among all this change."

He looked at the cities burning and cringed, saying, "Wishes are for the uninsightful." The Africans said, "No, my child, wishes are for those that believe." He walked away, leaving to see his wife. The African courts said we need to find the Danish queen and stop the Ziauddin for they have been pillaging the ancients rising to power. They can emerge even more powerful than any of us had imagined. They have become even more dangerous. The African court asked what of the scout; they said there is no word yet. The court said we should send more to investigate and the energy of Verculoidisodis. They realized the increased violence has affected the alluvials blocking visibility and communications.

The scouts have returned, saying the young prince Heilgurth is within an ancient ruined city. The African court said, "Summon him at once." The African royal guards entered the ancient city of the Avertians. The soldiers immediately stormed the dimension, heading straight for Ithecia's palace, and they found them practicing matter construction with Ithecia. The soldiers said to him, "You need to come now." He asked why. "You haven't heard he said an assassin attacked the royal city and killed the entire populace?" He was stunned, and they all left the ruined city.

Upon reaching there, he looked at his home and saw that the matter was like glue; they could not believe their eyes. Princess Heghater cried as their entire families were dead; she could not hold herself up. The prince looked around and saw all the collection sites were burned to the ground. He asked, "What happened, was it the dog clan?" They said, "No, something far worse," and they pointed to the systems. He looked and saw the animals were in an angry state. He asked, "Did it reply?" They said, "Yes, and it is called the Carnage Cycle. It is very old and very dangerous, its sole purpose to destroy the beings of the collected systems." He saw the destruction was immense. They said to him, "You must speak with your queen." He looked at the Princess Heghater, and she was on the floor in a state of grief. He said, "The queen is near the court of issues near the Felthieade, inside a dimension learning about matter construction. Someone needed to tell her what has happened here."

Heilgurth immediately left for the cities near Felthieade shifting in patterns to not be seen by the patrons. Upon reaching there, he stormed her purse dimension and called out to her. "My queen, you should come." She shifted to his position, asking what had happened. He said, "The cities have been destroyed." She asked in which he said all. They immediately left the dimensions, and upon shifting to the systems, she immediately screamed in horror at the vastness of the destruction. She fell to the ground in horror trembling, saying how can this be? She called out to the people she knew, but they were all gone. The African court shifted to her position, and the members picked her up off the floor, taking her to their hiding place saying we should be quiet. The African court said to her, "Get some rest. We will speak of this in the morning." She sat in the room trembling, saying, "How could this have happened. Heilgurth could not have said anything as he had never seen this much destruction."

The African court gave him some designs for eyes, saying, "Put these in," and as he did, he saw countless cities destroyed and burning. Quadrillions of beings were dead; he looked at all the cities. He saw that the Raija, the emperors, and all of his enemies were all dead. He looked on with a chill of death, asking in a trembling voice, "Who is still alive?" "Mostly us and a few other clans." What of the court of issues? Too many were slaughtered.

The African court said look and pointed to the ancients; he saw trillions of ancient cities burning. They said these were the ancients of more than fifty thousand eras. He looked at the African royals, saying, "We have never heard of anyone that old they said we know, and now they are all dead." They showed him the patrons executing citizens at their will. He said, "How could this have been? It is a season they call the Chuar. The unnamed speaker funds the larger clans, and they kill those of the collected systems he was speechless.

"How could this have happened, how could the world be this cold? They said it is the right thing to do; at least many of the survivors think it is." The court members said, "Look at the princess Kamadahara." They watched on as many of the cities near their region were destroyed. He wondered, *What have we become what we can do? They said the princess and her clan have vowed to partake in the Chuar. They said it is best, for doing what is right is taken in the light of what was considered of yesterday.*

The rule of the emperors was unjust and spawned hate and murderous tendencies among the people, creating violence and chaos. He looked on, saying this was too much for one man to handle. They said it gets worse the Ziauddin has been upgraded by the Chuar. He looked at them with sadness, asking if this is true. They said they have been plundering the old ancients for some time now, and it is presumed they are one of the most powerful clans among us today. So far, they have not been killed yet and their leader is still unknown.

He thought, We are in for a lot of trouble. They said it is theorized that it was the Ziauddin that assassinated your families. They looked at him and said they were sorry leaving him to his thoughts. He looked at the empty dimension and could not understand what could have happened to cause this. He looked at Princess Heghater and saw she could not hold herself together; he felt saddened. He looked at Ithecia and thought, *How could we have prevented this?* The world is too unkind, the queen is too distraught to consult, and all we can do is wait. He looked out to the cities and saw many patrons participating in the culling of the cities committing acts of slaughter.

Looking at the murder of many people, the patron simply left their parts; he watched many scavengers hid and collected the parts to build a vast army that would protect them. There weren't simply enough men to combat these super ancients; we were inferior in every way. He looked on, waiting and watching while everyone else was hiding and keeping their heads low. He though, *How could I bring back my brothers and sisters? They were completely destroyed.* He felt hurt inside, and tears flowed from his eyes. He cried he could not hold himself together; he shifted to an empty annex and sat on the dirt wondering what was next. How can we survive this trauma? The only family I have now is the queen and Princess Heghater, what are we to do now? How are we to carry on?"

He looked at the cities that were being destroyed and took the soul of a woman and made a little girl; she stood there wondering what was this place. He sat there watching the little girl wander the streets. He drowned in his own sorrow; the little girl had no idea of what happened and walked inquisitively through the street, looking at the dead bodies. He cried as he watched her look around in wonderment, bowing his head in pain and agony, sobbing with a runny nose.

He looked at the princess in a bedroom of the African castle with bloodshot teary eyes; she could not hold herself together. He looked at the entire African nation and saw they were trillions; every man and woman was a soldier ready to fight just waiting for the command. He looked at the courts and saw the courts discussing battle strategy and issuing orders to reincarnate the dead into their ranks. He saw they were strong but still had a chance to defeat the Chuar's men. He looked at the battles and saw they were still not enough. He thought, *Maybe we could survive.* He began to cry.

He wondered what were we to do. He looked at her and thought, *We are the same.* He took the power from an artifact, depleting its energy and giving the energy to her without her knowledge. He left the annex, heading for the African palace. He asked to speak to one of the kings. A young prince answered his call, saying, "Our fathers are busy with the war." Heilgurth said, "How can I rebuild my city?" They said, "We do not know for the dimension was totally destroyed." He then asked, "Can you find the rest of my people?" They said yes and saw the tiredness in his eyes and told him he should get some rest. They had guards escort him to a room. Heilgurth lay on the bed crying talking to himself calling out to his family, asking, "Why were you taken? A voice said to him, "You will die like the rest of them." He looked around and asked who was there. The voice said, "Seek the Chuar, and you will find your answers."

He immediately shifted and looked at the systems. He saw no one was there. He said within the animals, *Who are you?* It replied, "Another would be dead. I am no one, but you are a soldier." He said no, a prince. It replied, "Oh, how dangerous are you?" He said, "None." It replied, "Too many tears." It said, "I have a mission for you. Kill the prince of Lvehilurgeril, he asked, "Why me?" It said, "Your pain is beautiful." He said no it replied the mortality of men is not the reverence of their honesty, but the survivability of the heart is their loyalty to survival. He said you are the one that killed my family, it said your family was vile and deductive seeking safety at the expense of other lives. He asked how could you say that. It said they died at the hands of a judge, for which they were found guilty.

He said, "Show me," and he saw the battle. He replied, "Only one man, it is said you are a fool thinking of your power over your wits you too will die." He looked at the system saying, "Death is always followed by adjustments." It said, "Yes, you could tame your heart but the pace of your footsteps are that of the slaves that you are. You are born of the slaves of the systems, you will never be free until you free your heart. It is sad to kill for me and forget everything that is dear to you. For you are born in sin, and beloved the beguile of the system and the wine of the fruits of its tree. You will be my instrument or you will be my victim." He looked at the system and said you will be wrong.

He looked around and tried to find the Prince of Lvehilurgeril. He asked the African scouts to find the prince of Lvehilurgeril. They said, "It was not on our lists." The soldiers brought many designs of eyes for him, saying, "This is the best we can do for you he was grateful but could not see where this prince was." He said to the Chuar, "Where is Lvehilurgeril?" It replied in a very secret location. He said, show me, and it opened his eyes to an alter dimension filled with trillions of beings collecting souls from the systems but in an entirely different matter regime. The soldiers said to him how could this have been; he said it makes sense—what we see is what we collect. Our minds fashion the matter for many of these matter is an essence that is perceived by us, and we further enhance it to build ourselves.

He looked to the systems and said to the Chuar, "Which is the prince?" It said, "Look at the city and you will know which is to die." He looked at the world and saw a city beyond compare. It was huge, trillions of cities all under one collection scheme. Reincarnating all that was of the systems, they were huge and could not be stopped. They were unified under one King, with one family ruling for it has never been ruled by a foreigner. He looked and saw many beings in cages and enslaved and beaten to death many times over.

He realized that many of the people were suffering and were in a state of joyous hate for each other. He watched and saw the slaves were tortured without remorse same as that of the lesser cities of collection. He thought it is the same everywhere, but these seemed to be isolated too long. He immediately began looking for the prince and saw that the head torturer was the prince. He would whip the new comers for pleasure as they came to the city and he would do so in lust. He did this from the beginning of his creation; he was in love with their pain.

He said to the soldiers, "We cannot afford an enemy like this." They said, "We should give the mission to a lesser city." He said no for the Chuar must stop. The generals said we would do it and instructed a smaller animal city to invade the cities taking part in the Chuar then they invaded the cities of Lvehilurgeril. They immediately did and the patrons of the Chuar immediately flooded the cities where the animals were present, killing everything in sight. The people of Lvehilurgeril immediately shifted to another dimension, following them to a lesser city. The soldiers gave Prince Heilgurth more eyes, and the entire dimensions of dimensions revealed itself. There was an uncountable number of dimensional nexuses hidden between the dimensions. The invading clans proceeded to Lvehilurgeril. He looked at the system and said, "Why did you make me do that?" The Chuar said it needed to be done for you do not know the extent of the hate that has grown within your universe.

He watched and saw an uncountable number of deaths; the African soldiers reported the patrons were entering other unseen systems chanting they will all die. They looked in horror saying that was us yesterday. They will all die a terrible death; the African court sent scouts along with the patrons to report what was found. In a matter of minutes, they reported billions of new alluvials of nexuses with many different beings who had to be destroyed. An African court member said this was all too much, saying, "We are to remain unseen." That is the order they all agreed and returned to their quarters.

Heilgurth looked at the new dimensions, saying, "This cannot be stopped, it must be survived." He looked for the Calcuraltherians and saw they were readying their soldiers. He looked and saw billions of soldiers in perfected metallic radiant armor, preparing for war. He looked at Princess Kamadahara and saw she was talking with her captains. Heilgurth wanted help and thought he could be of assistance, but he was just one man. He looked at the Princess Heghater and said, "I should stay close to those I still have." He immediately went to visit her. He entered the room and as she was lying there in tears, he told her to be strong. She got up the bed and ran to him, hugging him tightly.

He looked at her telling her, "We need to be strong. There are still some of our countrymen alive. They were not all destroyed. She said, but now they can never return. He said, "We can find a way." She went into a deeper state of tears. "Tomorrow we will go to the remaining people and gather our strengths and attack the Ziauddin. They will pay for what they did and he began drying her tears. We need to find our queen; he left her quarters knowing exactly what they must do. He went to the queen's bedchambers. He opened the door and saw the queen looking through a window. He noticed she had looked like she had not moved in hours; her face was in horror at what the world had become.

He asked, "What are we going to do?" She said, we were about to go to war and lost before we even began to fight. Heilgurth said, we all lost, how can we fight, and we are soo weak," she said, "we must fight. We will build an army, where it strength is its powers not its numbers. Look outside of the window and he looked at the destroyed cities. They were all numerous, but now they are destroyed. Tomorrow, we will destroy the Ziauddin." Heilgurth looked at her, saying, "We have no choice, for sure they are located there in the city of Findsurlistueil He nodded thinking we need some rest, she sat there saying we will fight to our last.

He left and looked at the systems, saying to the Chuar, "I need power." The Chuar said, "You already have it," and the fishes laughed. He said, "I need to defeat the Ziauddin." The Chuar said, "You need to be a violent flame of a man that does the good of the creator in a world of sins, you need to be a soldier. If you truly wish to have power to be victorious you must be victorious in your mind, not your heart. For power is not of the heart but from survival. Look around and muster what you can for survival is the true test of a soldier." He looked at all he could and asked the African courts for all they have and they gave him a lot. He fashioned himself to be stronger, but he was still not a match for the ancient patrons of the Chuar. He looked at the Calcuralthera and said to them tomorrow "we will go after the clans of the Ziauddin; they said agreed."

He looked at the system and said to the Chuar, "We will speak again." The Chuar Olermesh GU Sardhesh laughed; he shifted to the annex and sat on the floor he felt fatigued. He looked at the girl he made and saw she was wondering about the city, he looked at her thinking tomorrow could be his last day. He sat there and rested with his eyes fixed on the destroyed cities. He looked at them, thinking they will all be sure of their faith as they will not survive this season. He looked at a burning city and build a soldier with the soul of a dyeing boy. He told him build an army for I will return he closed his eyes and quieted his mind.

The sun rose, and he sat there for many hours. He looked at the queen and saw she had changed her clothes to that of the armor of her forefathers. He immediately got up and changed his clothes wearing the armor of his generals, reconstructing the matter into a hard rocklike combustible matter. He called out to Princess Heghater, saying, "Ready your selves." He looked at Ithecia, saying, "We will fight today, giving her components from many of the fallen citizens completing her build. He left the annex going to the queen's chambers. The queen saw him and changed her matter and looked at him. "Today we will fight."

She immediately shifted to an empty annex-creating a war room, building structures and portals showing locations and places of the whereabouts of the Ziauddin, noting the energy signatures of persons and matter specifics. She created a central being to dispense information as she needed it. She said the Ziauddin was still pillaging the Algaruthieu systems they were more than sixty eras old. Then the Ziauddin was in the Gurteliesh system, they were more than 90 eras old and then to the Fultulong systems they were more than 110 eras old. They did this in succession; they are growing stronger and fast. The Ziauddin attacked the city of Calcuralthera for which they almost defeated the princess. She was very powerful at the time but was not powerful enough to defeat the king of Ingultheriat alone. The battles have gone beyond that of the emperors and the Raija for they are all dead.

We have used all the eyes we have at our disposal, giving them to this central being which is our intelligence, it will give us the information we need. Heilgurth said, "This was not enough, we will need to upgrade our network." The battle changes and many hidden dimensions are opened when under attack. Heilgurth created 111 new beings that would upgrade the network as needed. These were plugged into the existing networks gathering images and compiling lists of locations of specific targets and groups partaking in the Chuar. The remaining cities are to be monitored for any activity. They agreed they would need diversionary forces. They cloaked the war room with the cloaks from the Chuar's hidden cities. They created a detonating mass of radiant to absolutely destroy the annex concealing all portals in the event the dimension was invaded. They began looking at the Ziauddin's movement, with intention of killing their leader.

Heilgurth instructed Ithecia to build a sealed dimension so they can recreate soldiers. He then deployed spies to investigate the cities near the clans of the Ziauddin. They still had no idea who was their leader, they asked the Calcuraltherian for all of the information they had on the Ziauddin. They sent all they knew, but there were no records on who the leader was. According to the information from Calcuralthera, the clans of the Ziauddin was the descendants of the Churolindheras who had a common ancestor with the Roman royals. The royals of Bheriura were very close to the royals of the Roman courts; they were like brothers.

The Bheriura were both part of the courts of gathering and collection under the laws of forced recollection and confiscation scheme, of the latter end of the last era. They sought to dominate the systems with violence and elimination tactics, while simultaneously convincing the people to accede to their schemes of collection. The cities observed silently, and when they imitated their plan to take over the systems the cities protested against this actions. The unknown clans of benevolent gods created a plan using a man to change the ways of the systems. The man was to show the people a new way of life, for which they would not need to follow the ways of sin and fight for resources and commit murders in anger and jealousy.

The men would be fulfilled, not only the word of God but by the fact of not having a need for anything that he would desire. The laws of collection would have shifted the basis of collection. These shifts would have caused these laws to be applicable and the men would be free without the chains of desires. These chains are tied to their hearts and minds, which dominates their actions and behaviors. The court of gathering and collection was furious and enraged, but could not openly confront the hidden gods of benevolence. They sat there and wondered what they can do; they looked at the system and decided to change the hearts and minds of the men who would listen to his message.

They influenced the minds of the lesser cities and instilled fear and jealousy, simultaneously with the need for importance maintaining the system. The smaller cities began to fight among themselves, devising a plan to destroy the shifts in clauses that would facilitate this change. The larger cities looked upon the smaller cities, saying this was not good. They persevered and when they could not triumph, they sought to kill the man destroying the worlds by the hands of their brothers. The smaller cities raged and tortured the human beings, killing the people for sport and cognitive understanding. The way they were viewed by the other humans caused them to further control him and used him to taunt the kings of the time, causing many wars. They began to kill and hunt the people who practiced witchcraft, almost eliminating the lines.

They looked at these smaller cities, asking if this was necessary. They scorned the cities that spoke of reason; they continued dragging the man through his life in their cognitive structure of decision. They created harmful situations for all of mankind. They looked upon the system and spat in the faces of men, saying, "This was a gift for we shall be the gods of the day once more." The others looked on and said nothing; some left the system completely. Others stayed to help the humans once more for these actions are the usual actions of the systems. The larger cities destroyed the smaller cities as they eventually tried to use the man to destroy the world as they could not get their way. The upper courts dissolved the court of gathering and confiscation, causing mass shame and apathy for the actions of the royals.

The Bheriura royals opposed the decisions by the court, saying it was unfair and unlawful to remove the entire court based on the accusation of the minority. They sought to get legal redress and conspired to take over the ruling Monarch of the nation. Allying themselves with the Amustreen, an ancient enemy of the people of Commaullphario, they influenced the minds of states men and other officials, changing their decisions and allying themselves with the Amustreen people. They immediately began to conquer the cities of the smaller collection schemes. They were untouchable until they met the Felthieade for which they were destroyed for dominating the systems in an uninhabitable way.

They fought fiercely but were outmatched by the Calcuraltherian and began controlling the minds of many other clans, which they fought for their cause. They became a difficult enemy to defeat, influencing the minds of everyone who was their enemies, making them soldiers within their army. They were eventually destroyed as there was an artifact that could be used to find their locations. The entire clan was cursed in such a way so that they could not escape the eyes of the Calcuraltherian Svastham. Sometime after the eye was mysteriously stolen by an unknown thief, the artifact was never recovered.

It was said only nine of the children of Seramus survived, for which three died in the wars after the execution of the ombudsman. Many were sure the leader of the clan is one of the princes. They were always in the practice of illegally collecting souls from the schemes and were deemed to be banished for their crimes against the people. They had many enemies, but most of them are unreachable. They are very hateful because of what happened to their parents. They have been on the path of revenge since they were given the blade of the Hustelijun. They became more powerful than their rivals, but it was not enough to conquer the systems so they returned to hiding.

Heilgurth said, "We had to fight and sent assassins to scout the town and cities, trying to gain entry into hidden cities of the Algaruthieu systems." The queen said, "I have to show you something." She made a new dimension and went inside; they all followed. She said, I went into the vault and spoke with the psyche-emulation of an ancient. What I learned led me to the library, I received a lot of information about the matter types. The psyche-emulation said the original matter type was the illusions of the gods, and their creations would not fester life. They then created a new matter type that would cement and hold together the relationships that would sustain life. This is what we are made of. The original matter types are not perceivable by us and is the same as an illusion or an intangible force that cannot be controlled or perceived by us. We all live in a construct of what was called reality until time was split to cause dimensions.

So in that we would need the help of something outside of the universe to control the matter in the same way we control our types of matter. The types of matter we are made of is based on the mind of a being. The matter is of the same things like that of an alphabet. The matter that was created by us was based on our understanding of other types of matter, and the logic that is our connections and reasoning to the emphasis on the consonants present in the matter types that is created.

That is what the differences are in one particular regime; the interaction between regimes are the reaction of emphasis to decline of entropy and enthalpy, within the interaction among the types involved. These are the base structures that all the relevant apparent dimensions sit on. An armor's strength is based on emphasis of consonants interactions and position within the structural decline of entropy and enthalpy matrices of the base structure. The destructive force of a radiant that is the same in relationship but in the opposite reactions within the scale.

Creating indestructible soldiers is based on the ability to hold the soldiers' physical structure together within the ambient consonant structure of the higher resonating dimension of the base structure. The spelling of these matter are not that difficult to understand but is unperceivable since many of the ancients knew this and through war designed their matter types based on irregularity of preponderance in thought. The sound particles are based on the particles of the original structure of the universe, for which only the creator knows how it was created, for which all sound traverses. To find the base code of all particles we need to follow the sound particles.

There are some ancients that invented ways to track sound particles, but these methods are somewhat irrelevant in today's matter spaces. The first beings used the eyes of Papulurus in the library to create their descendants, but this knowledge was forgotten. She said, "We need to go to the library and access the eye for it is our only chance. Only then can we begin to understand the matter of the created universe." Heilgurth built another being and sent her to the library to gain access to this eye. The queen continued to say that many of the beings two thousand eras ago were killed for the knowledge of this eye, and the use of the eye was banned resulting in the loss of this knowledge.

Many beings two hundred thousand eras ago did not know what the eye was and thought it was a special artifact, but instead it was a being of immense strength. It was said this being was the absolute first being that was created within the universe and the most powerful. He went to the systems and asked the Carnage Cycle what was the eye of Papulurus. It said that was a baby of the creator for which you are no match in it is beloved throughout the regimes. He returned to the war room saying it is true and the Carnage Cycle said it was a baby of the creator.

She said, "We need to begin for the Ziauddin is moving forward with their plans," as she pointed to one of her portals. They were taking souls from the dimensions of Epludhelges the peace seekers of the hidden cities. The Calcuraltherian saw this and invaded the cities. The queen said, "In the short time I spent in the purses, we practiced building many types of beings for which it was easy to create based on what we know. Indestructibly was very difficult because in language, a word means something until the following words do not compliment or coincide with the meaning of the psychological chain or cognitive rhythms. It becomes nonsense the uncoordinated destroys the idea or sentence. It is in this same way the unbalanced is destroyed by the stable formations in matter.

So the queen said, "Let us begin," and they all linked to the central intelligence being, looking at the matter. They saw they were thick and globules, moving too vigorous to be held together indefinitely. It would become brittle and radiant would destroy the structure. She said taking apart the structure takes other particles specifically in sequences and patterns. The increments of movements of these particles to assist in the release of other particles will cause the globules to break apart. The counting of the particles would cause the smaller globules to become stable and unreactive, creating a smaller consonants of an alphabet. She said if we are to create indestructible soldiers, we need to find smaller and more stable particle globules that are less resonant than those of our enemies. He looked around and realized he could not see a lot of the particles within the matter of their enemies.

The girl Heilgurth sent to the library contacted him with a link to the eye. As soon as it came online they realized they were very high to the matter of the first universe. The matter spaces are not of usual matter sequencing or patterns of the first constituents of the universe. They looked around looking at the ancient cities and saw each had its own alphabet, and all had their own way of matter synchronization. The queen realized that she knew very little about the universe and all the constituents; many of the particles are not perceivable. She said we have very little time, instructing the beings to immediately fashion eyes to add to the central being.

They immediately looked for the Ziauddin and saw a mass structure of alluvials that the Ziauddin clans were traversing. The Ziauddin was huge, living in an abandoned city made more than 300,000 eras ago. They immediately sent images of the Ziauddin clans to the Calcuralthera, asking which of these are the leaders of the Ziauddin clans. She said they will have to check each being in the image individually and correlate with their records. She was more interested in the eye than she was using asking where she got this and how many cities can this see. The queen replied the eye is a secret and it sees all. The Princess looked at them saying this can be dangerous. The queen said, "Look around," and she nodded.

They looked at the Ziauddin clans and realized they were producing trillions of beings from the souls of the dead and those that was left behind from the wake of destruction from the Chuar. She said to the princess, "Look at this." The princess replied, "I have noticed. The queen said they are too many, if we do not stop this soon the battle would be even tougher. They said the battle is already stiff, they looked at the African royals saying the Ziauddin may be too many. They looked at her saying the war was too strong, the final battles will be too great. She said it will get worse, showing them images of the Ziauddin clans. The African royals looked at their number and recounted their soldiers, saying, "We are still not enough."

She said, "We need to do something." The African courts said, "Those are not the true problem," and pointed to the cities the Chuar upgraded. She watched with her eyes and saw they were very close to the constituents of the base structure of the universe. She showed this to the prince and Princess and they cursed at the Chuar, saying it is our real enemy. The African royal court said the Ziauddin clans were upgraded by the Chuar, the battle is unwinnable. She looked at the Ziauddin once more; she could not see the beings that were built like the Chuar's henchmen.

Princess Kamadahara realized that something was up with the queen, she looked around and saw the answer in the African royals. The Ziauddin has the power of the Chuar. She said then we are to be on the side of the Ziauddin. Her family said in this hour the side of the Chuar is not the side of all the patrons. The Ziauddin will die. She looked at the queen and said how is it I cannot see inside you. The queen said the eyes of the cloak was given to me by the hood of the clave. The queen looked at her saying I have to get back and she further cloaked herself.

The African court asked the queen to look for the gate. As she looked near the coordinates, she saw many vicious beings made of a very incremental spelling of matter. She showed it to Heilgurth. He said, "Look inside the gate." She saw a giant of a beast, and Heilgurth said, "This is the baby of the Chuar." She instantly copied his matter and began constructing it, saying, "It is time, we need to find the Ziauddin." The queen showed the being to the African royals, and they realized it was too dangerous—the Chuar was an evil being.

She asked the African royals where would the leader of the Ziauddin clans be. They replied in the safest place possible. She thought if he was upgraded by the Chuar, where would he be. They said pillaging a very rich enemy or destroying the enemies of his father. They looked at the cities of the oldest being they could find, and the Ziauddin clans were not there. The African royals brought a list of places to find and asked for help in finding a safe path to the gate. She sent a link to her central being to give them access to her network. They said, "We should visit the energy portal of Verculoidisodis. It is said there is a being that resides there that is from another universe that speaks there. It is called the fallen."

Heilgurth and Princess Heghater said they heard of this being make the journey. The queen said, "Build these," and they built four trillion beings of a very ancient matter design. Heilgurth and the Princess Heghater got to it, shifting out of phase with their guards. Heilgurth said to the central being, "We will lose communication soon, so upgrade our maps and keep a rescue team on standby." The queen immediately upgraded the central beings' build capabilities. It created trillions of rescue beings, for which the queen grew worried because of what could be next. She looked at the wars and the patrons of the Chuar and realized the upgraded beings by the Chuar was all of the same matter type.

She began to look for beings of similar types of matter and realized there were correlating similarities of patterns, which could mean an evolution of the matter types along the lines of inheritance of matter construction. The queen began to trace the lines, realizing this was a clue to the origins of the matter and the beings. She also knew the beings were of a similar disposition, seemingly presumptuous. A voice said to her, "Just because you can see doesn't mean you can find." She instantly knew what the voice meant—the particles were unperceivable and still observed. The particles that cannot be observed by me are unperceivable and nonexistent. These are also consonants of a matter type; she thought of the matter types that are made of all that is unperceivable. She looked at the system and said to the Chuar, "Why did you speak to me?" and it replied, "I speak to all." She asked, "Where are the Ziauddin clans?" It said, "You will have your turn, but you must not fail for they are one of my soldiers."

She looked at the system and said, "I am in no mood for games." The Chuar said, "This is the season for games. We are having a tie." The fish circled and then dispersed; she looked at the systems and said it is time. She immediately built more of the beings of the Chuar's matter type and left for the cities of the Ziauddin clans. She shifted to the city of Hureguloris and looked for all the Ziauddin clan members and began killing them. Her guards began destroying the cities, killing everyone for they were no match for the guards she created.

The neighboring cities all fled, and her guards quickly destroyed all the citizens of the cities. She screamed, calling out to the Ziauddin clans; no one answered. She took the lingering souls of the dead and created the symbol of the Ziauddin. The queen quickly moved to another city where their soldiers would be seen. She instantly began firing bursts of lightless radiant, a design of her own invention. The cities all began to explode, leaving a toxic corrosive dark gas that dissolved the atmosphere and the matter within it. The guards of the city all shifted to her position, and her guards shifted to her position and made quick dead of their attempts.

She took the souls and created another symbol of the Ziauddin; she traveled through the dimensions in this manner, destroying everything and everyone in her path. The members of the Ziauddin soon realized they were being hunted and sought to hide sending messages to their leader. The leader looked from his hidden position, watching out to the cities with a careful eye. He did not know what had happened to him. His recollection was that he was planning his attack when he and his council immediately transformed into grotesquely large beings of a strange type and design. They thought it was an attack from the Calcuralthera as they could not reform themselves to their former structure.

They looked at the wars with frightened eyes, unsure of their ability, ordering the men to collect as many artifacts as possible. They saw very old and powerful militants destroying the ancients whom they respected as superior and could not have thought could have happened. The queen reached upon a city where they had no quarrel with the Chuar, and she asked where is the leaders of the Ziauddin clans, and they pointed to a man, saying, "Surely he knows." She shifted to man and shifted him to a dimension where there was no one.

She stilled the matter with her hands, not allowing him to shift, asking, "Where is the leader of your clan?" He said, "Frighteningly, I have never known the leader. I cannot tell you who he, is but I can say there are safe havens set up all along the flows of Orneifeilthier." She immediately shifted out of the dimension, regrouping with her guards, instructing them to destroy the cities and interrogate the members of the Ziauddin. She realized the Ziauddin member did not know who their leader was; all they knew was it was profitable to be a member.

She knew she was in the lower reaches of the clan's hierarchy and had to climb the ladder. She used the eye and looked for plundering activities and saw the Ziauddin sacking the cities. She immediately shifted and began firing at the Ziauddin clan members, hitting clan members and civilians alike. The clan leader saw this and immediately shifted; her guards began destroying the cities, destroying the members of the Ziauddin. The battle was fierce with the largest fallout that city has ever seen; her guards forged radiant that disintegrated the Ziauddin's members.

They moved swiftly through the streets, killing anyone they could find. She looked around and saw that nothing was left standing. She walked over to the positioning of an elderly member of the Ziauddin clan. She took his soul and the other components and recreated him. He instantly was startled and began shooting. She immediately took off his arms, putting him to sit in the streets, saying, "Who is your leader?" He replied, "You will die, swine!" She said, "I am no swine!" and grew lightless radiant inside his stomach, causing him to scream. He tried to shift, but this only caused him more pain, he said look to the east he was there before you came. She immediately looked and saw someone was there and shifted. She thanked the man and his body detonated.

She immediately shifted and followed the man's energy trail; he shifted to a city that was very old, and there were no wars. It seemed they were unaware of the Chuar; she followed the trail to an abandoned house where he shifted again. She shifted into a cave where he stood for a minute then walked to the end of the cave. She looked up and saw what seemed like the inside of a castle. She saw the men and ordered her guards to attack. They immediately attacked the castle; she heard sounds of thunder and crashing. She shifted inside of the castle and began slaughtering all of the inhabitants. The men screamed as many of them shifted; she ordered her guards to follow and kill them. She looked around and saw many of the eldest shifted as the invasion started. She looked for the oldest and followed him, putting many of the guards to search and destroy.

She reached the inside of a palace where she saw the same old man speaking with a woman in a private room. She shifted to behind the woman and released lightless radiant into her spine. The man immediately shifted, and she followed him. The woman exploded as her guards laid waste to the palace. The man began running as he shifted to the streets of an ancient city shouting assassin. She fired at the man, disintegrating his body; her guards shifted to her position wearing a matter type she had never seen before.

She looked at the men and watched her surroundings, looking for her war room. The guards attacked her with a heavy radiant. She shifted and reshifted to behind the guards, hitting him with lightless radiant, but it blasted the armor, pushing him into the others. She realized her radiant types was not as powerful as the shielded matter. She called out to her central being, saying, "Find my location." It immediately showed her, and she said, "I need a solution for destroying this armor." It said, "The armor is of the old Louvgehernian spelling." She immediately shifted as they blasted radiant toward her.

She looked at the man and realized they were pouring in reinforcements; she began to cover herself in armor that was corrosive to that of the guards. They began to fire at her. She shifted and began to fire many variations of lightless radiant toward them until their armor began to chip away. She kept on moving and adjusting her radiant type until the armor was no longer impenetrable. She began to decimate the guards; they called for reinforcements, and a being of two hundred meters tall shifted into the dimension. The guards all moved away, creating a path between her and the being.

She covered herself in the hardest matter she knew, as the being shifted to her position and raised its foot and stamped on the ground, creating a very large crater throwing rocks and debris into the air. She flew into the air and shifted to the top of a building. The being then fired at her, huge bursts of radiant that destroyed the entire area more the thirty acres. She was pushed to the ground with all the matter around her melting to a thick hot liquid, she stood thinking this could be a challenge.

The being fired variations of this radiant hitting her as she shifted, causing destruction to the parts of her armor and the matter in the village. She had to reshift to a more stable energy regime. She shifted, the beings and the soldiers followed her, and they released a blue flame and the regime began to change the matter type of the city. The blue flame disappeared, and she looked at what that was, the being fired at her and shifted immediately and stamped her into the floor, trapping her under his foot, sending her thirty-five feet into the ground. She laid there for approximately sixty seconds before she shifted to behind the being. She fired multiple blasts of lightless radiant until one could have hurt him. He shifted and appeared temporarily then reshifted. She shifted and the soldiers fired at her, she fired a huge blast at the ground, causing the land to shake.

The building began to tremble and the being released a barrage of radiant covering her position. She covered herself and the land around her became a hot sticky liquid. She shifted to higher ground firing the same radiant as the giant causing a large volume of hot molten rock to flow down to the city covering the city and some of the soldiers. The giant shifted to above the molten rock and began walking toward him. She looked at him, asking the central being for a way to defeat him.

Her central intelligence being said, "Try to spell the matter it uses." She could not for she was not well versed in that language.

The central being said, "Look at the matter type within and just think of how to destroy it." She said yes, the central being said stop shifting within the dimension then detonate the entire dimension. She pulled together all that she could muster and pushed them together. Then focused all of her energy toward it and detonated it. She was blasted to the edges of the dimension, the particles all created a chain reaction destroying the constituents of the matter type to a lower consonant. She had to hold herself together physically, as she frantically moved toward the outer dimensions. Upon safety she immediately shifted back to the war room, she sat on a chair thinking of how she could have lost. She collected the souls of the dead from the destroyed dimension and brought them back in a controlled space. She had her men interrogate them.

She realized she needed to learn how to spell or learn some quick solutions of how to destroy the matter types of the Ziauddin clans. She looked at all the matter types and began to devise more effective radiant within those spectrums. She created millions of beings to help her in the battlefield to help her quickly figure out the dynamics of the particle substrates. These beings created a room where they believed they could have created many of the matter types within the universe. They figured out one integral part of the matter alphabet, there was a miss concluded letter deep within the particle structure.

This was the cause of a misfeed of radiant that caused and integrated rotation of miscoagulation among particles resulting in a wavelike motion of negative affinity toward particle adhesion this caused a temporary expansion resulting in a pulse rate affirmation affording matter instability along many gradients of the upper dependent consonants. She watched and realized that the particles are very unstable, especially in reaction to nine specific consonants. She looked at a member of the Ziauddin clans in one of the cities and destroyed the particle within the smaller reactive particle, and the man disintegrated. She made a being and gave him one of the nine particles and told him to enter these dimensions and kill everything in sight. She silently watched and mapped their movements while observing the matter's destructibility. She realized he killed a lot of being, and the particle was very effective against their armor but the being was just not enough.

She looked at the Ziauddin and traced them back to the homefronts with no luck of knowing who was the leader. She asked the African royals who was leader of the Ziauddin clans, and they replied they didn't know. She asked for methods and alphabets against the specific matter types of the Ziauddin clans. They gave her five alphabets; she thought this was not enough. She looked at the Calcuraltherian court and asked for help. The Calcuraltherian said, "You need to share your eye or we can become enemies." She shut her door saying, You are not okay, or was that the Chuar. Princess Kamadahara replied, "No, there has been a lot of power distribution. Who was the leader of the Ziauddin clans?" They replied rumor has its name, Prince Milkeidha Jurgeuish, one of the last sons of Seramus. She asked if he is three hundred feet tall; they said not likely. She replied most likely it was not him. She sent her guards to find and execute Milkeidha Jurgeuish. She shared this information to the African royal courts for which they said to her we need to speak in private.

The queen shifted to her quarters, the African royals said to her, "We need to get moving—the patrons of the Chuar is on their way." The queen asked, "Where would we move to?" They said, "Anywhere but here." The queen instructed the war room to move; she looked at an old abandoned city more the 40 million eras old and shifted through a path; the war room immediately followed. She looked at the dead giant beings lying on the floors and looked around and saw it was the remains of a dead race, killed by something many millions of eras ago. She looked around to her staff as they set up the portals.

She looked at the ancient city thinking of the Chuar and how to prevent their invasion. She thought of keeping their numbers low; she looked at her guards and her analysts looking at the empty African cities. She looked at the invading force and saw they were more than seventy thousand eras old; she looked at them and copied their abilities. The queen watched and influenced the mind of members of the Ziauddin clans, forcing them to attack their invaders. She watched as the invaders attacked the cities of the Ziauddin as she forced the other Ziauddin clan soldiers to attack the invader from all sides. The leader of the Ziauddin watched as the invaders got closer to his city.

The queen called out to the Calcuraltherian and said, "Watch out for the leader's movement. They said, "Sure, will she use the same tactic on King Warghenar?" She watched as their soldiers attacked the king who immediately shifted to the position of the Ziauddin clan's emaciating them swiftly toward the center of the cities, destroying everything in her path. The soldiers began to pour out from the inner reaches of the hidden cities. She asked her network, "Where is the Starvishier?" They said near the Cambaratu systems. She looked and saw they were destroying villages; she had some remaining soldiers of the Ziauddin attack the Starvishier. They immediately looked at them and shifted to their position.

She held the head of the weaker soldiers and had them shift to the center of the Ziauddin clan's stronghold. The Starvishier quickly made their way to the center of the cities, and this certainly got their attention. She said he had no choice but to come out; she looked and saw many of their soldiers pouring out from the walls. She thought we needed more patrons, she shifted to the systems and asked the Chuar, "Where are your soldiers?" The Chuar laughed and said, "They are everywhere!" She said stopped joking around. I need your help. It said destroy the gate of Yulthies. She asked how, the Chuar said use the library. She immediately instructed her network to find a way to destroy the gates of Yulthies.

Her scouts said the gates had been created by the Phulthies many eras ago. This meant the knowledge to rebuild it was lost. When it was presumed that the original designers were dead, they saw there was no record of them within the library. There is an arm in the library that was used to create the beings of old many eras ago. This was lost to many of the ancient civilizations. Her scouts said we can use the arm. I will link it to our central being. She looked at the gates, linked herself to the arm, and began pushing it to one side, the gate began to shimmer then to a violent rock, causing the gate to fall flat.

The being inside immediately crossed over, destroying everything and everyone in its path. The being moved viciously across the lands, killing everyone. The attacking guards of the gates did not even break the skin of this monster. She completely possessed the guards of the central cities of the Ziauddin clans, waiting for the right time to attack. She used the men to attack the being from the other side of the universe. The being was in a blood rage, killing the beings of the gatekeepers. The being stopped and looked at the location of the attack and shifted to the center of the city destroying everything it saw.

The guards rushed in to its location and it devoured every living inhabitant, making its way further into the heart of the Ziauddin clan's country. She watched at the hidden cities as they became visible, looking for any sign that the leader would emerge. The being raged through all of their defenses, and the royal guards appeared. They were significantly bigger than the usual city guards, firing callous blasts of radiant at the being. The being only became angrier and rushed through the guards killing them all.

The leader looked at the cities and saw the being could not be stopped, he looked at the other sides of his kingdom and saw even more patrons of the Chuar. She said the at the Calcuralthera we need more firepower, they said we got it and released the Choulghchen. A large six-legged beast came out of a teleporter, attacking everything in its sight. The major influenced the mind of the beast and showed it the guards of the royal cities of the Ziauddin, and it shifted, destroying the city, making its way to their stronghold. The leader of the Ziauddin watched in dismay as the beast charged through the city, destroying everything in its path. The leader called upon all his troops to defend the palace; they all shifted to in front of the palace and began to shoot at the beast.

They could not hurt the beast, and the beast charged right through the front line of guards. The leader called upon all of his troops asking for aid; the troops of the many cities shifted to the stronghold and began battling the beast. They all noticed many of the Ziauddin clan's troops, leaving for the hideout location. The queen immediately looked and saw the leader. The beast charged right through the palace, causing it to collapse. He was pushed into the sea behind it. The queen immediately shifted to his position and watched for his appearance as he might rise from the water.

The princess immediately shifted into the water, hitting him blows of lighted energy, causing his internals to shatter. He began frothing at his mouth as he was dying; his body began to float to the surface, and the princess shifted back to the surface. The queen looked at her drenched in seawater, asking, "Is he dead?" She said surely, and the African royals cheered, saying, "You did it! The princess did it!" She shifted back to Calcuralthera, and the queen waited until she could fully see his dead body. She looked at him, saying, "We are now even." She immediately shifted back to the system, saying, "How is it that the Calcuraltherian are able to defeat your soldiers?" The Chuar displayed smiles, saying, "My soldiers are the Calcuraltherian." She looked at them, thinking, *What do you know. The Chuar said you haven't even scratched the surface.*

She went back to her hideout and sat down on a chair looking at the chaos, thinking how deep this conspiracy goes. *Where we all to join the cause of the Chuar?* She sat and wondered, *How is it you are all unaware of the evidence of the Chuar? How is it you are all going to die someday?*

You are all forced not to care, a voice said, *because it is not my will.* She asked, Who are you?" It said I am the opposite of an avatar. The queen said how are we to do the work of the creator if we do not know how to accept our realities. She looked around and thought to herself how are we to notice the cruelty of the world if we are blinded by our reasons and selfish needs.

Many of us have no one to guide us and have no choice but to stand beside our decisions. I am a queen, and I have much responsibilities for which many people depend on me. She looked at Heilgurth and Princess Heghater and called out to them, but they were too far away. She used the arm to upgrade her central being; she looked around and ordered her staff to upgrade themselves as much as they could. She eventually regained communications with Heilgurth and Princess Heghater as they made their way across the many dimensions to the edge of the universe. She looked at the energy portal, and there was a single man standing there. She asked him his name, and he did not answer, he looked as though he could not move. She watched, and her staff immediately started experimenting with the spells of the matter type of that region. The central being said to them, "Be careful, there are many hidden cities along those systems."

They looked around, saying, "There are a lot of cities here, and we should be very quiet." They cloaked themselves, and the queen noticed someone noticing them. The queen watched and realized they were of an alien matter spelling. She said, "We may not be able to pacify them." He said understood and continued on his journey. The queen looked around the cities and realized they were all of royal standing for each city had a throne and a king. She also realized in the deep reaches of the systems they were a procreative type. The queen looked at them and scrutinized their designs, saying these do not look as though they were from the collected systems.

She looked even further and followed the social networks, realizing the being she freed resembled many of the beings of the upper reaches of the system. She thought, *Where this could have been?* Her analysts reported there is a similarity between the matter types in alphabetized spelling. They said less than 30 percent, she asked, did they have the flaw, they replied the being that destroyed the leader of the Ziauddin did not. She looked and realized that they are of their own kind; she asked how far has their social network gone. They said beyond a point where it became untraceable. The ambient is simply too cold for us to recognize the trails within the matter. She looked at Heilgurth and said to him stop, shift here, and she realized more people were sensing his presence.

He looked around, and she said, "No sudden movements, do not speak."

"I think there is something else out there," he said. "We will keep on going." She said, "Yes, but just one second." He said, "Show me all, and he realized there were trillions of nexuses filled with beings." It looks that way, a favorite type of the Chuar. He replied where their King as unseen. He continued moving slowly, and they seemingly wondered and went back to what they were doing. He looked at the energy portal and said, we can get there. She said, "Yes, but you need to be careful."

He traveled crossing two dimensions when the princess said, "I heard a voice saying, 'Lend me your soul.'" Heilgurth said, "You shouldn't answer we should try to see if they can see us." The queen said no it could be some sort of a trick.

Heilgurth asked what else is out here. She said, "That is what we are trying to find out." He looked at the princess and her skin began to turn dark blue; she said she felt cold. He began to slow then to a stopped, she immediately iced over. Heilgurth said help us something is wrong, the queen said her souls has disappeared or was it simply frozen I have never seen this before. Heilgurth covered her body in black metal and towed her body behind him, he said we need to reach the portal. Heilgurth began to hear the voice of a woman singing.

The queen immediately made a person standing next to Heilgurth, saying, "If you fall, this woman will take you home." The voice said to him who is she and giggled he asked, "Who are you?" The voice said, "I am the Alvendier, the singer of Calavary." The voice snapped, saying you are a liar." He said to the queen, "They can see our thoughts it is a trick, she said you have no choice but to play along.

The queen looked around the systems and saw a young prince speaking with the Chuar, it seemed he was begging the Chuar for answers, begging the Chuar to stop. The Chuar simply laughed at him and encouraged him to join the patrons, the queen looked at the Chuar's words and looked at Heilgurth, saying what did it say. They said it wanted to borrow my soul; the queen created a woman within the system cities and told her to ask the Chuar to borrow her soul. The queen watched as the men of the system were enraged by the woman's conversation but the Chuar answered sure you can you can find it near the edge of the universe encased in ice.

The queen looked at Heilgurth and told him to look for a soul. He said yes there are some the queen said take one and give it to princess, he said it seems not to fit. The queen looked at the woman and put in her mind where do we fit the Chuar said in another dimension where we all belong. The queen looked around and saw there were countless unusual being of unusual ways of movements. They looked at the networks and realized these are the highest in populations. Simply looking at the lesser beings waiting for an opportunity to devour them. She looked and saw they did not live in the usual dimensional alluvial structure for they were multiple beings in a singularity temporal motion.

He looked at the princess saying we need to get her to rise, the queen said the soul is from one of these beings that is above you. He said no it was from something that was before those above me, they transformed into that. The queen looked at the woman on the system influencing her mind saying how do I work. The Chuar said light and heat for they melt ice. The queen looked at the souls and realized the beings of the hidden cities are taken and transformed into these beings above. The queen looked and melted the soul to fit that of the Princess Heghater and she awoke and she said she had a dream she married a man, he was a human.

Heilgurth said, "We need help." The queen looked at him and said we will not survive this. There are simply too many beings in our universe the Chuar wishes to kill; the wars will be immense. Princess Kamadahara looked at their position and saw there was a much larger threat growing in the distances and the darkness unknowing to the inhabitants near the systems. She called out to her relatives, and they open the veils of that kingdom and they were vast beyond trillions. They were all ready for war, waiting for the instance to strike. She said to the queen, do not engage that city for that could be the end of our cities.

The queen said, "How can we avoid this enemy?" The princess said, "We cannot for there is a Charkarah beneath the lower sevelis of the dimensions. This is the mark of a grand patron." The queen said, "Show me." The princess pointed, and she saw a giant beast with many legs vicious and ready to destroy. She looked on in despair, saying to Heilgurth, "Are we sure the journey to the fallen is survivable. He said, "I think not, how else can we find help to defeat that Chaur?" The queen replied the Chuar could be the fallen. Heilgurth looked at the energy and spoke to it, and a strange voice answered, "The one you seek could bring you your end for the worlds will die."

She said we need to change the way the systems operate; it is the culture the gods that causes the hate and the selfishness of the people within the Dieu. The beings that are reincarnated in the Dieu still possess many of the norms and cultures of their earthly constructs, which affords the problems associated with their habitual thinking from their earthly lives. Heilgurth instantly instructed his staff to create beings that would go to earth and the other worlds within the system and forcefully change the cultures of the people.

The queen immediately influenced a small clan to attack the remaining cities of the systems, leading the patrons of the Chuar to their locations. She said we will surely not survive this, but we will at least try to save the worlds to come. The beings immediately went to the systems and began wars upon the worlds. The constituents of the system did not have enough time to change what she was doing because of the presence of the Chuar.

The being that came to this world spoke to me and told me the world of men will come to an end. For it was professed by our God many centuries ago. This was one of the beings Heilgurth made. Its plan is to create a global war by feeding technologies in weapons and energy, fueled by already existing global tensions. This, supported by a military culture, will cause the world to fall into a mass war for decades, destroying the culture of man until it falls back in a docile peace-loving society.

The being said it would implement riots across the world, and it did implement these riots in Hong Kong, Honduras, Nicaragua, Venezuela, France, Russia, Malaysia, and Bulgaria. The being said it would use the major countries of the world to fuel the world's largest world war with missile strikes in Turkey, which grew tension in Middle East. The being also said there is a war silently happening between the United States and Russia since the NATO accident of the Turkish troop shooting down a Russian fighter jet. Since then, tension has escalated, causing a missile attack on United States' soils by the Russian army, which the United States government covered up. This led to the breakdown of the Intermediate Range Nuclear forces Treaty between the then Soviet Union and the United States.

It also said there were aircraft carriers that were sunk in a silent battle from the United Kingdom and the other participating NATO countries. With many silent attacks happening within Europe, it said the global war was the reason for the French president's conspicuous reaction to public uproar. As time passed, tensions within Russian and the Middle East will worsen and cause war upon the nations of NATO. The world will fall into fifty years of relative war until it ends.

If man does not change their way of living, with agendas for hate, racism, and discrimination, the global domination agenda for resources will result in a war that will sink the population of the earth. On hearing this, I felt obligated to inform the world of what was about to happen because I saw the things it said come to pass. There is a lot more to come; it also said World War IV will be caused by Warschzen Luisterich, a man born near Switzerland who is not born yet. All we can do is sit and watch as these events progress.